A Complete Guide to the Spanish Subjunctiv

MW01029943

A Complete Guide to the Spanish Subjunctive is the most complete reference guide to the use of the subjunctive in Spanish. After an exhaustive review of published literature on the subjunctive, and a thorough discussion of all the uses of the subjunctive, including those that have generated much discussion, for example after 'el hecho de que', causative predicates and verbs of emotion, as well as after certain conjunctions, such as 'aunque' and 'después de que', the book presents a comprehensive theory of the subjunctive and provides practical rules for understanding, teaching and acquiring this linguistic structure. The book contains a wealth of authentic examples throughout drawn from linguistic corpora such as the Corpus de Referencia del Español Actual (CREA) and the Corpus del Español del Siglo XXI (CORPES XXI), large databases compiled by the Royal Spanish Language Academy and available on-line at http://www.rae.es/.

This book includes:

- A 'Synopsis' section that summarizes the content of the work and offers practical suggestions for teaching the subjunctive.
- An extensive alphabetical list of expressions used with the subjunctive or the subjunctive AND the indicative.
- An extensive and up-to-date bibliography of subjunctive literature.

Hans-Jörg Busch is Associate Professor of Spanish at the University of Delaware.

A Complete Guide to the Spanish Subjunctive

Hans-Jörg Busch

Routledge
Taylor & Francis Group

LONDON AND NEW YORK

First published 2017 by Routledge

2 Park Square, Milton Park, Abingdon, Oxfordshire OX14 4RN
52 Vanderbilt Avenue, New York, NY 10017

Routledge is an imprint of the Taylor & Francis Group, an informa business

First issued in paperback 2019

Copyright © 2017 Hans-Jörg Busch

The right of Hans-Jörg Busch to be identified as the author of this work
has been asserted by him in accordance with sections 77 and 78 of the
Copyright, Designs and Patents Act 1988.

All rights reserved. No part of this book may be reprinted or
reproduced or utilised in any form or by any electronic, mechanical, or
other means, now known or hereafter invented, including
photocopying and recording, or in any information storage or retrieval
system, without permission in writing from the publishers.

Notice:
Product or corporate names may be trademarks or registered
trademarks, and are used only for identification and explanation
without intent to infringe.

Library of Congress Cataloging-in-Publication Data
Names: Busch, Hans-Jèorg, author.
Title: A complete guide to the Spanish subjunctive / Hans-Jèorg Busch.
Description: New York : Routledge-Taylor & Francis Group, [2017] |
    Includes bibliographical references and index.
Identifiers: LCCN 2016048327 | ISBN 9781138963146 (hardback) |
    ISBN 9781315658940 (ebk)
Subjects: LCSH: Spanish language—Subjunctive | Spanish language—
    Verb phrases. | Spanish language—Modality. | Spanish language—
    Grammar.
Classification: LCC PC4290 .B87 2017 | DDC 465—dc23
LC record available at https://lccn.loc.gov/2016048327

ISBN: 978-1-138-96314-6 (hbk)
ISBN: 978-0-367-87532-9 (pbk)

Typeset in Goudy
by Apex CoVantage, LLC

I dedicate this book to my wife who shared me with the subjunctive over the past years. I am very grateful for her loving support.

I am deeply indebted to Ruth Tauber who proofread this book and corrected my English. (My native language is German.) If you find mistakes, they are mine and are due to the fact that I constantly added and changed things, even at the last minute.

Finally, I thank the reviewers of the manuscript and the publisher who helped me improve my initial project and gave me invaluable suggestions. I also thank my friends and colleagues who gave me feedback about the correctness of the Spanish and English examples.

Contents

1   Purpose and scope of this book

This book deals with the subjunctive as a grammatical category and its communicative potential. As you can easily see by just glancing at the bibliographical sources at the end of this book, there is a huge amount of literature regarding all aspects of the subjunctive. But despite all that has been written, there is no agreement if all the seemingly different uses of the subjunctive can be reduced to one basic grammatical meaning. On the one hand, there have been many attempts to find a single unifying semantic label, such as 'non-reality', 'uncertainty', 'subjectivity', 'virtuality', 'non-assertiveness', 'non-factuality' and others. However, there are always uses that seem to contradict these generalizations. On the other hand, partly because of the impossibility to point out one single meaning, some authors accept or claim that the subjunctive has no meaning at all and that it is just triggered or governed by subjunctive licencing contexts; for example, the meaning of the main predicate or other subjunctive indicators. Therefore what we find in grammars, practical subjunctive guides and textbooks today are often just descriptions of different uses, but not what distinguishes the subjunctive from other moods. This makes it is very difficult, let's say for language learners, to overcome this hurdle in the Spanish language. Due to the lack of a singular principle, Spanish teachers often resort to providing lists of expressions followed by the subjunctive, combined with semantic and pragmatic (over)generalizations, in an attempt to guide their students.

In this book, the subjunctive, as a **formal and systematic** manifestation of modality, particularly verb endings, is characterized as a set of morphemes with a general grammatical meaning. The latter cannot be explained in philosophical, semantic, or pragmatic terms, but as a notion that corresponds to all of the specific systematic manifestations in the language. Neither can it be defined as triggered by the meaning of other elements or just as the product of distribution rules.

In this book, the subjunctive is not treated as an object for elaborating or promoting certain grammatical or philosophic theories. The subjunctive is the main subject and focus. Different approaches are used to describe and attempt to resolve the real problems that we have in understanding, describing and effectively teaching the Spanish subjunctive to English speakers.

A common and widely accepted opinion today identifies the indicative with the semantic notion of assertion and the subjunctive with non-assertion of the occurrence expressed by a verb. From a linguistic standpoint, I will define assertion as a main characteristic of absolute statements about the world and an expression of the speaker's belief, state of mind and intention. The purpose of an assertion is to declare or state directly something that can be true or not. The mood of assertion by social agreement and convention is the indicative. I will show that the subjunctive, on the other hand, is a relative and dependent mode that cannot refer directly to a particular and specific situation but only indirectly through the deictic reference (ego, hic et nunc) of a subordinating predicate.

The discussion of more recent publications about modality and mood will be followed by a more detailed analysis of the syntactic contexts in which we find the subjunctive, that is, in (pseudo) independent, noun, adjective and adverb clauses.

In Chapter 11 I will try to refute the unsubstantiated claim that the subjunctive, especially in America, is disappearing by looking at empiric data and research about mood variation throughout the Spanish speaking world.

At the end of the book, I will outline strategies and practical step-by-step instructions for the teaching of the subjunctive. In the appendix, you can find an alphabetic list of conjunctions that are used with the subjunctive or both moods. There is also an extensive subjunctive bibliography.

2   About the empiric material and the examples used in this book

Most of the authentic examples in this book are taken from the Corpus de Referencia del Español Actual (CREA) between the fall of 2013 and the fall of 2016. The CREA is a collection of texts originating from a variety of sources and all Spanish speaking countries. They are digitized and searchable according to certain criteria on-line through the Royal Spanish Language Academy website at http://www.rae.es/recursos/banco-de-datos/crea.

The last version from June of 2008 contains a little bit more than 160 million word stems. The material, mostly written texts, but also transcriptions of oral samples, date from the period 1975–2004. The written texts are from books, newspapers and magazines. The content is divided into 100 categories. Most of the oral examples are from radio or TV programmes. The written part of the corpus consists of 140,000 documents with more than 154 million word stems: 49% of the written corpus comes from books, 49% from newspapers and magazines and 2% from other sources. Fifty percent of the material is from Spain and the other 50% from the different regions in America, the Andes, the Caribbean, the Chilean region, the United States, Mexico, Central America and the Rio de la Plata region.

All the examples in the book taken from the Corpus de Referencia del Español Actual are marked with <CREA>.

A smaller amount of examples are taken from the Corpus del Español del Siglo XXI (CORPES XXI), http://www.rae.es/recursos/banco-de-datos/corpes-xxi, which also consists of written texts and oral samples from Spain, America, the Philippines and Equatorial Guinea. It has 25 million word forms from each year starting 2001 and ending 2012.

All the examples in this book that are taken from the Corpus del Español del Siglo XXI are marked with <CORPES XXI>.

All the basic examples without an indication of origin are my own.

3   Overview of the subjunctive literature

As already mentioned, there is no shortage of literature regarding the subjunctive.[1] A closer look, however, paints a more accurate picture:

(1) The bulk of literature consists of theoretical articles that describe partial aspects of the subjunctive from the perspective of a specific linguistic theory in vogue at a given time.[2] They are mostly written for linguists or 'insiders' who are familiar with these theories. They are not usually accessible to 'outsiders' and have very limited practical value for teachers and students of Spanish. Published more recently, the collection of articles in Becker/ Remberger (2010), Bosque (1990a), Bosque/Demonte (1999) and Rothstein/ Thieroff (2010) also fall under this category.

(2) A second source of information about the subjunctive is Spanish grammar books.[3] Grammars as well are written with a specific theory of language in mind and reflect an underlying ideology, the state and trends in linguistics and other sciences (such as metaphysics, psychology, psycholinguistics, structuralism, ethnography, logic, etc.) of the time. Grammars are usually descriptive, if we ignore the attempts to come up with 'generative' grammars. Many of them are also written with the intention to prescribe a certain norm in the use of grammatical structures, particularly the one of the motherland, Spain. This was especially the case of the Grammar of the Royal Spanish Language Academy, until 1931. The descriptions of the subjunctive in Spanish grammars differ in length, but they all have one thing in common: they only give the reader examples of the correct uses from the past. None of them provide readers with clear instructions for generating correct sentences and preventing unacceptable ones. They only list different uses of the subjunctive. None of them, not even the *Nueva Gramática de la Lengua Española* (NGLE), published in 2009 and different in many respects from its predecessors, can pinpoint the abstract systematic meaning of this mood. After considering everything that had been written about the subjunctive until 2009 and after looking at all the uses of the subjunctive mood, the authors of the NGLE came to the conclusion: "From all this we shouldn't deduce that the merger of the various contexts determining the choice of mood is impossible. It only means that, for now, this integration has not yet been achieved" (2009:

1870).[4] Obviously, none of the grammar books can be used for teaching the language without a methodological and pedagogical adaptation.

(3) A third source is book-length monographs. Examples are: Ahern (2008), Fente Gómez (1972), Fernández Alvarez/Fente Gómez (1992), Haverkate (2002), Hummel (2001) and Martinell Gifre (1985). They are also written with specific linguistics theories in mind. In monographs, however, the theoretical limitations are often overcome and tend to be secondary in an effort to describe and explain all the different and sometimes contradicting uses of the subjunctive, as well as to extract rules and regularities from them. Many monographs are purely descriptive and lack the methodological and pedagogical tools that are necessary for teachers and learners. However, some do offer practical exercises at the end of the book inviting the reader to apply what they have learned from the analytical part (Borrego et al., 1985: 187–256; Molina, 2006; Navas Ruiz, 1986: 157–201; Porto Dapena, 1991: 259–311; Sastre Ruano, 1997: 245–387). The book by Manteca Alonso-Cortés (1981) doesn't fall into this group because, according to the author, his study is just an outline of the subjunctive syntax within the confines of Chomsky's Standard Theory of 1980. A different kind of monograph is the *Diccionario de uso del subjuntivo* by Pérez/Süss (2010), which is conceived as a reference manual and lists, by alphabetical order, subjunctive indicators with examples and explanations as well as rules and mood terminology.

(4) A fourth source is manuals that are written solely for the purpose of giving simple and clear rules for the use of the subjunctive. This goal is often achieved by oversimplifying and neglecting all or part of the more theoretical linguistic literature about the topic (Anderson, 1995; McKay, 1976; Vogt, 2008). Borrego et al. (1985: 8) explicitly warn anyone who studies the subjunctive to be suspicious of simplified explanations.[5] Unfortunately, the chapters about the subjunctive in most Spanish textbooks fall into this category.

(5) Since the 1980s, there has been a rapid growth in research on first and second language acquisition and learning (for example Blake, 1985; Collentine, 1995, 1998, 2002, 2003, 2010; Farley, 2001, 2002, 2004; Gragera, 2000, 2002; Jegerski/VanPatten, 2014; Kirk, 2013; Krashen, 1990; Lee, 1987; Lee/VanPatten, 1995; Pérez-Leroux, 1988; VanPatten, 1995; VanPatten/ Dvorak/Lee, 1987; VanPatten/Lee, 1990). However, this research does not "automatically translate into pedagogy" (VanPatten, 1995: 179), nor do second-language researchers necessarily have "some special insight into what should happen in the classroom" (VanPatten, 1995: 179). According to VanPatten:

> Second-language acquisition research can help instructors understand why their students often perform the way they do, and certain *general* principles for the language-teaching enterprise can be gleaned from the research . . ., but second-language acquisition research per se is not about language teaching.
>
> (1995: 179)

(6) There are relatively few articles that use the results of the subjunctive and second-language-teaching research to study their potential for pedagogical purposes. Some examples are Fukushima (2014f), Gregory/Lunn (2012), Klein-Andreu (1994), Rosemond (1996), Ruiz Campillo (2007, 2008), Stokes (1988), Stokes/Krashen (1990), Stokes et al. (1988) and Tyo (1993).

(7) There are also studies about the diachronic (historic) and diatopic (regional) variation of Spanish, such as Cano Aguilar (1990), Carbonero Cano (1990), Ferrell (1999), Fontanella de Weinberg (1997), Fukushima (1981a, 2001a), Gordon (1964), Guitart (1987), Jensen/Lathrop (1973), Knauer (1998), Lehner (2009), Metz (2013), Nieves Vázquez Núñez (1999), Oro (1975), Puente-Schubeck (1992), Ramirez Luengo (2001), Renaldi (1977), Serrano Montesinos (1996) and Veiga (1989, 1992b, 1993, 1996a).

Notes

1 See: Castronovo (1984) and Navas Ruiz (1990).
2 See the bibliography at the end of the book.
3 Zamorano Aguilar (2005) offers a history of the subjunctive in Spanish grammars between 1771 and 1973.
4 Original quote: "De ello no se deduce que sea imposible el análisis integrador de todos los contextos que determinan la elección del modo, sino más bien que, por el momento, esa integración no se ha conseguido."
5 Original quote: "que desconfíe de exposiciones simplistas que dan cuenta del subjuntivo español recurriendo a una pareja de conceptos."

4 The subjunctive

An expression of modality

The subjunctive is an expression of modality which has always attracted the interest of philosophers, grammarians, linguists and anyone trying to understand the mechanisms governing language use. The Greek philosopher Aristotle, for example, distinguished 'apophantic' or 'assertiv' from 'semantic' types of statements. This distinction reflects the characteristic of attributive statements, such as: 'All dogs are mammals.' These statements are universally true or not true and are logically attributed to their subjects. The truth value of a statement has always been the main concept in defining mood and modality, until today.

Mediaeval scholastics distinguished between the 'dictum' – the relation between subject and predicate – and the 'modus' – the specification whether the statement is true or false. For the German philosopher Kant, modality was the degree of truth or certainty that the speaker attributes to a statement. Bally (1944: 27–54), and other linguists before him, distinguished between the propositional content of an utterance or what we say, the DICTUM, and its formal realization or how we say it, the MODUS. Obviously, there are many ways to modify the content of a proposition, such as by changing the intonation and rhythm or by adding all kinds of modifiers to characterize the message as a question, an exclamation, a command, an indirect command, a possibility, an obligation, etc. Let's take the simple sentence *Paul and Mary eat your dinner*. Variations could be:

- Paul and Mary eat your dinner.
- Paul and Mary eat your dinner?
- Paul and Mary, eat your dinner!
- Paul and Mary, I want you to eat your dinner.
- Paul and Mary must eat your dinner.
- Paul and Mary have to eat your dinner.
- Paul and Mary may eat your dinner.
- Paul and Mary will eat your dinner.
- Paul and Mary would eat your dinner.

And so on. In general, modality is seen as a reflection of the speaker's attitude towards propositional contents. The *Esbozo* (1973: 454), for example, defines the two terms in the following way: "In several occasions we have distinguished the content of what is said (*dictum*) from how we present it in relation to our psychic attitude (*modus*)."[1] The *Nueva gramática de la lengua española* (NGLE) (2009: 1866) follows this tradition and adds:

> Traditionally, it has been said that a characteristic feature of mood is to inform about the speaker's attitude toward specific information, and particularly about his/her point of view towards the content of what is presented or described. The concept of 'modality' is clearly wider than that of 'mood', but the connection between both notions is very close.[2]

Based on the division by Bally and other French linguists, the NGLE (Manual) distinguishes two kinds of modality: first 'modalidades de la enunciación' [intersubjective or illocutionary modality] and second, a 'modalidad proposicional' or 'modalidad del enunciado' [subjective or logical modality]. Among the first, the NGLE lists an imperative, interrogative, exclamative, optative, desiderative and assertive modality. In the second group there is mention of an epistemic (known as true, false or undecided), a deontic (being mandatory, permitted or prohibited), an alethic (being necessary and probable) and a volitive modality.

Notes

1 Original quote: "En varias ocasiones hemos distinguido el contenido de lo que se dice (*dictum*) de cómo lo presentamos en relación con nuestra actitud psíquica (*modus*)."
2 Original quote: "Tal como se ha señalado en la tradición, un rasgo característico del modo es informar sobre la actitud del hablante ante la información suministrada y, en particular, sobre el punto de vista que este sostiene en relación con el contenido de lo que se presenta o se describe. El concepto de 'modalidad' es, ciertamente, mucho más amplio que el de 'modo', pero la conexión entre ambas nociones es muy estrecha."

5 The subjunctive

The morphosyntactic manifestation of mood

Moods are **formal and systematic** manifestations of modality. In other words: There could be, theoretically, infinite ways to present something (manifestations of modality), but only the most basic and universal concepts have a systematic grammatical expression in the language system. In Spanish and many other languages, moods are represented by verb endings that have the function to characterize the speaker's attitude with respect to what s/he communicates. Other categories of the verb such as tense and aspect are expressed with the help of verb endings or morphemes as well. Morphemes consist of phonemes, the smallest building blocks that make up our languages. Phonemes by themselves don't have meaning. However, their distinguishing features can be used to build and differentiate meaningful linguistic units, such as morphemes and words.

Because verb endings are grammatical morphemes, they can only have a very general grammatical meaning that is much more abstract than the meaning of words or lexicon items, which is just an abstraction of the specific uses in different contexts.

In the 1931 edition of the *Gramática de la lengua española*, the Royal Spanish Language Academy still listed five moods: the infinitive, the indicative, the conditional (potential), the subjunctive and the imperative. In the edition of 1973, the infinitive and the conditional disappeared. The same goes for the NGLE of 2009.

6 Attempts to define the meaning of the subjunctive

There has been no shortage of labels to describe the meaning of the subjunctive. Depending on the theoretical linguistic and philosophical model as well as on the linguistic material used for the description, the subjunctive has been called 'el modo de la no-realidad' [the mood of non-reality] (Alarcos Llorach, 1994: 153–154), 'modo de la incertidumbre' [mood of uncertainty] (Badía Margarit, 1953), 'modo de la subjetividad' [mood of subjectivity] (Hernández Alonso, 1984: 291–296), 'modo de la futuridad indefinida' [mood of indefinite futurity] (Beardsley, 1925), etc. Sastre Ruano (1997) defines the indicative as the 'modo de la factualidad y de la imposición objetiva de los fenómenos' [mood of factuality and objective imposition of phenomena] and the subjunctive as the 'modo de la virtualidad, de lo hipotético, de la valoración subjetiva de la realidad' [mood of virtuality, of hypothesis, of subjective assessment of reality]. In the 1970s and 1980s, the generative grammar and its sequels used the subjunctive to prove the universality of their formalizations and transformations and introduced new sets of binary distinctive features. One example is Lozano (1972, 1975) with his features [optative] and [dubitative] and his discussion with Bolinger (1974, 1976) about whether there is only one subjunctive or whether there are two. Terrell/Hooper (1974) point out the problems of the traditional generative-transformational theory and the syntactic feature approach. They use semantic and universal logic concepts, such as truth value, presupposition, assertion and anticipation (1974: 484) to distinguish moods. Bell (1980) summarizes the discussions in the 1970s and comments on the approaches of Bergen (1978), Bolinger (1974, 1976), Goldin (1974), Lozano (1972, 1975), Rivero (1970, 1972, 1975) and Terrell/Hooper (1974) without reaching any practical conclusions. The concept of truth value plays an important role for many linguists, such as Bustos Tovar (1986), who writes that with the indicative, the speaker commits to the truth of what s/he is saying and with the subjunctive s/he doesn't. A similar description can be found in Porto Dapena (1991: 31). Asencio/Prieto (1985: 8) think that with the subjunctive, the speaker suspends his commitment with the truth of the sentence because s/he doesn't want to confirm it or because it is not necessary. Starting in the 1990s, Mejías-Bikandi (1993, 1994, 1998a, 1998b, 2002, 2009, 2014, 2016) continued the work of Terrell/Hooper (1974).

6.1 What happens when you explain the use of the subjunctive (only) with generalizing semantic and pragmatic terms?

Usually, when we try to explain the use of the subjunctive in concrete examples we use some variation of the labels discussed. How do you answer John, who is a very good and inquisitive student in these specific situations, when he asks: 'Why do I have to use the subjunctive?' Here are some hypothetical examples and answers:

- *Quiero que <u>compres</u> este libro sobre el subjuntivo.* [I want you to buy this book about the subjunctive.]

  - [TEACHER] It's a **wish**. It **hasn't happened yet** and therefore it is **not real or factual**.

- *Me alegro que <u>compres</u> el libro.* [I am glad that you are buying the book.]

  - [TEACHER] It's the expression of an **emotion**. It hasn't happened yet and therefore it is not real or factual.

- [STUDENT] If someone is showing me a book, can I say: *Me alegro que <u>hayas comprado</u> el libro.* [I am glad that you have bought the book.]?

  - [TEACHER] Yes, because it's the expression of an emotion.
  - [STUDENT]: But it has happened already. Isn't it real?
  - [TEACHER] Yes, it is, but because of the verb *alegrarse* we still have to use the subjunctive. It's **subjective**.

- [STUDENT] Profe, I found this example with *alegrarse* in the newspaper *El Mundo* from Spain: *Edgar se alegraba de que al menos su abuela le <u>compraba</u> todos los caprichos que le pedía: una moto, ropa, una consola de videojuegos, etcétera.* [Edgard was happy that at least his grandmother bought him all that he wanted.] Why is there no subjunctive?

  - [TEACHER] That's an **exception**.

- [STUDENT] Profe, I found a lot of examples with *temerse* using the indicative, even more than the subjunctive. Here is just one example: *La verdad es que me temo que no <u>seremos capaces</u> de cumplir nuestra parte de los compromisos* [The truth is that I fear (think) that we will not be able to fulfil our part of the agreement]. Isn't this an expression of emotion, and doesn't *seremos capaces* describe something that hasn't happened yet?

  - [TEACHER] Here, *me temo* **means something different**, it means *creo que*.
  - But isn't it also **subjective**?
  - [TEACHER] Yes, but *creo que* is never followed by the subjunctive, only *no creo que*, because it means *dudo que*.

- [STUDENT] Profe, I found this example with *no creo que* followed by the indicative: *No creo que tus padres saben la verdad.* [I don't think your parents know the truth.] Is this wrong?

  - [TEACHER] No, it's not wrong. **Sometimes** *no creer que* can also be followed by the indicative. The speaker in this sentence might have thought that the other person assumed that his/her parents knew the truth. S/he, however, says that s/he doesn't believe that.

- [STUDENT] Profe, I found an example with *creo que* followed by the subjunctive: *¿Crees que Juan esté enfermo?* Do we always use the subjunctive after *creer que* in questions?

  - [TEACHER] No, it **depends** if the **speaker believes** that Juan is sick **or not**.

- [STUDENT] Profe, when do you use the subjunctive or the indicative after *aunque*?

  - [TEACHER] We use the subjunctive to indicate a **possibility** or that something is **uncertain** or **hypothetical**, for example: *Aunque llueva mañana, iremos a la playa.*

- [STUDENT] Profe, yesterday my friend from Spain, referring to his brother, said something like: *Aunque sea mi hermano, no le voy a perdonar esta mentira.* [Even though he is my brother, I am not going to forgive him this lie.] Didn't you say that the subjunctive after *aunque* indicates that something is a possibility or hypothetical? But it's the reality.

  - (TEACHER) Yes, but here the subjunctive is used to refer to something that is **known to both the speaker and listener**. It's has **low information value**.

These are just a few examples of the mixed and contradicting signals (**bold**) that we are sending John, and that will confuse him rather than enlighten him. If a student is told that the subjunctive expresses uncertainty, it shouldn't surprise if s/he says, **Creo que Juan no tenga muchos amigos* to express that s/he is not sure about it. Bolinger (1974: 466) formulated the problem as follows: "The traditional rules of thumb – willing, emotion, indefinite antecedents, unreality, unrealized future, etc. – are hints at the underlying semantic tendencies, . . . , but neither they nor any refinement of them will serve as rules in the formal sense."

6.2 Attempts to negate the meaning of the subjunctive

The difficulties in finding a universal meaning that incorporates all the different uses of the subjunctive or other motives led some people to claim that the subjunctive doesn't have any meaning at all and that a "much better approach is to concentrate on learning *when* to use the subjunctive rather than on asking *why* one uses it or what it 'means' " (Butt/Benjamin, 2011: 241). Another author (Vogt, 2008: viii) writes: "First of all, it is important to accept something many books don't openly declare: the subjunctive doesn't mean anything!" For this author, the subjunctive is just "a set of verb forms required in clauses of certain types". He adds a fourth type that he calls "hypothetical or contrary to fact statements" (2008: 3). But because, clearly, the predicate of noun, adjective and adverb clauses can be in indicative and subjunctive, he needs what the NGLE calls mood indicators. If the main verb expresses "assertion of belief" (2008: 28), the verb in the subordinated clause will have to be in indicative, otherwise in subjunctive. This is also how many textbooks explain the use of the subjunctive, after they have characterized the subjunctive as the mood of unreality, subjectivity, virtuality or any of the other semantic generalizations that we have seen before.

This may work with noun clauses that depend on the verb *querer que* and similar expressions, where the subjunctive is the only choice. However, with many other verbs, there are at least two problems with the idea that the main verb completely determines the mood selection in subordinated noun clauses:

1   Many verbs that indicate how information or facts are transmitted – for example *comunicar, decir, dejar saber, escribir, informar, notificar*, etc. – can also be used to express wishes and orders. On the other hand, verbs such as *admitir, advertir, proponer* and *sugerir* can be used to express an intention of the speaker, but also as communication verbs.

    •   Te digo que <u>encuentres</u> (SUB) un buen trabajo.
        [I am telling you to find a good job.]
    •   Te digo que <u>encontrarás</u> (IND) un buen trabajo.
        [I am telling you that you will find a good job.]

    The argument of those who claim that the main verb completely determines the mood selection in the subordinated clause is that, in the example with the subjunctive, the meaning of *decir* is similar to that of *desear* and, in the other example with the indicative, similar to *comunicar*. Therefore, we have to use the subjunctive in the first example. If the different verb endings don't mean anything and are only triggered by the meaning of the main verb, the implication is that we must have stored all the specific meanings that a word can acquire in different contexts separately in our mind, which wouldn't be very economical and is rather unlikely. It is much more plausible to assume that we have a somewhat abstract representation of the lexical meaning of a word, which is the average of all its uses in all the different contexts where we have seen and heard it. It is the context again which determines and creates the actual meaning of a word. Because the only elements in the two examples that are different are the verb endings, it seems logical to assume that they DO have a function, which I call a grammatical or structural meaning.

2   The second problem, which is closely related to the first one, can be seen with main verbs that seem to have the same meaning, and that can be used not only with the subjunctive, but also with the indicative. Good examples are the expressions of emotions, such as *alegrarse (de que), temer que, temerse que, enojarse de que, molestarle que*, etc. The use of the indicative has also been documented

and commented on by Bolinger (1953), Hunnius (1976), Lope Blanch (1958) and many others. In Old Spanish, verbs of emotions were mostly used with the indicative because the object clause was not fully subordinated by the governing verb and had the status of a causal clause.[1] Bolinger concluded that in modern Spanish "the indicative probably went underground, but never disappeared in familiar speech" (1953: 460). This might also be the reason for the more frequent use of the indicative in Latin American Spanish, which often conserves forms that are extinct or considered archaic in Spain. If it were so, it would contradict the theory that the use of the subjunctive is dying, which is often documented with examples from Latin America that contain expressions of emotions. Lope Blanch (1958) shows that the use of the indicative is not only limited to Latin America (Mexico), but that it can also be found in modern Spanish literature. The same goes for adjective clauses. The mood in the subordinated clause is seen as triggered exclusively by "an indefinite, vague, or nonexistent (unreal) antecedent" (Vogt, 208: 37), a noun or pronoun that is modified by the adjective clause. Again, the question is: How would the reader know in which one of the following two sentences the antecedent is indefinite, undetermined and vague or definite, determined and specific?

- dime lo [antecedent] que sepas (SUB), porque quiero saber quién es, no para denunciarla, sino para agradecérselo;
  [tell me whatever you (might) know, because I want to know who she is, not to speak out against her but to thank her for it;]
- dime lo [antecedent] que sabes (IND), porque quiero saber quién es, no para denunciarla, sino para agradecérselo;
  [tell me what you know, because I want to know who she is, not to speak out against her but to thank her for it;]

Have we stored two meanings of *lo que*, one equivalent to *whatever* and the other equivalent to *that what*? Isn't it more plausible to assume that the mood of the verb in the adjective clause causes the different interpretation of the antecedent, assigning the mood a more active and meaningful role? The other question is, if in the example with the indicative, we can say that the antecedent is definite, determined and specific, how can the pronoun *lo* be definite and specific?

The theory that the subjunctive doesn't mean anything falls completely apart when it comes to adverb clauses because most adverbial conjunctions can be followed by a clause in indicative or subjunctive. Vogt uses the example of *aunque*:

- Aunque Juan sea (SUB) rico, no lo parece.
  [Even if Juan is rich, he doesn't look like it.]
- Aunque Juan es (IND) rico, no lo parece.
  [Even though Juan is rich, he doesn't look like it.]

In the absence of any indicator in the main clause, the only solution is to say what has been repeated throughout history, that the "indicative or the subjunctive depends entirely on the attitude – or the degree of confidence – a speaker has about his or her assertion" (Vogt, 2008: 49). In other words, moods do have meaning, even if it is a very general one.

6.3 The concept of assertion

The nature of assertion, which can be traced back to Aristotle, has always intrigued logicians, mathematicians, philosophers and linguists. It is a basic concept used to describe human interaction. When it comes to assertion, modern linguistics usually quote the German philosopher, logician and mathematician Gottlob Frege, who lived from 1848 to 1925, especially his assertion sign (⊢) and its importance for the analysis of human languages. He devised techniques that took him far beyond Aristotelian syllogistic and stoic propositional logic. His scattered philosophical treaties, especially his 1892 paper "Über Sinn und Bedeutung" ['On Sense and Reference'] are often referred to in contemporary linguistics.

In mathematical logic, a logical assertion is a statement that affirms that a certain premise is true and is useful for statements of proof. In linguistics, 'assertion' is used

> to denote a basic speech act or speech-act category with two key characteristics: it commits the speaker to the truth of the proposition expressed and it has the function of informing the hearer of that proposition (note that there is a third feature implicit in these: an asserted proposition is one which is explicitly communicated).
>
> (Jary, 2004: 237)

A common and widely accepted opinion today identifies the indicative with the semantic notion of assertion and the subjunctive with non-assertion of the occurrence expressed by a verb.

Already in 1765, J. Harris wrote:

> If we simply **declare**, or **indicate** [bold added by the author of this book] something to be, or not to be (whether a Perception or Volition, it is equally the same) this constitutes that Mode called the Declarative or Indicative. . . . If we do not strictly **assert** [bold added by the author of this book], as of something absolute and certain, but as of something possible only, and in the number of Contingents, this makes that Mode, which Grammarians call the Potential; and which becomes on such occasions the leading Mode of the sentence.
>
> (Harris, 1765: 140–141; emphasis added)

6.4 Newer studies that use the concept of assertion and related concepts to describe the meaning of the subjunctive

In 1974, Terrel and Hooper used the semantic concepts of assertion, truth value, presupposition and anticipation, which they found in Lenz (1935), as a reaction to the shortcomings of the 'syntactic feature approach' (Terrell/Hooper, 1974: 484) of the generative-transformational theory in vogue in the 1970s. In generative grammar "the subjunctive verb forms themselves [had] no real semantic function; they appear purely on the basis of a co-occurrence relationship" (Terrell/Hooper, 1974: 484). This approach, which is often attributed to A. Bello, is also followed in most Spanish textbooks. Students are taught that they have to memorize long lists of verbs and expressions if they want to learn the correct use of the subjunctive. Bello (1981: 327) wrote: "The verb endings that are influenced or ruled by a word or phrase to which they are or can be subordinated, are called MOODS."[2] Those who quote Bello (for example R. Lenz (1935: 452), who criticizes the Venezuelan author and writes: "[Bello] assumes that the forms depend or could be dependent upon certain dominant verbs")[3] often forget to mention that, in the first four editions of his grammar, Bello also mentions the contrast between assertion and non-assertion. Here he writes: "The indicative mood is used for affirmative and negative judgements by the speaker or by another person mentioned in the predicate upon which the verb depends"[4] (330) and, "The forms, in which we don't affirm or negate are called subjunctive"[5] (337). This idea disappears in the last edition, which became the starting point for all subsequent editions of his grammar.

The question of whether the subjunctive forms have their own meaning or whether they are just a morphological reflex, determined almost exclusively by another subordinating predicate (=matrix), has been a central issue in the subjunctive debate throughout history. In their article, Terrel and Hooper defend the idea that the mood of the embedded or subordinated predicate 'can be freely chosen' and carries meaning. Their 'hypothesis' is "that there are several basic attitudes that a speaker can adopt toward a proposition" and that "these attitudes govern the choice of verb form and the choice of matrix" (1974: 485). Obviously, this is not a new theory either and has been commonplace in Spanish grammars for a long time.[6] We can also find it in Porto Dapena's comprehensive description of the meaning and uses of indicative and subjunctive in Spanish. He writes: "the indicative presupposes the affirmation or negation of a fact; this means the speaker commits to the truth of what s/he says. The subjunctive, on the other hand, lacks such a presupposition; the speaker adopts a neuter attitude about the truth of what is said"[7] (1991: 33).

The three main concepts Terrell/Hooper (1974) chose to develop their hypothesis are 'assertion', 'presupposition' and 'truth'. For them, asserting something means saying or stating that it is true. Independent main clauses can only be assertions. Indicative verb forms correlate directly with assertion whether they are used in independent main clauses or dependent and subordinated clauses. Dependent clauses in indicative are associated with assertive matrixes; for example *saber que, creer que, ser seguro que, parecer que*, etc. Dependent clauses in subjunctive are therefore associated with non-assertive matrixes; for example *quiero que, espero que, ser bueno que, dudar que, no ser cierto que*. The second element in their equation, mainly to explain the use of the subjunctive after expressions of emotions and other types of comments (for example value judgements), is the notion of 'presupposition'. A dependent clause is presupposed if it is assumed by the speaker to be true. The truth value must be preserved when the matrix upon which it depends is negated.[8] The idea is influenced by Kiparsky/Kiparsky (1971) who distinguished factive matrixes (that require presupposed complements) from non-factive matrixes (that don't). For the authors, dependent clauses that are both asserted (stated to be true) and not semantically presupposed to be true are asserted and therefore appear in the indicative mood. Accordingly, dependent clauses that are not asserted (stated not to be true) but presupposed, and that are neither asserted nor presupposed, appear in subjunctive. They illustrate their hypothesis with the English example *It is interesting that Mary studies so much*, in which, according to the authors, "the speaker accepts the fact that *Mary studies so much* and his purpose . . . is to comment on that fact" (485). The dependent clause (*Mary studies so much*) must be true or presupposed because the negation of the matrix – *It is NOT interesting* – does NOT change the truth of *Mary studies so much*. On the other hand, in the example *It is true that Mary is beautiful*, the truth of '*Mary is beautiful*' would not be presupposed because the negation of the matrix DOES affect the truth of the embedded clause.

The Terrel/Hooper article, especially the logical notion of 'presupposition', its usefulness and status, as well as the notion of 'truth', triggered a variety of reactions and comments. For example, is it correct to say that in *It is interesting that Mary studies so much*, the speaker accepts the proposition *Mary studies so much* to be true? Don't we often say that something is interesting just to relativize or politely rebut a statement, such as in the following dialogue? Isn't this the reason why the subjunctive is mostly used in this context in Spanish?

- [Mother to her neighbour] "My daughter Mary studies every night for the exams, and now she is exhausted."
- [Neighbour] "It is interesting that you say that because my daughter told me that she sees Mary out at parties all the time. [Es interesante que diga (SUB) eso porque mi hija me dijo que ve a Mary andando de parranda todo el tiempo.]

All we can say is that the neighbour acknowledges what the mother said and that she refers to it, but not that this is presupposed to be a true statement, as her reaction shows. It would even sound strange if the neighbour repeated the mother's statement literally and said:

- [Neighbour] "It is interesting that your daughter Mary studies every night for the exams, because my daughter told me that she sees Mary out at parties all the time.

This shows that with 'es interesante' and many other expressions we can refer to something already mentioned or old information, which doesn't have to be necessarily true or considered to be true. It would even sound as if the neighbour accused the mother of lying if she quoted literally what the mother said. 'It is interesting that you say that' clearly sounds more polite. Furthermore, even though in Spanish, *es interesante que* is mostly used with the subjunctive, it is not difficult to find examples with the indicative as well:

1) Los resultados, según las estadísticas ofrecidas por el servicio gratuito de Vantage, fueron los siguientes: Confesamos nuestra particular sorpresa ante los 71 visitantes (equivalente a 33 %) que respondieron no conocer libros digitales gratuitos. Sin embargo, es interesante que esto coincida (SUB) con lo que expresábamos en nuestro editorial del número 89 de Letralia: "Antes del modelo King era escaso el respaldo al libro electrónico 'blindado', ese que requiere de software adicional en función de resguardar los derechos de autor." <CREA> [It is interesting that this coincides with what we wrote in our editorial in number 89 of Letralia.]

2) Por otro lado, el mismo editorial puede servir como material informativo a las personas que no conocen el concepto de libro digital, de las cuales 28 participaron en nuestra encuesta. También es interesante que 44 personas afirmaron (IND) no poder leer de la pantalla, lo que podría tener diversas razones, desde problemas de la vista hasta limitaciones de tiempo. <CREA> [It is also interesting that 44 people said that they couldn't read from the screen.]

3) Yo creo que son tres las cuestiones que debe hacer, ordenadamente. La primera de ellas es aclararse, o lo que es lo mismo tratar de definir de la forma más exacta posible qué tipo de trabajos son los que le convienen, los que le quedan bien, los que puede, de acuerdo a su formación, a su cualificación, a sus posibilidades. Para eso, para no equivocarse, entre otras cuestiones es interesante que se ponga en contacto (SUB) con personas que conozca, que en este momento puedan estar relacionadas con ese trabajo. <CREA> [it is of interest (for the applicant) to get in touch with people that s/he knows and that in this moment could be working in this area.]

4) El propósito, como se ve, es anterior a la fecha de publicación de la novela, 1871; escrita en 1868, cinco años antes de Trafalgar, primero de los Episodios, es interesante que Galdós, al iniciarlos, da marcha atrás (IND) y se remonta a 1805, todavía en el "antiguo régimen", cuya caída va a historiar en los volúmenes siguientes. <CREA> [it is interesting that Galdos . . . retracts and goes back to 1805]

In example (1), the subjunctive use has nothing to do with logical presupposition, but rather with the larger context and the intention of the speaker to tie the content of the proposition to something that the speaker thought impossible (*nuestra particular sorpresa ante los 71 visitantes (equivalente a 33 %) que respondieron no conocer libros digitales gratuitos*). In example (3) *es interesante que* is used similar to *es necesario que* and the proposition is a recommendation. In examples (2) and (4), *44 personas afirmaron no poder leer de la pantalla, da marcha atrás* and *se remonta* are absolute statements, 'assertions'. The negation of the main predicate (**No** *es interesante que*), which wouldn't make a lot of sense here, would not change the meaning of the noun clause or negate its 'truth'. This means that the content would be presupposed. Why is it then that we can find the subjunctive

AND the indicative in this case? The answer is that the expression *to be interesting* has nothing to do with the truth of the dependent noun clause. The same goes for *It is true that Mary is beautiful*. According to the authors, here, the negation affects the truth of the embedded clause, which is saying that the speaker thinks that Mary is not beautiful, and, hence, that it is not presupposed. Logically, *no es cierto que* would be followed by subjunctive. A quick look at the CREA, however, reveals that this is not necessarily the case. It is very easy to find examples with 'no es cierto que' followed by indicative:

5) Urtecho estuvo tres horas declarando en la oficina de la fiscal, Doris Aguilar, y a su salida indicó que únicamente llegó como testigo a esclarecer que no es cierto que de su despacho sacó 14 cajas conteniendo documentación concerniente a la defraudación fiscal, descubierta en las aduanas. <CREA> [he pointed out that he only came as a witness to clarify that it is not true that he removed 14 boxes with documentation related to the tax evasion]

This means that negation has nothing to do directly with assertion or presupposition. It doesn't matter if we say *Mary is beautiful* or *Mary is not beautiful*, *(él) sacó 14 cajas* or *(él) no sacó 14 cajas*. In each case the speaker asserts that the content of the embedded clause is true, independently from his/her personal perspective or attitude.

Another argument against the hypothesis that dependent clauses that are both presented as true and not semantically presupposed are asserted, and therefore appear in indicative, is the subjunctive use in the complements of causative predicates such as *hacer que* in Spanish.[9]

Ruiz Campillo (2007) categorically excludes the ideas of 'truth value' or extralinguistic reality which have nothing to do with the subjunctive. Predicates never refer directly to extra-linguistic situations, events or actions; something that happened, happens or will happen; or short extra-linguistic facts. They are always tied to the belief, the intention and the perspective of the speaker and/ or grammatical subject. Their extra-linguistic truth value cannot be determined without extra-linguistic elements. This does not only refer to predicates in the subjunctive, but also in indicative:

* *It is raining*. (Statement made by whoever uttered this sentence; it can be true or not.)
* *Yesterday I saw a UFO*. (Statement made by someone identified as first person, who therefore is identical to the speaker; it can be true or not.)
* *Yesterday Pete saw a UFO*. (Statement of 'Pete'; it can be true or not.)
* *Tomorrow it will rain*. (Statement made by whoever uttered this sentence; it can be true or not.)

Later it was argued that the notion of presupposition was pragmatic, rather than semantic, and related to the notion of old versus new information. One example is Ahern (2008: 83) who writes that the subjunctive is used when the speaker refers to (1) a potential situation or possibility and (2) a situation that is known by the speaker and listener. Based "on relevance-theoretic notions on the interaction between the roles of semantics and of pragmatics in the interpretation process", she argues that the semantic content of the matrix, the subordinating expression, "plays a less prominent role in interpretation than is normally assumed" (2005: 212).[10] This idea is also rejected by Ruiz Campillo (2007) on the ground that it mixes the pragmatic meaning, which is just an update and manifestation of the actual systematic grammatical value of the subjunctive.[11]

The idea that the notion of presupposition was pragmatic rather than semantic is also the tenor of an article by Mejías-Bikandi (1994). He writes:

> Thus, whether a proposition is asserted or not depends not so much on whether that proposition is true or false, but on what are the intentions of the speaker when s/he decides to present the information expressed by the proposition to a particular audience.
>
> (1994: 892)

A proposition is asserted if the speaker indicates that it "describes the world as s/he or some other individual perceives it" (1994: 892). However, the intention of the speaker when uttering *Me alegro de que María venga mañana* is not to describe the world as s/he perceives it, but to express that the proposition belongs "to the mutual knowledge of speaker and hearer" (2014: 896), which boils down to the notion of old/new information.

In another article Mejías-Bikandi concludes that logical and semantic truth conditions are less important than illocutionnary and pragmatic (the relation between speaker and listener, the speaker's intention) notions to understand the use of the subjunctive. He establishes the following rules of mood use in Spanish:

> (i) matrices whose complement represents old information trigger the use of the subjunctive in the complement, (ii) complements that refer to information that is not presented as true (for the speaker or the matrix subject) appear in the subjunctive, (iii) information that is pragmatically asserted appears in the indicative.
>
> (1998a: 947)

In a more recent article he comes back to the notions of assertion and informative value. Based on Stalnaker's (1978) "notion of context set, which is defined as the set of possible worlds compatible with what is presupposed in a particular conversational setting" (2016: 117), Mejías-Bikandi reiterates that the subjunctive mood is used in clauses that lack informative value or that are "lower in a scale of assertability" (2016: 107).

However, there seems to be at least one group of verbs that cannot be explained with the concepts of assertion and presupposition, and they are causatives. Mejías-Bikandi (2014: 651) examplifies this with the sentence: *La lluvia hizo que se desbordaran los ríos.*[12] Here the embedded proposition (*que se desbordaran los ríos*) is asserted (true) – the rivers did overflow – and not presupposed, because according to the rules of logic, the truth value is not preserved under negation: *La lluvia no hizo que se desbordaran los ríos*. This means, "the complement is not presented as necessarily true" and the rivers might not have overflown in the negative example (2014: 653). To explain the subjunctive in this case, Mejías-Bikandi uses the concepts of 'grounding', particularly that of 'clausal grounding', and 'subordination' taken from Langacker (1987, 1991, 2008, 2009) that were also employed in the crosslinguistic functional (=notional, cognitive, semantic/pragmatic) study of subordination by Cristofaro (2003). "The term ground is used in CG (= cognitive grammar – HJB) to indicate the speech event, its participants (speaker and hearer), their interaction, and the immediate circumstances (notably, the time and space of speaking)" (Langacker, 2008: 259). The lexical and morphosyntactic structures that are used in a specific speech event are called "grounding elements" (Langacker, 2008: 259). Langacker distinguishes 'nominal grounding' elements, such as articles and pronouns, and 'clausal grounding' components, verb endings and modal verbs that "situate(s) the profiled relationship with respect to the speaker's current conception of reality" (Langacker, 2008: 259). Cristofaro's notion of subordination that is based on Langeacker's cognitive grammar is defined solely in functional terms. Subordination is

> regarded as a particular way to construe the cognitive relation between two events, such that one of them (which will be called the dependent event) lacks an autonomous profile, and is construed in the perspective of the other event (which will be called the main event).
>
> (Cristofaro, 2003: 2)

Mejías-Bikandi (2014) shows that the complement clauses of causative predicates in Spanish are not independently grounded, which means they are not independent absolute statements and therefore non-assessments, because the temporal relation to the speech situation is not established with the complement clause but via the matrix predicate. Because of their meaning, causative predicates always situate the event of the dependent predicate after the main predicate: the overflowing must logically happen after the rainfall. This makes causative predicates very similar to predicates expressing wishes, recommendations, etc. that are always followed by the subjunctive in Spanish and by an infinitive construction in everyday English: *Quiero que vengas.* = *I want you to come.*

The reason why the negation doesn't have a direct effect on expressions that are always followed by the subjunctive, is that, by definition, it is impossible to assert the truth with the subjunctive. With reference to Togeby (1953: 118), as well as large amounts of empirical data, Borrego et al. (1985: 8) came to the same conclusion when they wrote:

> With the subjunctive, the speaker suspends any compromise with the truth of the sentence because he doesn't want and thinks that it is not necessary to affirm it, . . . , or because he is not in a situation to do so.[13]

The subjunctive characterizes a subordinated predicate as semantically and pragmatically dependent upon the main subject and originator. The complements of causative predicates are always presented as dependent upon what the subject or originator of the utterance considers or not to be the cause of the overflow. Without the negation (*la lluvia hizo*), the overflowing is presented as a direct consequence of the rain. With the negation (*la lluvia no hizo*), the speaker doesn't say that the rivers didn't overflow. It is still possible that they did. However, if they did, it was not due to the rain.

The main idea of Achard in an article from 2000 is that the indicative and subjunctive endings have a proper meaning which must be compatible with the main verbs (154). This is nothing new. He also uses the idea of 'grounding' taken from Langacker (1991), but combines it with the Maldonado's interpretation of 'dominion', which consists of the "conceptualizer's capacity to control actively and to manipulate a circumstance in order to assess its status with respect to elaborated reality" (Maldonado, 1994: 406). 'Elaborated reality' in this model is someone's conception of what is real or what has the potential to be real. According to Achard, the abstract meaning of the indicative is that someone has complete dominion or active control of the content of a complement/noun clause, which is grounded completely in the conceptualizer's elaborated reality. Clauses in subjunctive, on the other hand, are not grounded in reality, but with respect to some 'mental space' (see: Fauconnier, 1985), introduced by the subject of the main or matrix clause. The content of the complement clause only exists in this mental space (Achard, 2000: 159). Neither the speaker nor any other conceptualizer has direct access to the relation that exists between the main subject and the dependent clause (Achard, 2000: 159). Therefore, the meaning of the subjunctive consists of indicating the mental space in which the complement is located.

De Jonge (2001), using the concept of a 'contextual alternative', defines the subjunctive with the feature "contextual relevance of an alternative for the occurrence expressed by the verb".[14] The idea of 'contextual alternative' is also used by Villalta (2008). She writes:

> In Spanish, a predicate selects the subjunctive mood in its embedded proposition if the proposition is compared to its contextual alternatives on a scale introduced by the predicate. In this proposal, predicates that select the subjunctive mood are thus analyzed as gradable predicates.
>
> (2008: 468)

This makes her a defender of the idea that the subjunctive is triggered by the semantics of a subordinating predicate and her "goal is to develop a first proposal for a common semantics of the predicates that select the subjunctive mood in Spanish" (2008: 470). Her article is inspired by Heim (1992) and his analysis of desire predicates, which builds on Stalnaker's (1984) idea that every desire report contains a hidden conditional. Villalta argues "that such a conditional semantics should be extended to all predicates that select the subjunctive mood in Spanish" (2008: 470). What distinguishes predicates that select the subjunctive mood "is that they establish a comparison" and "introduce an ordering relation or scale" (2008: 475) which "is contributed by the lexical meaning of each predicate" (2008: 476). What distinguishes her from Heim is that her analysis "involves comparison of the embedded proposition p with contextually available alternatives" (2008: 476) that are more than just the negation of this proposition. She then argues that the "reference to the subject's beliefs can be replaced with the set of contextually available alternatives" (2008: 476). Villalta applies her formal logical approach to semantics to directive, desire and emotive predicates; predicates expressing likelihood and doubt; and – to a lesser degree – causative predicates. There is no doubt that the use of the subjunctive always entails the concept of alternative. However, Villalta's attempt to tie the subjunctive directly to the meaning of specific fields of verbs or expressions doesn't answer the question of why verbs of emotion, for example, can be used also with the indicative in specific contexts and why, for example in German, communication verbs (*to say*), commissives (*to promise*) and fiction verbs (*to dream*) called for the subjunctive (Konjunktiv) in the past, which would limit the universality of this model. Furthermore, abandoning the reference to the speaker's belief would question the general consensus that moods characterize the speaker's attitude with respect to what s/he communicates.

Similarly, Hummel (2001) calls the indicative 'Existenzmodus' and the subjunctive 'Inzidenzmodus'. This classification is based on the observation that language can abstract from the existence or non-existence of an event in the real world, and that the main function of the subjunctive is to present events, no matter if they actually happened or not, as possible alternatives to their realization.

Ruiz Campillo (2007) considers the term 'assertion' too narrow because it can only be applied to events following verbs and expressions such as *saber, ver, ser evidente, estar seguro*, etc., but not *creer, suponer, parecer* and similar verbs. He replaces 'assertion' by 'declaration' which includes both 'assertion' (knowing something for sure; 'declaración positiva') and 'supposition' (an approximate declaration).

6.5 The definition of assertion in this book

From a linguistic standpoint, I define assertion as a main characteristic of absolute statements about the world and an expression of the speaker's belief, state of mind and intention. The purpose of an assertion is to declare (state directly) something that can be true or not.

The mood of assertion per definition/social agreement/convention is the indicative. Predominantly, the indicative is found in independent main clauses. In an independent clause a speaker directly expresses a belief, state of mind, an intention, etc. Objectively, what s/he says can be true or false. The listener can accept it or not. This is dependent upon the communicative situation, which includes many things, such as prior knowledge of the things and participants mentioned, familiarity between speaker and listener, the actual linguistic context and all kinds of circumstances in which the assessment is made. Langacker (2008) shows this with the sentence My *cat is hungry*:

> If I say My *cat is hungry*, I would normally be interpreted as indicating that I accept the profiled occurrence (my cat be hungry) as part of immediate reality. However, this default is easily overridden:
>
> (50) (a)   *Let me guess why you're phoning. My cat is hungry.*
>   (b)   *My cat is hungry. Sure. Tell me another one.*
>   (c)   *My cat is hungry. And if you believe that, there's a bridge in Brooklyn I want to sell you.*
>
> Even when it stands alone as a sentence, a finite clause is not always intended as a true statement, nor does its grounding invariably reflect the speaker's epistemic stance. The proposition it expresses might be used for any number of discourse purposes.
>
> (2008: 448)

According to Langacker, if the speaker doesn't intend to make a true statement, s/he "merely **entertains** the proposition, without necessarily **embracing** it" (2008: 448).

The indicative can also be used in subordinate noun, adjective or adverb clauses. The content of the dependent clause is now a dependent statement and must be interpreted through the prism of the main predicate and its subject.

- *Yo digo que Pablo va al supermercado.*
  [I say that Paul goes to the supermarket.]
- *Ricardo dice que Pablo va al supermercado.*
  [Richard says that Paul goes to the supermarket.]

The first example is my statement and the second, Richard's statement. Whoever utters the second example doesn't assume any responsibility for the truth of the statement which now lies completely with Richard (i.e. with the subject of the subordinating main clause).

Because it is generally assumed that assertion is a very fundamental linguistic and philosophical concept that is not language specific, I am going to use a cross-linguistic approach to analyze the relation between assertion and subordination.

6.6 Assertion and subordination in German

In German, in the past, the present subjunctive, which in the German grammar is called Konjunktiv I, was used to indicate that the speaker distances him/herself from the truth of someone else's (*Richard's*) statement (*of Paul going to the supermarket*):

(1) Richard sagt, Paul gehe (SUB) zum Supermarkt.
     [Literally: *Richard says, Paul go to the supermarket.]

Without distancing him/herself from Richard's statement, the speaker would
have said:

(2) Richard sagt, Paul geht (IND) zum Supermarkt.
     [Richard says, Paul goes to the supermarket.]

This is equivalent to quoting directly what Richard said:

(3) Richard sagt: "Paul geht (IND) zum Supermarkt."
     [Richard says: "Paul goes to the supermarket."]

German also has the systematic possibility to start the dependent noun clause
with the subordinating conjunction *dass*. The following example would be more
or less equivalent to example (1):

(4) Richard sagt, *dass* Paul zum Supermarkt gehe (SUB).
     [Literally: *Richard says, *that* Paul to the supermarket go.]

Notice that the subordinating conjunction *dass* causes a different word order in
the clause that follows, with the verb now in final position, marking the noun
clause formally as a subordinated clause.
    Accordingly, example (2) would be equivalent to the following example (5):

(5) Richard sagt, dass Paul zum Supermarkt geht (IND).
     [Literally: *Richard says, that Paul to the supermarket goes.]

Today, particularly in spoken German, the use of the present subjunctive – there
is also a past subjunctive in German (= Konjunktiv II) – has fallen into disuse.
By using the indicative instead of the subjunctive, the listener no longer knows
whether the speaker endorses Richard's proposition or not. With the disappearance of the subjunctive as a systematic morphologic marker, the possibility for the
speaker to distance him/herself from the truth value with morphological means
is fading. In order to do that now, the speaker has to resort to lexical means, for
example, with the choice of the main verb:

(6) Richard *gibt vor*, *dass Paul zum Supermarkt geht* (IND).
     [Literally: *Richard alleges/claims/pretends that Paul to the supermarket
     goes.]

In the last example, however, it is not possible to quote the originator (Richard)
of the initial statement *Paul geht* (IND) *zum Supermarkt* directly in the form of a

direct statement, with the typical word order for declarative sentences – subject/verb/object:

(7)   *Richard gibt vor, Paul geht (IND) zum Supermarkt.*
      [*Richard alleges/claims/pretends Paul goes (IND) to the supermarket.]

This means *to allege/claim/pretend*, in addition to communicating a statement, also characterizes the speaker's attitude towards a proposition that can include joy, doubt, regret, surprise, wish, etc., a common characterization of the subjunctive in Spanish.

   Consequently, the following sentences in German would not be correct either:

(8)   *Richard freut sich, Paul geht (IND) zum Supermarkt.*
       [*Richard is happy Paul goes (IND) to the supermarket.]
(9)   *Richard zweifelt, Paul geht (IND) zum Supermarkt.
       [*Richard doubts, Paul goes (IND) to the supermarket.]
(10)   *Richard bedauert, Paul geht (IND) zum Supermarkt.
       [*Richard regrets Paul goes (IND) to the supermarket.]
(11)   *Richard ist überrascht, Paul geht (IND) zum Supermarkt.
       [*Richard is surprised Paul goes (IND) to the supermarket.]
(12)   *Richard will, Paul geht (IND) zum Supermarkt.
       [*Richard wants Paul goes (IND) to the supermarket.]

So, how is it possible that the use of a subjunctive form in German has the effect to distance the speaker from a proposition? My explanation is that the subjunctive – compared with the indicative – is a relative and dependent mode that cannot refer directly to a particular and specific situation, but only indirectly through the deictic reference (ego, hic et nunc) of a subordinating predicate. In Langacker's terminology (2008) we could say that predicates with the subjunctive are not independently grounded. *Paul gehe zum Supermarkt* in our initial example (1) cannot be interpreted as an independent, but only as *Richard's* statement. By using *gehe* (SUB), the speaker says: this is not my statement, but Richard's and by doing this, the speaker distances him/herself from it. If the speaker and the sentence subject are the same, it is not possible to use the subjunctive in this case:

(13)   *Ich sage, Paul gehe (SUB) zum Supermarkt.
       [Literally: *I say, Paul go (SUB) to the supermarket.]

Example (4) with the verb in subjunctive is similar. The difference is that the noun clause, the proposition that *Paul goes to the supermarket*, is marked three times as subordinate and dependent: with the subjunctive, with the conjunction *dass* and with the word order for subordinated clauses. The noun clause in example (5) is only marked two times as subordinate and dependent with the conjunction *dass* and with the word order for subordinated clauses. This means the proposition is still clearly attributed to *Richard*. This is also the case in example (6), but with the addition that the speaker distances him/herself with the choice of the verb in the main clause. Here it is not possible to use the indicative and the word order for an absolute and independent statement. This suggests that this kind of structure is not compatible with the meaning of the main predicate which prevents the syntactically dependent clause to be presented as an independent statement versus assessment. This prompts me to think that the grammatical function of the subjunctive is subordination under the meaning of another predicate and its subject and non-assertion.

6.7 Assertion and subordination in English

There is no doubt that in English you can express anything you can say in Spanish, German or other languages. The possibility to express the speaker's attitude is no exception. You can do that by lexical means, such as adverbs and adverbial expressions:

- The play <u>presumably</u> will be produced on Broadway.[15]
- S/he is <u>probably</u> still in Madrid.
- <u>I bet you</u> that s/he is still in Madrid.
- Do you think s/he is still in Madrid? <u>I have my doubts</u>.

All the following Spanish noun clauses can be translated into English without any problems.

- Quiero que <u>termine</u> (SUB) la guerra. → I want the war to stop. / I want that the war stops.
- Exijo que <u>esté</u> (SUB) en mi casa a las tres. → I demand that s/he be at my house at three. / I demand that s/he should be at my house at three.
- Insisto en que me <u>traiga</u> (SUB) los papeles. → I insist that s/he bring me the papers. / I insist that s/he brings me the papers. / I insist that s/he should bring me the papers.
- Dudo que <u>pueda</u> (SUB) estar en la estación a las cinco. → I doubt that s/he can be at the station at five.
- Me alegro de que <u>venga</u> (SUB) mi hija. → I am glad that my daughter comes tomorrow.
- Espero que <u>venga</u> (SUB) a verme mañana. → I hope s/he will come see me tomorrow.
- Siento que <u>venga</u> (SUB) a verme mañana. → I am afraid s/he will come see me tomorrow.
- Me imagino que él sólo <u>quiere</u> (IND) impresionarte. I guess (that) s/he only wants to impress you.
- Sé que ya <u>está</u> (IND) en Madrid. I know (that) s/he is already in Madrid.

It is my understanding that moods are morphosyntactic categories which indicate semantic and pragmatic subordination or coordination in Spanish as in other languages. Because in modern English the systematic possibility to mark semantic subordination under the meaning of the main predicate or other contextual elements with the help of verb endings is very limited, English resorts to other linguistic means to mark subordination. The most popular, especially after *want*, is the typical infinitive construction with direct object: *I want you to open the book* which is the source of the infamous **Yo te quiero a abrir el libro*. The other is to mark subordination with a noun clause introduced by the conjunction *that*, which is more similar to Spanish. However, there only is the possibility to mark semantic subordination under the main predicate in the endingless third person singular. And even this possibility is used less and less, giving way to the use of the third person indicative instead:

- Insisto en que me <u>traiga</u> (SUB) los papeles. → I insist that s/he <u>bring</u> (SUB) me the papers. / I insist that s/he <u>brings</u> IND) me the papers.

Of course we can always use modal auxiliary verbs, such as *should, would, may, can, could*, etc. in English to express the modality 'request':

- I insist that s/he <u>should bring</u> me the papers.

Modal auxiliaries, the same as infinitives, lack any inflections and are therefore not able to form independent meaningful statements or, if allowed, only under very specific context conditions. This creates a stronger dependence upon the main predicate and subordinates it under its meaning.

   Even though the conjunction *that* only subordinates clauses syntactically, its presence or absence can be an indicator of a stronger dependence of the subordinated verb on the meaning of the main verb. In the following sentences, which in Spanish are followed by the indicative, *that* is often omitted because it sounds superfluous and unnecessary:

- Me imagino que él sólo <u>quiere</u> (IND) impresionarte. → I guess [that] he only wants to impress you.
- Sé que ya <u>está</u> (IND) en Madrid. → I know [that] s/he is already in Madrid.

The reason for this is that both the main and subordinated clause are semantically independent and rather coordinated than subordinated. Even though the subordinated clauses mentioned previously are semantically necessary to complete the main verbs, there are situations where *imaginar* could well stand alone, especially in everyday speech:

- Pero el brazo, te pesa bastante ¿no? <u>Me imagino</u>. Pero lo mueve. Dice que la duele, pero lo mueve. Pero si lo llevas en el cabestrillo es más fácil. <CREA> [But I imagine the arm is pretty heavy, right? But she can move it ….]
- Ese negocio del periódico, por ejemplo, fue un negocio malísimo. <u>Me imagino</u>. Luego, otro negocio que hay dos tipos de definitivamente de negocios. <CREA> [I imagine the newspaper deal, for example, was a bad deal ….]

This wouldn't be possible with *saber*. The situation in English is similar. It is much easier to use *to guess* without a complement than *to know*:

- S/he only wants to impress you. I guess. OR S/he only wants to impress you, I guess.
- *S/he is already in Madrid. I know./*S/he is already in Madrid, I know.

Most importantly, however, the subordinated clauses are only syntactically subordinated. Semantically they are coordinated and independent. They carry the main content of the sentence, a declaration or statement about something. The 'main verb' only confirms the statement and specifies that it is based on the speaker's imagination or knowledge.

This is different with verbs that are followed by the subjunctive in Spanish, where the conjunction *that* cannot be omitted because this would create a semantic contradiction:

- *I want the war stops. (If the war stopped, why would I still say that I want it to happen?)

Generally, the same goes for the sentence with 'I doubt':

- *I doubt s/he can be at the station at five.

English speakers, however, might not reject the last sentence as categorically as the one with *I want*. Again we can see the parallels with Spanish where the subjunctive after *quiero que* is mandatory, while, semantically, there is the possibility to use the indicative as well after *dudo que*:

- fue elegido 'Mejor Jugador Novato del año' y comenzó a asombrar aquellos que dudaban que alguien sería capaz (IND) de hacer sombra a los Bird, Magic, Kareem y compañía. <CREA> [and he surprised all those who doubted that someone would be able to eclipse Bird, Magic, Kareem and others.]
- Hubo un tiempo en que dicen que los ladinos dudaban que nosotros éramos (IND) gente. <CREA> [There was a time when the Ladinos doubted that we were people.]

The reason for this is that the subordinated clause after *dudar que* can reflect the attitude of the main subject (*los ladinos*), but the speaker can also choose to present it as an absolute statement representing his/her attitude. If the subordinated clause expresses the attitude of the main subject, then *dudar que* must be followed by the subjunctive:

- Dudo que (yo) pueda (SUB) estar a las cinco.
  [I doubt that I can be there at five.]

If the subordinated clause expresses someone else's attitude, the indicative sounds more acceptable, even though the norm calls for the subjunctive:

- ?Dudo que (Juan) puede (IND) estar a las cinco.
  [I doubt that Juan can be there at five.]

After 'I hope' and 'I am afraid' American speakers prefer the future tense with the auxiliary *will* because the content of the dependent clause is in the future:

- Espero que venga (SUB) a verme mañana. → I hope s/he will come see me tomorrow.
- Siento que venga (SUB) a verme mañana. → I am afraid s/he will come see me tomorrow.

None of the following variations are usually accepted:

- *I hope s/he come see me tomorrow.
- *I hope s/he comes see me tomorrow.
- *I hope that s/he comes see me tomorrow.
- ?I hope that s/he will come see me tomorrow.
- *I am afraid s/he come see me tomorrow.
- *I am afraid s/he comes see me tomorrow.
- *I am afraid that s/he comes see me tomorrow.
- ?I am afraid that s/he will come see me tomorrow.

This would suggest that the content of the subordinated clause after *I hope* and *I am afraid* in English is understood as a declaration of the main speaker/subject rather than a wish for something uncertain to happen. This is confirmed by the definition in the dictionary as "to look forward to something with confidence or expectation".[16] It is precisely this meaning of *esperar* that would also be used with the indicative in Spanish:

- "lo que dije la pasada noche creo y espero que expresa (IND) los puntos de vista del señor Slobodan Milosevic" <CREA> [I wish and hope that what I said last night expresses the point of view of Mister Slobodan Milosevic.]
- Yo espero que él sabrá respetarlo (IND). <CREA> [I hope (that) he will know to respect it.]
- Ludo esperó que cruzarían (IND) los rieles por esa zona inquieta de La Victoria. <CREA> [Ludo hoped (that) they would get across the rails in this troubled zone of La Victoria.]

There is a similar situation in French where *espérer que* is always followed by the indicative. In the song 'J'espère que tu va bien' by Patrick Fiori from the Canadian movie with the same title, it says:

J'espère que tu vas bien
Que rien ne t'enchaine depuis
J'espère que tu vas bien
Que rien ne manque à ta vie

To express in English that one feels that something desired may happen, we should probably say:

- I hope s/he may/can come see me tomorrow.
- I wish for him/her to come see me tomorrow.

The sentence *I am afraid s/he will come see me tomorrow* is similar to *I am pretty sure s/he will come see me tomorrow* and could be translated with *Me temo que vendrá a verme mañana.*

Notes

1 See for example Jensen/ Lathrop (1973).
2 Original quote: "Llámanse MODOS las inflexiones del verbo en cuanto provienen de la influencia o régimen de una palabra o frase a que esté o pueda estar subordinado."
3 Original quote: "[Bello] parte de la base de que las formas estén o puedan estar dependientes de ciertos verbos dominantes"
4 Original quote: "El Modo indicativo sirve para los juicios afirmativos o negativos, sea de la persona que habla, sea de otra persona indicada en la proposición de que dependa el verbo."
5 Original quote: "Llámanse subjuntivas las formas verbales en que no se afirma ni se niega"
6 The authors of the *Esbozo*, for example, write: "Entre los medios gramaticales que denotan **la actitud del hablante respecto a los que se dice**, se encuentran las formas de la conjugación conocidas por antonomasia con el nombre tradicional de *modos*" (454). "En la realidad del habla, los términos de esta clasificación se confunden entre sí, porque el modo depende **de la actitud del hablante**, es decir, de cómo viva en cada caso los matices y grados de la duda, el deseo, etc., y consiguientemente prefiera el indicativo o el subjuntivo" (455).
7 Original quote:"el indicativo presupone la afirmación o negación de un hecho, esto es, el hablante se compromete con la verdad de lo que dice, en tanto que el subjuntivo carece de semejante presuposición, el hablante adopta una postura neutra acerca de la verdad de lo dicho."
8 This logical concept is taken from Frege.
9 Mejillas-Bikandi (2014).
10 See also Guitart (1991), Laskurain (2010) and Lunn (1989a, 1989b, 1995).
11 Ruiz Campillo writes: "Yo creo que este punto de vista tiene la ventaja indiscutible de separar netamente la realidad lingüística de la extralingüística. . . . Pero también creo que tiene limitaciones evidentes que se deben, en mi opinión, al hecho de que la valoración que efectúa es de naturaleza discursiva, y estos valores no solo residen en la forma en sí misma, sino que se manifiestan en un nivel de actualización del significado gramatical bastante avanzado, donde ya es inevitable la influencia de múltiples factores ajenos al valor de operación propio de cada forma" (2007: 308).
12 Translation: The rain caused the rivers to overflow.

13 Original quote: "con el subjuntivo el hablante suspende todo compromiso con la verdad de la oración porque no quiere o no es necesario afirmarla, . . . , o porque no está en condiciones de hacerlo."
14 See also De Jonge (1999, 2004, 2006).
15 The example is taken from Worrall Brown/Brown/Bailey, *Form in Modern English.* Oxford University Press, 1958: 171.
16 Source: http://www.thefreedictionary.com/Hope.

7 The function or systematic grammatical meaning of the indicative, subjunctive, and imperative moods in Spanish

By defining moods as the **formal and systematic** manifestations of modality, they are characterized as grammatical structures with a general modal meaning. This meaning cannot be explained in philosophical, semantic or pragmatic terms, but as a notion that corresponds to all the specific systematic manifestation in the language. Neither can it be defined as triggered by the meaning of other elements or just as the product of distribution rules.

7.1 The formal distinction between indicative and subjunctive in Spanish

The basic mood in Spanish is the indicative. Its verb endings and uses distinguish it from the subjunctive and the imperative.

The formal distinction between the present indicative and subjunctive is minimal. It is just based on the distinction between the phonemes versus allophones /a/, /e/ and /i/. The same goes for the difference between the imperfect and the imperfect subjunctive (past subjunctive) of regular -ar verbs that are only distinguished by the phonemes [b] and [r]. This is similar to how we use phonemes to distinguish words with different meaning, such as *fAn* and *fUn*, *bOOt* and *bOAt*, *haPPy* and *HaRRy*, etc.

Therefore, it is important for teachers to train their students to hear the phonetic difference between [a] and [e] and to point out the importance of this phonological distinction in the Spanish language.

The subjunctive paradigm is in many ways more limited and restricted when compared to the indicative:

1 There are only two simple subjunctive conjugations – if we ignore the differences between the two imperfect subjunctive forms *hablara/hablase*:[1] the present and past subjunctive. However, there are five simple indicative conjugations: the present, preterit, imperfect, future, conditional indicative.[2] (We can neglect the analytic forms consisting of *haber* + past participle because they basically add an aspectual dimension to the other conjugations.)
2 There is no formal distinction between the first and third person singular.

If we compare the indicative and subjunctive paradigms, we come up with the following parallelism:

INDICATIVE	SUBJUNCTIVE
Present: *hablo*	Present: *hable*
Future: *hablaré*	
Present Perfect: *he hablado*	Present Perfect: *haya hablado*
Future Perfect: *habré hablado*	
Imperfect: *hablaba*	Imperfect: *hablara/hablase*
Preterit: *hablé*	
Conditional: *hablaría*	
Past Perfect: *había hablado*	Past perfect: *hubiera/*
Conditional Perfect: *habré hablado*	*hubiese hablado*

7.2 The indicative

The indicative mood in Spanish consists of five simple tenses: the present (*hablo*), preterit/pretérito perfecto (*hablé*), imperfect/pretérito imperfecto (*hablaba*), future (*hablaré*) and conditional (*hablaría*); and five compound tenses: the present perfect/pretérito perfecto (*he hablado*), past perfect/pretérito pluscuamperfecto (*había hablado*), pretérito anterior (*hube hablado*), future perfect (*habré hablado*) and conditional perfect (*habría hablado*). The mood and tense system in Spanish also show an aspectual differentiation, represented by the perfective and imperfective aspect.

The indicative is used in simple declarative, interrogative or exclamative sentences:

- Juan va a venir mañana. (declarative)
- ¿Juan va a venir mañana? (interrogative)
- ¿Va a venir mañana Juan? (interrogative; yes/no question)
- ¡Juan va a venir mañana! (exclamative)

What distinguishes declarative from interrogative sentences is intonation and word order.

The indicative is used in

a)   simple sentences,

- Juan está enfermo. [Juan is sick.]

b)   syntactically coordinated clauses

- Juan está enfermo y no puede ir a clase. [Juan is sick and cannot go to class.]

c) and syntactically subordinated clauses

- Puedo ver <u>que Juan está enfermo</u>. [I can see that Juan is sick.]
- Pienso que <u>Juan está enfermo</u>. [I think (that) Juan is sick.]

Even in subordinated and syntactically dependent clauses in indicative, the clause keeps its declarative intonation and word order. It is only syntactically subordinated with the conjunction *que*. Semantically and pragmatically, however, it keeps its independence and declarative character. In both of the above sentences under c), we are stating *Juan está enfermo*. The part that syntactically represents the main predicate, *puedo ver*, just adds information about how the content of the syntactically dependent clause is acquired. Bolinger noted:

> "Superordinate verbs, such as *digo, declaro, pienso, creo, sé, veo,* etc. add information on how we acquired the intelligence (*esta mañana yo leí que . . .*), what vehicle we are using for its expression (*le escribí que . . .*), what universe of reality it exists in (*anoche yo soñé que . . .*), what part of our own storage it comes from (*me imagino que . . ., predigo que . . .*), and other similar ideas; but the underlying meaning of 'intelligence' remains the same, embodied in the indicative mode.'" (The word 'intelligence' here is synonym with 'information' – HJB).
>
> (1974: 464)

We can also say that, pragmatically – understood as where the focus of what we want to communicate is – *Juan está enfermo* would be the main clause, while *puedo ver* only functions as some kind of circumstantial element. The fact that 'Juan está enfermo' is an independent declaration can be shown by fronting it, which means moving it to the beginning of the sentence:

- Juan está enfermo. Lo puedo ver. [Juan is sick. I can see it.]
- Juan está enfermo y lo puedo ver. [Juan is sick and I can see it.]

There are interesting and not coincidental parallels with English. Bolinger wrote:

> In English our freedom to move the performative [which I would call the explicit declarative verb or expression] . . . away from the beginning of the sentence, and to place it in the middle or at the end, mirrors exactly the choice of mode in Spanish.
>
> (1974: 466)

The following examples are taken from Bolinger (1974: 466):

English	Spanish
The "main verb" is postposable	= The "subordinate" verb is in indicative
The "main verb" is not postposable	= The "subordinate" verb is in subjunctive

English	Spanish
I think s/he is coming. → S/he's coming, I think.	= Creo que viene. (Indicative)
I insist that it stop. → *It stop, I insist.	= Insisto en que pare. (Subjunctive)
I see you know each other. → You know each other, I see.	= Veo que se conocen. (Indicative)
It's probable that they know. → *They know, it's probable.	= Es probable que sepan. (Subjunctive)

Bolinger also notes that the function of the superordinate verbs is comparable with sentence adverbs and illustrates this with:

- I suppose s/he is coming. → S/he's coming, I suppose. → S/he's coming, supposedly.
- I don't doubt s/he will do it as soon as s/he can. → S/he will do it, I don't doubt, as soon as s/he can. → S/he will do it, undoubtedly, as soon as s/he can (1974: 466).

We can establish the following rule:

> **The indicative is primarily an absolute mood. It can be found in simple sentences with one predicate or syntactically subordinated noun, adjective or adverb clauses. However, each predicate, even if it is syntactically subordinated, contains an absolute statement that is semantically and pragmatically independent from the main clause and its subject.**

The NGLE (2009) gives the following list of superordinate verbs and expressions that are followed by noun clauses in indicative:

1. Verbs and verbal expressions that express **that something happens**. Examples: *acontecer, ocurrir, suceder*, etc.

   - Sucede que Juan está enfermo.
     [It happens that Juan is sick.]

2. **Speech and communication** verbs and expression: *afirmar, aludir (a), apuntar, asegurar, comentar, conversar (sobre), decir, describir, gritar, hablar (de), indicar, informar (de), mencionar, poner de manifiesto, pregonar, referir(se) (a), repetir, revelar, señalar, soltar, sostener, sugerir*, etc.

   - Afirmo que Juan está enfermo.
     [I affirm that Juan is sick.]

3.   Verbs and expressions of **certainty**: *ser/considerar cierto, claro, evidente, obvio, palmario, patente, seguro, ser de sentido común, saltar a la vista, resaltar,* etc.

- Es cierto que Juan está enfermo.
  [It is true that Juan is sick.]

4.   Verbs and expressions that refer to kinds of **perception**: *advertir, caer en la cuenta (de), encontrarse (con), mirar, notar, observar, oír, percibir, recordar, reparar (en), tropezar (con), ver,* etc.

- Veo que Juan está enfermo.
  [I see that Juan is sick.]

5.   Verbs and expressions that refer to **possession, acquisition,** and **loss of information** or **knowledge**: *aprender, averiguar, convencer (de), creer, enterarse (de), estar al tanto (de), leer, saber, olvidar, tener noticia (de), tener la impresión (de),* etc.

- Sé que Juan está enfermo.
  [I know that Juan is sick.]

Because it is not possible to mention and group all the verbs and expressions that are followed by the indicative, the NGLE (2009: 1878–1879) summarizes them as **predicates whose arguments express what is communicated, known, accepted, believed or perceived.**

The three types of subordinated clauses are:

- Noun clauses:
  - They function syntactically as nouns and are the grammatical object of a main predicate: *Juan dice que vendrá mañana.* [Juan says (that) he will come tomorrow.]; *Te voy a explicar cómo se llega a mi casa.* [I am going to explain to you how to get to my house.]; *Te voy a presentar a quien me salvó la vida.* [I am going to introduce you to the one who saved my life.] They stand for something (what?) or someone (who or whom?).

- Adjective or relative clauses:
  - They function syntactically as adjectives and modify a noun (what kind of?), and are introduced with a relative pronoun: *Este es el color que me fascina.* [This is the colour that fascinates me.] *Estos son los problemas a los que me refiero.* [These are the problems I am referring to.]

- Adverb or circumstantial clauses[3]:
  - They modify a predicate and answer the questions How?, When?, Where?, Why?, Under what conditions?, etc.: *Cuando era niño, siempre jugaba con mi hermano.* [When I was a child, I always used to play with my brother.] *Si tengo tiempo, iré a España.* [When I have time, I will go to Spain.]

In each of the three types, the clauses in indicative keep their declarative intonation and word order. Furthermore, even after deleting the 'main clause', the message, now only represented by the lexical meaning of the elements in the noun clause and the indicative, remains the same: *Juan vendrá mañana; (asi) se llega a mi casa; la persona me salvó la vida; el olor me fascina; me refiero a estos problemas; siempre jugaba con mi hermano; tengo tiempo.* Even without the explicit declarative expressions *puedo ver, dice, te voy a explicar*, etc., the declarative character doesn't disappear. Therefore, I can formulate the rule:

> **The general meaning of the indicative mood is DECLARATION.**
> **With the indicative we can only communicate that something is known, accepted, believed or perceived as true, which doesn't mean that it is indeed known, accepted, believed or perceived as true. The speaker just presents it as such.**

A declaration has nothing to do with the truth of what we are saying. Truth is not a linguistic, but an extra-linguistic concept. Words or grammatical structures can't lie. Only people using words and grammatical structures can lie. With the indicative we can also express things that haven't happened yet, because they are in the future, even if they are unbelievable or wrong. Nevertheless, with the indicative, they are declared by the speaker as if they were real facts:

- Juan vendrá mañana. [Juan will come tomorrow.]
- Ayer vi un ovni. [Yesterday I saw a UFO.]
- En este mundo nadie muere de hambre. [In this world nobody dies of hunger.]

7.3 The subjunctive

The subjunctive mood in Spanish consists of three simple tenses: the present (*hable*), past/pretérito de imperfect (*hablara/hablase*) and the future, which has disappeared almost entirely from modern Spanish (*hablare*); and three compound tenses: the present perfect (*haya hablado*), the past perfect (*hubiera hablado*) and future perfect (*hubiere hablado*), which has disappeared as well. The subjunctive mood in Spanish also shows an aspectual differentiation, represented by the perfective and imperfective aspect.

Compared with the indicative, the subjunctive morphemes always signal an unfinished and dependent predication that cannot be used without an explicit or implicit main predicate:

- Sé que <u>tienes</u> (IND) razón. → Tienes (IND) razón.
  [I know that you are right. → You are right.]
- Quiero que <u>tengas</u> (SUB) razón. → *Tengas (SUB) razón.
  [I want you to be right. → *Be right.]

The subjunctive is used in <u>dependent</u> or <u>subordinate</u> noun (subject or object), adjective or relative, and adverb or circumstantial clauses:

- Dudo <u>que Juan esté enfermo</u>. (noun clause)
  [I doubt that Juan is sick.]
- Me alegro (de) <u>que Juan no esté enfermo</u>. (noun clause)
  [I am glad that Juan is not sick.]
- Busco un libro <u>que explique el uso del subjuntivo de forma sencilla y lógica</u>. (adjective/relative clause) [I am looking for a book that explains the use of the subjunctive in an easy and logical way.]
- Te lo digo <u>para que lo sepas</u>. (adverb/circumstantial clause)
  [I am telling you so that you know.]

The conjunction *que* and other connectors are indicators of syntactic subordination, and the subjunctive is a marker of semantic and pragmatic subordination under the meaning of the main clause. The subjunctive indicates that the dependent clause doesn't refer to something that is independent from the meaning of the main clause (its predicate or subject), but that is part of it and subject to specific conditions dictated by it.

In my view, the subjunctive forms occupy an intermediate position between indicative conjugations and infinitive verb forms. With the latter they share the characteristic that they are unable to form independent statements, if we neglect very specific pragmatic situations in which we could use infinitives independently from finite verb forms, such as in commands and instructions such as in textbooks or signs (*Llenar los espacios en blanco*; *No abrir las ventanas*; etc.). Its verb forms characterize the subjunctive as a dependent and relative mood.

Neither in English nor in Spanish can we move the main verb which expresses the attitude of the speaker or the sentence subject away from the beginning of the sentence and place it in the middle or at the end. If we do, it will make it some kind of circumstantial element or modifier and convert the dependent clause into a main clause. However, the subjunctive can never stand in a main clause. The fronting of the main verb produces nonsense sentences:

I want you to come tomorrow. → *You come tomorrow I want.	Quiero que venga mañana. → *Venga mañana quiero.
I insist that it stop. → *It stop I insist.	Insisto en que pare. → *Pare insisto.
I wish it were summer. → *It were summer I wish.	Deseo que fuera verano. → *Fuera verano deseo.
It's probable that they know. → *They know is probable.	Es probable que sepan. → *Sepan es probable.
Harris was determined that the film be authentic. → The film be authentic Harris was determined.	Harris estaba determinado de que la película fuera auténtica. → *La película fuera auténtica, Harris estaba determinado.
It is imperative that we eat soon. → We eat soon is imperative.	Es imperativo que comamos pronto. → *Comamos pronto es imperativo.

I like for you to stay longer. → For you to stay longer I like.	Me gusta que se quede más tiempo. *Se quede más tiempo me gusta.
I doubt that s/he will pay today. → S/he will pay today I doubt.	Dudo que vaya a pagar hoy. → *Vaya a pagar hoy dudo.

Some of the sentences, however, sound much better if we add the conjunctions *that* and *que* or *el que*, and some are even correct:

It's probable that they know. → ?That they know is probable.	Es probable que sepan. → (El) Que sepan es probable.
It is imperative that we eat soon. → ?That we eat soon is imperative.	Es imperativo que comamos pronto. → (El) que comamos pronto es imperativo.
I doubt that s/he will pay today. → That s/he will pay today, I doubt.	Dudo que vaya a pagar hoy. → (El) que vaya a pagar hoy dudo.

Except for the last example, the English sentences are probably not accepted as correct. By adding *que* or *el que* in Spanish, we are marking the clause as a subordinate clause where the use of the subjunctive is allowed. Whenever we can use *el que*, we can also use *el hecho de que*.[4] This shows that *hecho* here doesn't mean 'fact' in the sense of 'reality'. Here it only has a grammatical function.

Utterances in subjunctive – as well as imperatives and infinitives – are per definition **non-assertions**. Rather than referring to independent or absolute facts, they characterize the embedded predicate as representing the **personal attitude (opinion, intent, purpose) of the main subject, the effect or result of the main predicate, its cause or condition.**

So, even if the other person is standing in front of me, *que hayas venido* in *Me alegro que hayas venido* cannot be interpreted as an assertion, as me communicating that obvious fact, but primarily as an expression of my attitude with reference to this fact. Whether the person is actually there at this moment is not relevant. Without seeing the other person and just picking up what another person said, I would have used the same structure: *Me alegro que la persona haya venido*, even if I doubted it, as in *Me alegro que la persona haya venido aunque lo dudo*.

The same goes for causative predicates, such as *causar que* or *hacer que* that are always followed by the subjunctive in Spanish:

- La lluvia <u>hizo</u> que los ríos se <u>desbordaran</u> (SUB).[5]
  [The rain caused the rivers to overflow.]

It doesn't matter that the rivers actually overflowed. The reason why we are using the subjunctive here is to present the overflowing not as an event that exists independently from the main subject (*la lluvia*), but as being caused by it. In other words, in causative structures we are focusing on the cause and the originator and not on the result or the effect. In the example

- Juan <u>dijo</u> que los ríos se <u>desbordaron</u> (IND).
  [Juan said that the rivers overflowed.]

the overflowing has nothing to do with Juan. He is just communicating it as an independent fact and independently from whom or what caused it.

Some people say that the subjunctive sentences such as

- Quiero que se desborden los ríos.
- No quiero que se desborden los ríos.
- Dudo que se desborden los ríos.
- Es posible que se desborden los ríos.

are redundant and meaningless because they only repeat what is already contained in the lexical meaning of the main verbs (*querer, dudar, ser posible*). This might be true to a certain extent in these specific examples. (Even though I wouldn't call this redundancy, but rather consider it a form of agreement.) However, the combination of the subjunctive conjugation with these and other verbs has the effect that, over time, the subjunctive endings are able to express everything that these particular verbs have in common and distinguishes them from other words or phrases that are usually combined with the indicative (for example *asegurar, estar seguro, informar, saber, creer, mostrar*, etc.) in a very abstract but not less meaningful way. This can also be seen in sentences with communication verbs such as *decir*, which can be used either with the indicative or the subjunctive depending on whether we just want to inform or formulate a wish or request:

- Te digo que encontrarás (IND) un buen trabajo.
  [I tell you that you will find a good job.]
- Te digo que encuentres (SUB) un buen trabajo.
  [I tell you to find a good job.]

Most words are polysemous or homonymous. Moods are one way to select their specific meaning:

- Siento que Juan está (IND) enfermo.
  [I have the feeling/I think (that) Juan is sick.]
- Siento que Juan esté (SUB) enfermo.
  [I am afraid that Juan is sick.]
- Me temo que Juan está (IND) enfermo.
  [I am afraid/I think (that) Juan is sick.]
- Me temo que Juan esté (SUB) enfermo.
  [I am afraid that Juan is sick.]

Wishes, however, can only be used with the subjunctive in Spanish:

- Quiero que me digas (SUB) la verdad.
  [I want you to tell me the truth.]
- *Quiero que me has dicho la verdad.
- *Quiero que me dices la verdad.
- *Quiero que me dirás la verdad.

In this case, we can talk about semantic incompatibility with indicative forms. Many other verbs and expressions, however, are used with the subjunctive for social, conventional and historical reasons. Knowing the rules and conventions assures that we understand what others are saying and that we are being understood. One example is verbs of emotions. All newer grammars and textbooks tell us to use verbs and expressions of emotions with the subjunctive. This, however, was not always the case. In Old Spanish, they were usually followed by the indicative. And even today this is more common in Latin American Spanish that often has retained linguistic features which once existed in Spain and are no longer used there. There are no semantic reasons why expressions of emotions should only be used with the subjunctive, only conventional reasons.

Because the subjunctive forms do have meaning (syntactically, semantically and pragmatically), however, it is not the same to say:

- Me alegro que Juan está (IND) en Francia. OR Me alegro (de) que Juan esté (SUB) en Francia.
  [I am glad (that) Juan is in France.]
- No creo que Juan está (IND) enfermo. OR No creo que Juan esté (SUB) enfermo.
  [I don't think (that) Juan is sick.]

With the indicative, there are always two statements:

- Juan está en Francia. AND (Yo) me alegro de ello.
  [Juan is in France. AND I am glad about it.]
- Juan está enfermo. PERO (Yo) no lo creo.
  [Juan is sick. BUT I don't believe it.]

With the subjunctive there is only one statement in which the speaker/sentence subject (in cases where the speaker and the sentence subject are identical) comments on something that is the object of his/her personal attitude; one cannot be separated from the other:

- Me alegro [ATTITUDE OF THE SPEAKER/SENTENCE SUBJECT] (de) que Juan esté (SUB) en Francia [CONTENT OF THIS ATTITUDE].
- No creo [BELIEF OF THE SPEAKER/SENTENCE SUBJECT] que Juan esté (SUB) enfermo [CONTENT OF THIS BELIEF] (= Juan NO está enfermo).

In cases where the speaker and the sentence subject are different, the content of the dependent clause always reflects the attitude of the sentence subject (*Pablo*):

- Pablo se alegra [ATTITUDE OF THE SENTENCE SUBJECT] (de) que Juan esté en Francia [CONTENT OF THE OPINION].
- Pablo no cree [BELIEF OF THE SENTENCE SUBJECT] que Juan esté enfermo [CONTENT OF THIS BELIEF] (= Juan NO está enfermo).

We can formulate the following rule:

> **The grammatical meaning of the subjunctive is SUBORDINATION under the main predicate and sentence subject.**
> Clauses in subjunctive are dependent upon other propositions (states, events or actions) that bring them about. Therefore, we can find this mood in combination with wishes, orders, aspirations, hopes, needs, suggestions, advice, opposition, disagreement, doubts, but also feelings and other attitudes of the speaker or sentence subject, as well as the effect or result of the main predicate, its cause or condition.

The existence of conventions also allows us to go against these rules in order to achieve certain pragmatic effects, but of course only if we stay within the limits of their communicative potential. We can, for example, use the future tense for speculations, questions for requests, infinitives for commands, but also the subjunctive where we would expect the indicative:

- -¿Qué hora es? -Serán las nueve.
  [-What time is it? -It's around nine.]
- ¿Te importa quitar los pies de la mesa?
  [Do you mind taking your feet of the table?]
- Abrir el libro en la página 100.
  [Open the book to page 100.]
- -¡Pero ella es tu hermana! -No me importa. Aunque sea mi hermana, no la quiero ver.
  [-But she is your sister! -I don't care. Even though she might be my sister, I don't want to see her.]

7.4 The uses of the subjunctive in (pseudo) independent clauses

Even though the subjunctive is a marker of subordination and dependence, and precisely for that reason, it can also be found in sentences with only one predicate; for example, in formal positive commands, negative commands, 'let's do it' commands, expressions of hope and exclamations with or without *ojalá* or introduced by *que*, and after certain adverbs expressing possibility, such as *acaso*, *probablemente*, *tal vez* and *quizá(s)*.

These 'independent' uses of the subjunctive, together with the fact that they can also be found in grammatically subordinated clauses, are the main arguments for those who reject the assumption that the subjunctive is the mood of subordination. However, rather than backing up their position, these uses clearly show the contextual dependence of the subjunctive, which can only be used to express the intent or desire of an overarching subject. Only because of this, these utterances can be understood or interpreted:

> Whether such expressions of desirability are then interpreted more specifically as suggestions, commands, exhortations, or wishes (optatives), depends only on the conditions of the actual situation: principally on who it is that is expected or called upon to bring about the event (the hearer, or someone else), and on whether or not the speaker is in a position of authority to force this person to do so.
>
> (Klein-Andreu, 1994: 424)

Even though the imperative is considered a separate mood with certain syntactic, semantic and pragmatic particularities (for example, the use of enclitic pronouns with positive commands, the inventory of forms that is limited to the second person and others), it is obvious that formal and negative commands, on the one hand, and noun clauses that express wishes, influence, suggestions, preference, permission, concession, admission, possibility, necessity, as well as prohibition and opposition, on the other, are closely related. The latter could be called indirect commands:

- ¡Venga a verme mañana! (≈ Quiero/digo/exijo/ . . . que venga a verme mañana.) [Come see me tomorrow. (≈ I want you to/tell you to come tomorrow. / I demand that you come tomorrow.)]
- ¡No venga a verme mañana! (≈ No quiero/prohíbo/no es necesario/ . . . que venga a verme mañana. [Don't come see me tomorrow. (≈ I don't want you to/I forbid you to come tomorrow. / It is not necessary for you to come tomorrow.)]

The same goes for exclamations, wishes, orders and instructions with or without *ojalá* or *que*:

- ¡Viva la república! (≈ Queremos que viva la república.)
  [Long live the republic! (≈ I want the republic to live long.)]
- ¡Ojalá (que) venga a verme mañana! (≈ Quiero/digo/exijo/ . . . que venga a verme mañana.)
  [I hope s/he comes see me tomorrow. (≈ I want him/her to come see me tomorrow. / I tell him/her to/expect him/her to come see me tomorrow.)]
- ¡Que venga a verme mañana! (≈ Quiero/digo/exijo/ . . . que venga a verme mañana.)
  [If s/he came see me tomorrow. (≈ I want him/her to come see me tomorrow. / I tell him/her to/expect him/her to come see me tomorrow.)]
- ¡Qué te vaya bien!
  [Fare well! / Have a nice day. / See you/ . . .]
- ¡Qué pase!
  [Come in!]

- ¡Qué alguien me ayude!
  [Help!]
- ¡Qué lo saquen de aquí!
  [Get him/her out of here!]

Used as an exclamation, **así** is also used with the subjunctive:

- ¡Así te <u>parta</u> un rayo!
  [May you get hit by lightning!]

The past subjunctive forms or the verbs *querer*, *deber*, *poder* and *valer* are often used instead of the present indicative and the conditional to express polite wishes and petitions:

- <u>Quisiera</u> hablar, por favor, con don Gabriel Gil Amador. (= Querría/Quiero)
  [I <u>would</u> like to talk to Mr Gabriel Gil Amador, please.]
- <u>Debieras</u> confesarte, llevas tiempo sin hacerlo. (= Deberías/Debes)
  [You <u>should</u> confess. It has been a while since the last time.]
- <u>Pudieras</u> volverte decente y dejar de contar mentiras. (= Podrías/Puedes)
  [You <u>could</u> become a decent person and stop lying.]
- Y más <u>te valiera</u> casarte. (= te valdría/te vale)
  [It <u>would</u> be better if you got married.]

All 'independent' uses of the subjunctive must be interpreted as wishes, commands, suggestions, permissions, etc. In order to express the concept of personal feeling about something, possibility or probability, the subjunctive alone is not enough. In this case we must use additional lexical means, such as *lástima que, acaso, a lo mejor, posiblemente, probablemente*, etc.

Lástima que is based on *es una lástima que* and therefore the predicate that follows it can be considered clearly as a dependent predicate. It is always used with the subjunctive:

- <u>Lástima</u> que no se <u>hayan conservado</u> estas cartas.
  [It's a pity that these letters have not been treasured.]

Acaso, a lo mejor,[6] **posiblemente, probablemente, tal vez** and **quizá(s)**[7] are more or less equivalent to impersonal expressions such as *es posible que* and *es probable que*. They can be followed by the indicative or the subjunctive. The subjunctive can only be used with these expressions if the adverb precedes the verb and there is no pause between them:

- <u>Quizá</u> vendrá/venga a verme mañana. BUT Vendrá/*venga a verme mañana, quizá. [May be s/he will come see me tomorrow. BUT S/he will come see me tomorrow, may be.]

The subjunctive instead of the indicative is used to express that the event is more unlikely than likely to happen. If the event has not happened yet, the present subjunctive and, less frequently, the future indicative is used. However, the present indicative is not used.

The expression **puede que** is always used with the subjunctive:

- Si yo paso, <u>puede que</u> me <u>insulten</u>, me <u>amenacen</u>, o algo más.
  [If I come in, it is possible that they insult and threaten me or something else.]

In some countries,[8] the adverbs *igual* and *lo mismo* to express doubt or the meaning of 'perhaps' are used in colloquial speech, but always with the indicative:

- Por eso me vine anoche a dormir contigo, claro que <u>igual</u> te <u>molesta</u>.
  [That's why I came last night to sleep with you, but maybe it bothered you.]

Many pseudo-independent uses are formulaic and lexicalized. This means they have to be learned as complex vocabulary units. Some examples are:

- Pase lo que pase
- Pese a quien pese
- Sea cual sea
- Diga cuanto diga
- Andes por donde andes
- Le gustara o no

7.5 The imperative

Some linguists and grammarians (such as Bello, Alarcos Llorach) don't want to give the imperative the same status as the indicative and subjunctive.[9] The reasons that they put forward are the specific context conditions for its use as well as the reduced inventory of forms, which overlap with the subjunctive forms; for example, for formal commands (*hable, hablen*), negative informal commands (*no hables*), 'let's do it' commands (*hablemos*) and even with the indicative (*habla*). In reality, there is a very close relationship between the forms and functions of subjunctive and imperative. After all, the meaning of the imperative is to tell someone (*you*, singular and plural, sometimes including oneself) to do something. And this is also the function of the subjunctive after expressions of wish and will, where the use of the subjunctive is mandatory:

- ¡Hable (IMP) con ella! → Quiero que hable (SUB) con ella.
  [Talk to her! → I want you to talk to her.]
- ¡Coman (IMP) con él! → Quiero que coman (SUB) con él.
  [Eat with him! → I want you to eat with him.]
- ¡No subas (IMP) al primer piso! → Quiero que no subas (SUB) al primer piso.
  [Don't go up to the first floor! → I want you not to go up to the first floor.]

Even if there are several formal differences between the imperative and the subjunctive (for example, the position of pronouns and the difference between formal and informal commands), it is very likely that small children and second-language learners of Spanish first hear the 'subjunctive' forms as part of direct commands, instructions, orders, directions, advice, etc. before they hear them in indirect commands, disguised as expressions of will and wishes. Taking into account the similarities in meaning and form, it would be foolish not to use this parallelism and combine the following pairs of direct and indirect commands, such as in teacher talk that is meant to prepare Spanish learners for the more sophisticated uses of the subjunctive.

- ¡Abren los libros! → Quiero que abren los libros.
  [Open your books! → I want you to open your books.]

7.6 The conditional

Some authors, such as Porto Dapena (1991: 52), assign the conditional, also called potential, the status of secondary moods. Others consider it part of the indicative paradigm. However, there are good reasons to consider the conditional as halfway between the indicative and the subjunctive. First of all, the conditional is mostly used in subordinated clauses, and is considered a relative tense by the NGLE/M (2010: 449) and in other grammars.[10] Its main use is in conditional if-clauses and as a 'past future' ('pospretérito' in Bello's tense system) or a future seen from the past:

- Te ayudaría si tuviera tiempo. (condicional)
  [I would help you if I had time.]
- Juan me dice que vendrá mañana. → Juan me dijo que vendría mañana. (pospretérito) [Juan tells me that he will come tomorrow. → Juan told me that he would come tomorrow.]

Only rarely it is used in stand-alone sentences:

- ¿Qué hora era cuando vino Juan? → Serían las tres. (≈Probablemente eran las tres.) [What time was it when Juan came? → It must have been around three. (It was probably at three.)]
- Yo no diría eso.
  [I wouldn't say that.]
- Deberías trabajar más.
  [You should work more.]

As with the subjunctive, by using the conditional, a speaker expresses a certain attitude. S/he presents an event as dependent on a condition, as potential or as a possibility. Rather than considering the conditional as representing a separate mood by itself, many authors prefer to speak about a modal use of the conditional.

The same could be said about the future that can also be used to express uncertainty, possibility or approximation, such as in:

* ¿Qué hora es? → Serán las seis. (≈ Probablemente son las seis.)
  [What time is it? It's probably six o'clock. (≈ It is probably six o'clock.)

The closeness with certain uses of the subjunctive is probably the reason why, mostly in colloquial or regional speech, the conditional is used instead of the past subjunctive. According to the NGLE/M (2010: 449–450), in some varieties of conversational Spanish in Chile, in the Rio de la Plata region, in the Andes, in southern Colombia and parts of northern Spain, it is not rare to hear *si llovería pronto* instead of *si lloviera pronto* and the conditional instead of the subjunctive in final and adverb clauses of time such as *para que sería más cómodo* and *Se lo diría cuando tendría la ocasion.* Outside of these areas, the use of the conditional in this kind of clause is not recommended.

Notes

1 For the differences, see Bejarano (1962), Bolinger (1956), Carbonero Cano (1990), DeMello (1993), Goldberg (1991), Hermerén (1992), Lemon (1925), Lunn/Cravens (1991), Mallo (1947), Merrill (1987), Rodriguez-Ford/ Georgalas (1983), Rojo (1996), Schmidely (1992), Serrano (1996), Wright (1926a, 1926b, 1929, 1933), etc.
2 See NGLE (Manual) (2010: 455ff).
3 There is an ongoing discussion about the nature and status of adverb clauses in the contemporary literature. The NGLE, for example, doesn't have a separate chapter about modality in adverb clauses and treats them under the heading 'Elección del modo con las partículas – Elección del modo con las conjunciones subordinantes' (NGLE [Manual], 2009: 487).
4 Alarcos Llorach (1978: 262) remarks that if the clause is not in subject position, *el hecho de que* sounds more natural than *el que.*
5 This example is taken from Mejías-Bikandi (2014: 651).
6 In Mexico, the form *a la mejor* is also common. According to Butt/ Benjamin, *a lo mejor*, which means 'perhaps', "virtually never takes the subjunctive in Spain, and only occasionally in Latin America. It is heard everywhere on both continents, but it is confined to spoken language or informal writing" (2013:248).
7 Both forms can be found.
8 According to Butt/ Benjamin (2013: 248), only in Spain. They also mention *de repente* (especially in Peru) and *por ahí* (Argentina).
9 For the treatment of the imperative by the Real Academia de la Lengua Española, see also Fukushima (2013: 31–48).
10 For the treatment of the conditional by the Real Academia de la Lengua Española, see also Fukushima (2013: 31–48).

8 The sequence of tenses of the subjunctive

The subjunctive is a relative and dependent mood. Therefore, which subjunctive tense is used in the dependent clause is due particularly to the tense of the main verb and the chronology of events in the main and dependent clause. Nevertheless, there are cases where the subordinated verb refers directly to time, such as in relative clauses.

Logically, the event in the dependent clause can be before, after or at the same time as the main event. However, there are other factors that predetermine the relation between the main and subordinated event, such as the actual meaning of the main and subordinate verb, as well as other contextual elements (i.e. adverbs and other expressions of time).

After verbs of volition, order, request, advice and similar expressions, which are always followed by the subjunctive, and which can be considered the centre of expressions requiring the use of the subjunctive, the most common being *querer*, the chronology is clear: logically, the tense of the subordinated verb must always signal posteriority.

- Quiero que usted <u>sea</u> (SUB PRES) el director.
  [I want you to be the director.]
- Quería que usted <u>fuera</u> (SUB PAST) el director.
  [I wanted you to be the director.]

All other expressions triggering the subjunctive (for example *dudar*, *esperar*, *preferir*, *alegrarse*, *lamentar*, *ser posible*, etc.) can be combined with events that happen simultaneously, after and before the main event.

- Dudo que <u>compren</u> (SUB PRES) ropa el domingo en Vallirana. (AFTER) <CREA> [I doubt that they buy clothes on Sunday in Villarana.]
- Dudo que <u>haya</u> actualmente un cantante con más capacidad de comunicación emocional que Cecilia Bartoli. (SIMULTANEOUSLY) <CREA> [I doubt that there is a singer with more emotional communication skills than Cecilia Bartoli.]

- "Dudo que pudiera hacerse algo para impedir el accidente." Gonzalo vio el cadáver de su hermano, traje gris. (BEFORE) <CREA> [I doubt that anything could be done to prevent the accident.]
- Dudo que la fama haya afectado mi trabajo. (BEFORE/SIMULTANEOUSLY) <CREA> [I doubt that fame has affected my work.]

The present subjunctive (*hable*) covers the domains of simultaneity and posteriority. Because the present subjunctive can refer to both the present and future, it sometimes is difficult to distinguish both.

- "Esperamos que sea así, como dice el alcalde." (PRESENT/FUTURE?) <CREA> [We hope that it is/will be as the mayor says.]
- Esperamos que sus hermanos lo repitan. (FUTURE) <CREA> [We hope that his brothers will repeat it.]

The imperfect subjunctive (*hablara/hablase*) has only very limited reference to time and can be combined with events that happen simultaneously, after and before the main event. The present perfect mostly signals anteriority, but can also be combined with events that happen simultaneously and after the main event. Finally, the past perfect subjunctive signals anteriority. Only under very specific conditions can it indicate posteriority.[1]

The possible relation between the tenses in the main clause and the four subjunctive tenses is summarized in Table 8.1:

Table 8.1

Tense in the main clause	Tense in the subjunctive clause	Example	Chronology with respect to the main clause
Imperative	Present	• dile que suba a darme un beso en la frente y que se vaya [tell him to come up and give me a kiss … and to leave] <CREA>	posterior
	Present	• Supongamos que en Chile cambie la estructura tributaria y algunos impuestos suban. [Let's suppose that the tax code in Chile changes and that some taxes go up.] <CREA>	posterior/ simultaneous
	Past	• Supongamos que la única regla del concurso fuera la de atenerse a criterios reales y sencillos. [Let's suppose that the only rule in the contest was to stick to real and simple criteria.] <CREA>	posterior/ simultaneous
	Present	• Supongamos que en vez de planetas estemos hablando de naciones de la Tierra. [Let's suppose that instead of planets we are talking about nations on Earth.] <CREA>	simultaneous

Tense in the main clause	Tense in the subjunctive clause	Example	Chronology with respect to the main clause
	Past	• Celebra que ganaras el premio.[2] [Be happy that you won the price.]	anterior
	Past Perfect	• Supongamos que hubiera muerto de repente.[3] [Let's suppose that s/he has died suddenly.]	anterior
Present	Present	• Dudo que Juan venga mañana. [I doubt that Juan is going to come tomorrow.]	posterior
	Present Perfect	• Espero que hayas leído el libro dentro de una semana. [I hope that you read the book within one week.]	
	Past	• Dudo que su marido llegara a ganar tanto en un mes. [I doubt that her husband has managed to win that much in one month.]	posterior
	Present	• Dudo que Juan esté enfermo hoy. [I doubt that Juan is sick today.]	simultaneous
	Past	• A cambio, le regalé una pluma de mi pavo real. Dudo que hubiera una pluma más linda que ésa. [In exchange, I gave him a feather from my peacock. I doubt that there is a nicer feather than that one.] <CREA>	simultaneous
	Present Perfect	• Dudo que Juan haya venido ayer. [I doubt that Juan came yesterday.]	anterior
	Past	• El PP niega que intentara un contacto con ETA tras el atentado. [The PP denies to have contacted ETA after the attack.] <CREA>	anterior
	Past Perfect	• Dudo que Peckinpah hubiera filmado Duelo en la Alta Sierra o Grupo salvaje, tal y como las conocemos. [I doubt that Peckinpah has filmed Duelo in the Alta Sierra...] <CREA>	anterior
Future	Present	• Los padres querrán que vuelva a casa pronto. [The parents will want him/her to come back home soon.]	posterior
	Present	• Lo que ocurre es que a esta gente también le gustará que haya programas formativos, si no para ellos sí para que los vean sus hijos. [What happens is that these people also like that there are educational programmes...] <CREA>	simultaneous
	Present Perfect	• El señor González negará que nos haya aconsejado eso. [Mr. González will deny that he has given us this advice.] <CREA>	anterior

(*Continued*)

Table 8.1 Continued

Tense in the main clause	Tense in the subjunctive clause	Example	Chronology with respect to the main clause
	Past Perfect	• Les apenerá que por aquel entonces ya te hubieras quedado sin dinero.[4] [They will be sorry that back then you were already broke.]	anterior
Present Perfect	Present	• Chillida ha querido que su obra, la que le represente en el tiempo, quede aquí, en su País Vasco. [Chillida wanted his work . . . to stay here . . .] <CREA>	simultaneous/ posterior
	Past	• Dios ha querido que yo viviera después de ese accidente. [God wanted me to live after this accident.] <CREA>	simultaneous/ posterior
	Present Perfect	• el consejero. . . , ha negado que. . . se haya dicho que exista una clasificación de la mascota. [the adviser denied that someone said that there would be a classification. . . .] <CREA>	anterior
Past (Preterit, Imperfect)	Present	• Alvarez Cascos señaló que es necesario crear una comisión parlamentaria que investigue a fondo los casos de soborno denunciados recientemente y dudó/dudaba que el PSOE consienta en ello. [Alvaez Cascos . . . doubted that the PSOE agreed to it.] <CREA>	posterior
	Past	• cuando llamó con los nudillos a la habitación número veintiuno dudó que verdaderamente fuera a abrirle Lucrecia. [s/he doubted that Lucrecia really was going to open him.] <CREA>	posterior
	Present	• El letrado dudó/dudaba que la Interpol se dedique a buscar al sacerdote, ni que Sanabre pueda verse afectado por una posible petición de extradición. [The attorney doubted that Interpol was going to look for the priest and that Sanabre would be faced with the possibility of an extradition request.] <CREA>	simultaneous
	Past	• Julio López Hernández le consideró un pintor "bien dotado", aunque dudó/ dudaba que mereciera el galardón. [Julio López Hernández considered him a 'well endowed' painter even if he doubted that he deserved the recognition.] <CREA>	simultaneous

Tense in the main clause	Tense in the subjunctive clause	Example	Chronology with respect to the main clause
	Present Perfect	• Otro experto en interceptaciones dijo que el trasmisor parecía algo de la década de los 70 y dudó/dudaba que algo tan antiguo haya sido usado por los servicios de seguridad en los últimos años. [Another expert . . . doubted that something that old had been used by the security services in the last years.] <CREA>	anterior
	Past Perfect	• El general . . . dudaba que hubiera tenido el valor de tomar la iniciativa y dirigirse al Presidente. [The General doubted that he had had the courage to address the president.] <CREA>	anterior
Conditional	Present	• ayer insistía en que sería bueno que el presidente despeje hoy mismo esa incógnita. [yesterday s/he insisted that it would be good if the president resolved this mystery today.] <CREA>	posterior
	Past	• sería bueno que los partidos se pusieran de acuerdo. [it would be good if the parties agreed.] <CREA>	posterior
	Past	• desearía que Selena aún estuviera viva. [I wished Selena were still alive.] <CREA>	simultaneous
	Present Perfect	• -Me alegraría que Nieves no se haya equivocado -dijo mamá Paulina. [I would be happy if Nieves were wrong.]<CREA>	anterior
	Past Perfect	• Pero le gustaría que el club le hubiera firmado la ampliación de contrato. [But s/he would be happy if the club had signed the extension of the contract.] <CREA>	anterior
Past Perfect	Present	• Hasta hace poco esa prueba había hecho que lo procesen por traficar drogas. [Until recently, this evidence had caused that they processed him for drug trafficking.] <CREA>	posterior
	Past	• el Gobierno español había querido que esta primera reunión bilateral fuera precisamente con Francia. [the Spanish government wanted this first bilateral meeting to be precisely with France.] <CREA>	posterior
	Past Perfect	• nadie había negado que el Pentágono haya entrenado a oficiales del batallón 3–16. [nobody negated that the Pentagon trained officers of battalion 3–16.] <CREA>	anterior

Table 8.1 Continued

Tense in the main clause	Tense in the subjunctive clause	Example	Chronology with respect to the main clause
Conditional Perfect	Past	• No di el paso que habría hecho que se abrieran las puertas automáticas del vestíbulo. [I didn't take the step that would have caused the automatic doors of the lobby to open.] <CREA>	posterior
	Past Perfect	• cosa que habría hecho que las "cosas no hubieran ido tan lejos." [a thing that would had caused that 'things didn't go that far'.] <CREA>	anterior

Notes

1 This is only the case in (pseudo)independent uses, such as 'Ojalá el año que viene hablara español con soltura' and certain counterfactual adverb clauses, such as 'Aunque saliera ahora mismo, no le podría abordar.'
2 Example from Borrego et al. (2003: 22).
3 Example from Borrego et al. (2003: 22).
4 Example from Borrego et al. (2003: 23).

9 The grammatical function of dependent subjunctive clauses

By now it should be clear that we will fail when we try to define the subjunctive in purely semantic and pragmatic terms. I have tried to show that moods are morpho-syntactic categories and that the subjunctive is the mood of subordination. Therefore, it is important to teach learners the exact structure and functions of dependent noun, adjective and adverb clauses so that they don't make the following mistakes:

- *Me sorpresa la paciencia que usted <u>tenga</u> (SUB). OR
  *[I am surprised about the patience that you having.]
- *Probablemente Juan <u>esté</u> (SUB) enfermo. OR
  *[Probably Juan be sick.]
- *Si <u>tenga</u> (SUB) dinero, iré a España.
  *[If I having money, I will go to Spain.]

9.1 Noun clauses

Noun clauses have the function of direct objects, prepositional objects or subjects of verbs and are embedded in main clauses. Together, both form complex sentences.

- Lamento <u>que hayas fracasado</u>. [I am sorry that you have failed.] (**What** do I lament? = **direct object**)
- No se satisface **<u>con que solo apruebe la mitad de los alumnos.</u>** [S/he is not satisfied with only half of the students passing.] (**With what** is s/he not satisfied? = **prepositional object**.)
- Le fastidia <u>que reaccionemos así</u>. [It bothers him/her that we react this way.] (**What** does bother him/her? = **subject**)

The conjunction '*que*' signals that the clause has the same function as a noun, and therefore it can often be replaced by a noun:

- Lamento <u>tu fracaso</u>. [I am sorry about your failure.]
- No se satisface **<u>con la mitad de los alumnos.</u>** [S/he is not satisfied with half of the students.]
- Le fastidia <u>nuestra reacción</u>. [S/he is bothered by our reaction.]

Syntactically, semantically and pragmatically, the noun (clause) is part of the main predicate. Without the noun (clause), the sentence is incomplete:

- *Lamento. (What?)
- *No se satisface. (With what?)
- Le fastidia. (What?)

The interdependence and close relationship is the reason why the noun clause is under the influence of the main clause:

- Es indudable que Juan está enfermo. [It is undeniable that Juan is sick.] (As an object of 'ser indudable', 'Juan está enfermo' is presented as a fact.)
- Es posible que Juan esté enfermo. [It is possible that Juan is sick.] (As an object of 'ser posible, 'Juan esté enfermo' is presented as a possibility and not as a fact.)

Noun clauses are different from adverb/circumstantial clauses where the dependent clause is optional and only adds additional information:

- Me alegro de que hayas venido. [I am glad that you came.] → *Me alegro de. [*I am happy about.] (missing necessary information= what?)
- Me alegra que hayas venido. [I am glad that you came.] → *Me alegra. [*Pleases me.] (missing necessary information= what?)
- Me alegro porque has venido. [I am glad because you came.] → Me alegro. [I am happy.] (additional optional information = why?)

The contextual meaning of *alegrarse* in the first two sentences is 'Your coming makes me happy' and in the third 'I am happy because you came.' In the last one, a fact is presented as the reason for my state of mind, and in the first two, the coming is the subject or object of my state of mind. Without it, there is no such state of mind. Let's take another example. The noun clause in the next example is the object of *quiero* and necessary to complete the action of the verb. At the same time, *quiero* characterizes the dependent clause as a wish and not as a fact. *Que vengas a verme* only exists as the object of *quiero* and without it, it is non-existent.

- Quiero que vengas a verme. [I want you to come see me.] → *Quiero. [*I want.] (missing necessary information= what?)
- Te quiero porque vienes a verme. [I like you because you come see me.] → Te quiero. (additional optional information = why?)

The interdependence is also the reason for the different contextual meaning of the verb *decir* in the following examples:

- Le digo a Juan que vaya a limpiar el baño. (Le mando que limpie el baño.) [I tell Juan to go and clean the bathroom. (I order him to clean the bathroom.)]

- Le digo a Juan que va a limpiar el baño. (Le informo que va a limpiar el baño.) [I tell Juan that he will clean the bathroom. (I inform him that he will clean the bathroom.)]

The difference between noun clauses and circumstantial clauses also explains the mood choice in the following examples:

- Me molesta que siempre fumes. [It bothers me that you always smoke.] (NOUN CLAUSE)
- Me molesta si siempre fumas. (Siempre fumas. Esto me molesta.) [It bothers me if you always smoke. (You always smoke. This bothers me.)] [CIRCUMSTANTIAL CLAUSE]
- Le enfada que siempre le critiquen. [It makes him/her mad that they always criticize him/her.] [NOUN CLAUSE]
- Le enfada porque siempre le critican. (Siempre le critican. Eso le enfada.) [It makes him/her mad because they always criticize him/her. (They always criticize him/her. This makes him/her mad.)]. [CIRCUMSTANTIAL CLAUSE]

9.1.1 Verbs and expressions that are followed by the subjunctive in noun clauses

Because it is not the abstract meaning of a verb, noun or adjective that can prompt the subjunctive, but its actual meaning and how it is used in a specific (con)text, it is difficult to group verbs and verbal expressions according to semantic categories. There are no clearly defined limits between the following groups and many intersections.

Generally speaking, all verbs and expressions that characterize the content of a subordinated noun clause, not as absolute and independent statements or declarations of the speaker and sentence subject about some parcel of reality, but as only belonging to and being originated by the sentence subject, can theoretically be used with the subjunctive. The use of the subjunctive indicates that there is a difference between what is assumed and manifested by the sentence subject versus what other people assume or may think; for example, opposition in combination with *dudar* and *no creer*, but also with *querer*, which expresses the wish of the sentence subject that the content of the noun clause be different. This includes expressions of emotions which state that the content of the noun clause is not an independent fact, but the very personal feeling of the sentence subject. This means we can find the subjunctive not only in combination with wishes, orders, aspirations, hopes, needs, suggestions, advice, opposition, disagreement, doubts, but also with feelings and other attitudes of the sentence subject. Here are some examples:

- Sé que Juan vendrá mañana. → Juan vendrá mañana. [I know that Juan will come tomorrow. → Juan will come tomorrow.] (INDEPENDENT STATEMENT)
- María cree que Juan vendrá mañana. → Juan vendrá mañana. [Maria thinks that Juan will come tomorrow. → Juan will come tomorrow.] (INDEPENDENT STATEMENT)

- Estoy convencido de que Juan <u>vendrá</u> mañana. → Juan <u>vendrá</u> mañana. [I am convinced that Juan will come tomorrow. → Juan will come tomorrow.] (INDEPENDENT STATEMENT)
- Quiero que Juan <u>venga</u> mañana. ≠ Juan <u>vendrá</u> mañana. [I want Juan to come tomorrow. ≠ Juan will come tomorrow.] (WISH)
- Dudo que Juan <u>venga</u> mañana. ≠ Juan <u>vendrá</u> mañana. [I doubt that Juan will come tomorrow. ≠ Juan will come tomorrow.] (DOUBT.
- Es posible que Juan <u>venga</u> mañana. ≠ Juan <u>vendrá</u> mañana. [It is possible that Juan will come tomorrow. ≠ Juan will come tomorrow.] (POSSIBILITY)
- Temo que Juan <u>venga</u> mañana. ≠ Juan <u>vendrá</u> mañana. [I am afraid that Juan will come tomorrow. ≠ Juan will come tomorrow.] (NEGATIVE FEELING, NEGATIVE WISH)
- Me alegro (de) que Juan <u>venga</u> mañana. ≠ Juan <u>vendrá</u> mañana. [I am glad that Juan will come tomorrow. ≠ Juan will come tomorrow.] (POSITIVE FEELING, POSITIVE WISH)

Accordingly, verbs or expressions that rule the subjunctive are often divided into the following categories:[1]

9.1.1.1   Wishes and orders

The prototypical verb of this group is **querer**. It is not only the archetype of the group because of its frequency, but also because *querer que* is **always** followed by the subjunctive.

- Raúl quiere que María se lo diga a sus amigos.
  [Raul wants Maria to tell it to her/his friends.]

If there is only one subject in the sentence, it means that the main and the dependent subject are the same. In this case, instead of a noun clause with *que*, **the infinitive is used**. However, not all the verbs in this group can be used with the infinitive:

- Raúl quiere ir al cine. [Raúl wants to go to the movies.] (Raul wants it and he carries it out.)
- Ellos desean ir al cine. [They wish to go to the movies.] (They wish it and carry it out.)

Other verbs and expressions in this group are:

---

aconsejar que, dar el consejo que, aspirar a que, autorizar que, la autorización de que, azuzar a que, confiar en que, contentarse con que, estar contento con/ de que, decidirse a que, estar decidido a que, demandar que, desear que, estar deseoso de que, (con/tener) el deseo de que, disponer que, empeñarse en que, (con/en) el empeño de que, encantar que, estar encantado de que, esforzarse por que, esperar que, (con/tener) la esperanza de que, exigir que, (con/tener) ganas de que, gustar que, ilusionar que, estar ilusionado con que, (tener) la ilusión de que, ser importante que, intentar que, (con/tener) la intención de que, insistir en que, luchar por que, mandar que, necesitar que, ordenar que, (con) el orden de que, ser partidario de que, pedir que, (aceptar/con/hacer/mantener/ser/ . . .) la petición de que, permitir que, preferir que, pretender que, procurar que, proponer que, estar resuelto a que, recomendar que, requerir que, resolver que, rogar que, satisfacer que, estar satisfecho de que, solicitar que, la solicitud de que, sugerir que, (ante/con/emitir/oír/ser/ . . .) la sugerencia de que, suplicar que, tratar que, urgir que, el visto bueno de que, (con/tener) la voluntad de que, etc.

They all share the element **<Intention>** of the speaker or subject

Most of the verbs in this group are polysemous, which means they can acquire slightly different meanings in different contexts. *Admitir,*[2] *advertir, proponer, sugerir* and others, for example, can also be used to simply communicate a fact and not an intention of the speaker. On the other hand, many verbs that indicate how information or facts are transmitted (for example *comunicar, decir, dejar, saber, escribir, informar, notificar,* etc.) can be used to express wishes and orders:

- Y luego voy yo, que soy la tercera, que tengo veinte años, aunque la gente dice que no los aparento. <CREA> (COMMUNICATION = FACT) [And then I will go. I am the third one and I am twenty, even though people say that I look younger.]
- Le digo: . . . ¿y usted lo metió ahí? Sí. no, entonces usted maneja muy bien. Que si el señor me dice que lo saque, ahí estuviéramos todavía. <CREA> (COMMAND = NOT A FACT) [If the man hadn't told me to get him out, we would still be in it.]
- Muchos de estos pacientes informan que a veces se hallan ellos mismos en un círculo repetitivo de acciones o pensamientos. <CREA> (COMMUNICATION = FACT) [Many of these patients tell us that they themselves are sometimes in a repetitious cycle of thoughts.]
- Atención compositores, nos informan que estén atentos para que puedan recoger las bases del Festival de la Amazonía que se desarrollará en la segunda semana de julio. <CREA> (COMMAND/SUGGESTION = NOT A FACT) [we were informed that you should be attentive.]
- El plan advierte que EEUU enfrenta la peor escasez de energía desde los embargos petroleros de la década de los setenta. <CREA> (COMMUNICATION = FACT) [The plan says that the United States is facing the worst shortage of energy since the oil embargos of the seventies.]

- Los amigos le adverten que cuide su prestigio profesional, y le recomiendan que haga lo que casi todos sus compañeros de cuerpo: compatibilizar el puesto en la Administración con los negocios particulares. <CREA> (COMMAND/SUGGESTION = NOT A FACT) [Friends tell him to look after his professional reputation.]

The intersection with speech or communication verbs shouldn't surprise anyone because communication is the essence of language use. It is not very frequent, but possible to combine the element <Intention> with other expressions that are normally only used to transmit facts (things that are independent from the intention of the speaker), such as *pensar, estar pensado, tener la idea de, (tener) la opinión de, considerar, opinar, tener en cuenta*, etc.

- En este caso ha sido el Betis quien ha ofrecido un pulso a la organización, ya que inicialmente estaba pensado que participaran los dos equipos sevillanos con un tercer rival de por medio. <CREA> [initially the idea was that both teams from Sevilla plus a third one would participate.]
- La operación se aprovecha para fijar la pintura donde sea preciso y reforzar la pieza, pues se tiene la idea de que una vez llegue a su nueva ubicación se tenga que hacer sólo un repaso y alguna restauración muy concreta, según explicó Juan Bolet, jefe de restauración del museo. <CREA> [because the idea is, once it reaches its new location, all that has to be done is to inspect it and do some specific restoration]
- En su lugar, alza la característica más elocuente de su pensamiento: el pragmatismo. Así, por ejemplo, frente a la opinión de que se vayan los americanos de las bases, posición compartida por mucha gente en España, González considera que esa idea puede ser "rentable electoralmente." <CREA> [So, for example, faced with the opinion that the Americans should leave the bases, ... González thinks that]
- -Voy a traspasarle a ella algunas otras instituciones que dirijo, que está considerado que sea la señora del comandante en jefe del Ejército la que las dirija, porque están ligadas absolutamente al Ejército. <CREA> [I will transfer some of the institutions that I direct to her, because it is appropriate that the army chief's wife should run them]

Some of the verbs in this group that admit a direct and an indirect object (such as *aconsejar que, dejar que, mandar que, ordenar que, pedir que, permitir que, proponer que, recomendar que, sugerir que*, etc.) can also be followed by an infinitive if the subject of the dependent clause (s/he who is supposed to do what the main subject wants) is mentioned with a noun and/or pronoun in the main clause:

- Hierro reconoció que los técnicos le sugirieron estudiar los impactos del plomo en las pinturas y los juguetes. <CREA> [Hierro admitted that the technicians suggested that he study the impact of lead in paintings and toys.]

9.1.1.2 *Opposition, prohibition, denial, doubt*

The prototypical expression of this group is **no querer**.

- Raúl no quiere que María se lo diga a sus amigos.
  [Raúl doesn't want Maria to tell it to her/his friends.]

  Other verbs and expressions in this group are:

> *advertir que, la advertencia de que, estar asustado que, estar cansado de que,* *contrario a que, desconfiar de que, desmentir que, dudar de que, (tener) duda(s)* *de que, ser (un) error que, fastidiar que, estar harto de que, ignorar que, impedir* *que, negar que, negarse a que, la negativa a que, objetar a que, oponerse a que,* *oposición a que, (ante/correr/existir/haber/sobre/. . .) el peligro de que, preocu-* *parse de que, estar preocupado de que, prohibir que, rechazar que, rechazo a que,* *renunciar a que, resistir(se) a que, reticente a que, reticencia a que, sospechar de* *que, ser sospechoso de que, etc.*

- López, veterano jugador del equipo y verdadero corazón de la modesta junta
  directiva, que se niega a que desaparezca el equipo. <CREA> [López
  who opposes that the team may disappear.]

This group is very similar to 9.1.1.1. The only difference is the additional element
<Negation>, which explains why many verbs and expressions that normally
trigger the indicative can be used with the subjunctive if the main predicate is
negated:

- "Para ser franco, no estoy de acuerdo (con Dole)", dijo McCaffrey en una
  conferencia de prensa sobre los esfuerzos de Estados Unidos para interceptar
  cargamentos de drogas. "Yo no creo que el problema de las drogas vaya a ser
  resuelto por ningún ejército", agregó el general retirado. <CREA> [I don't
  think any army can resolve the drug problem.]
- La juventud no admite que se le esconda información y, además, es una
  cuestión de responsabilidad. <CREA> [The younger generation doesn't
  allow anyone to hide information from it.]
- Lamentablemente en el Partido Revolucionario Institucional, cuyos militantes gobiernan por hoy en la mayoría de los municipios de México, no sabemos
  que exista honestidad en esa política doctrinaria. <CREA> [Unfortunately,
  in the PRI we cannot tell if there is truth in this doctrine.]
- Y no digo que no tengan derecho a hacer eso. <CREA> [I am not saying they
  have no right to do that.]

The combination of a negation with verbs of THINKING and JUDGEMENT (such as *creer, parecer, pensar, suponer, ser probable*, etc.) causes what has traditionally been called 'negación anticipada' (anticipated negation) in Spanish grammars. With this term they describe the use of the adverb *no* in the main clause, while actually negating the dependent predicate. Instead of negating the main verb, we could also place the negation before the dependent verb:

- Yo no creo que el problema de las drogas vaya a ser resuelto por ningún ejército. (≈ Yo creo que el problema de las drogas **no va a ser resuelto** por ningún ejército.

The message of the subordinated clause would be the same: *no se va a resolver el problema.*[3] This is not the case with other verbs, such as *saber, decir* and other speech verbs:

- no sabemos que exista honestidad en esa política (≠ sabemos que no existe honestidad en esa política)
- La juventud no admite que se le esconda información (≠ La juventud admite que no se le esconde información)

The negation of expressions of opposition, prohibition, denial and doubt creates the semantic conditions for the use of the indicative, the combination with something that is represented as a fact.

- Para este banco empieza un tiempo nuevo. Y no dudo que será un tiempo de trabajo duro y de éxitos. <CREA> [I have no doubt that it will be a time of hard work and of success.]

   Still, the use of the subjunctive is not excluded:

- La imagen de los africanos hacinados y apaleados en Ceuta, . . . , parece la versión moderna de la parábola del pobre Lázaro y del rico Epulón. . . . la frontera que la separa de Marruecos con un alambrado, . . . , calificada por IU y la Asociación Pro Derechos Humanos como nuevo "muro de la vergüenza". . . . El problema – la creciente bolsa de inmigración ilegal de la ciudad norteafricana – es extraordinariamente complejo. Nadie pone en duda que se deban establecer mecanismos de control sobre el flujo de africanos que llegan, pero levantar una frontera de alambre, instalar focos y cámaras térmicas y desplegar agentes no es la solución idónea y generará, además, nuevos y graves problemas de orden público. ¿Alguien puede creerse que los desesperados inmigrantes no tratarán de cruzar la frontera? <CREA> [Nobody questions that we have to establish mechanisms to control the influx of]

Logically, if you don't question something, then you consider it true. Does that mean that the use of the subjunctive here is wrong or atypical? The answer, of course, is no. There is a reason why the author chose 'nadie pone en duda' + subjunctive instead of 'todos están de acuerdo' or 'piensan' + indicative. With the indicative – that the author could have used as well – both the noun and the main clause would have been presented as two independent and absolute statements: (1) 'Se deben establecer mecanismos de control' and (2) 'Nadie lo pone en duda.' With the subjunctive, on the other hand, the author characterizes the content of the noun clause as dependent on 'duda' or 'poner en duda'. This creates the effect of a rhetorical question, such as: '¿Hay alguien que pone en duda que se deban establecer mecanismos de control?' which is then negated. The difference between the indicative and the subjunctive could be represented as follows:

Indicative: (Nadie pone en duda) (se deben establecer mecanismos de control.)$_1$)$_2$

Subjunctive: (Nadie (pone en duda (se deban establecer mecanismos de control.)$_1$)$_2$)$_3$

9.1.1.2.1 NEGATIVE MODIFIERS IN THE MAIN CLAUSE

§1 Negative words are very powerful modifiers. They can cause many predicates that would otherwise be followed by a clause in indicative to enable the subjunctive:[4]

1) Sus miembros <u>no creen</u> que la temática <u>sea</u> exclusiva de los adultos, aún así reconocen que es un reto para cualquier artista. <CREA> <u>[Its members don't believe that the topic is exclusively an adult subject]</u>

2) Lamentablemente en el Partido Revolucionario Institucional, cuyos militantes gobiernan por hoy en la mayoría de los municipios de México, <u>no sabemos</u> que <u>exista</u> honestidad en esa política doctrinaria. <CREA> <u>[Unfortunately, in the PRI, we cannot tell that there is honesty in this doctrine.]</u>

3) Yo <u>no digo</u> que la gente <u>esté dispuesta</u> a lanzarse a una movilización armada ya, <u>no estoy diciendo</u> que la población mayoritaria <u>esté dispuesta</u> a lanzarse a la actividad guerrillera. <CREA> <u>[I am not saying that the majority of people is ready to join the guerrillas]</u>

§2 The use of the subjunctive indicates dependence of the subordinated clause upon the main clause, its predicate and subject. Its content is marked as the object of the main clause and only as an expression of the point of view of the speaker or main subject. The speaker doesn't say anything about the existence or non-existence of the content of the dependent clause. However, the negation expresses the negative attitude of the speaker. The reading in 3), for example, is: I am not SAYING that people are inclined to stage a military mobilization. Maybe they are; maybe they are not. All I am SAYING is that I am NOT SAYING that. It's the same in example 4), where the reading is: I am not SAYING that no matter of state is involved. Maybe there is, maybe there isn't. All I am SAYING is that in the brief, I don't SEE that.

4) No me afecta la cuestión de Estado, entre otras cosas porque en los hechos que conozco – y admito que puede haber muchos que desconozco – es decir, en los sumarios, no veo que esté implicada ninguna cuestión de Estado. <CREA> [in the brief I don't see that any matter of state might be involved]

§3 The same examples could also be used with the indicative, but then the reading would be: the members do NOT believe that this is a fact; we do NOT know that this is a fact; I am NOT saying that this is a fact or I am NOT saying that I see that as a fact. This implies that there IS someone who believes, knows or claims that this is a fact. The content of the subordinated clause is presented as existent independently from the (attitude, belief, wish, will, etc. of the) main subject, or as 'objective'. Here are other examples:

5) Porque si no creemos que Cristo es el Dios Hijo hecho hombre por amor al género humano, si no creemos que murió en la Cruz para pagar por los pecados del género humano, si no creemos que Cristo murió por ti y por mí y que resucitó y fue a preparar morada celestial para cada uno de los creyentes. <CREA> [Because, if we don't believe that Christ is the Son of God]

6) Esta imbécil no se cree que van a matarme. <CREA>[5] [This idiot doesn't believe that they are going to kill me.]

7) Lo que pasa es que las convenciones no saben que Guatemala es un país de 8.500.000 de personas y está enfermo. <CREA>[6] [What happens is, they don't know that Guatemala is a country of 8.500.000 people]

8) no veo que está implicada alguna[7] cuestión de Estado. <CREA> [I don't see that any matter of state might be involved.]

§4 Without the negation, only the indicative is possible:

- Sus miembros creen que la temática es exclusiva de los adultos, ...
- . . ., sabemos que existe honestidad en esa política doctrinaria.
- Yo digo que la gente está dispuesta a lanzarse a una movilización armada ya, estoy diciendo que la población mayoritaria está dispuesta a lanzarse a la actividad guerrillera, . . .
- . . ., veo que está implicada alguna cuestión de Estado.

§5 The meaning of *digo* in the previous examples is: 'communicating a fact' and of *veo* 'communicating a perception'. Both meanings are incompatible with the interpretation of the noun clause as non-factual, non-existent or uncertain.

§6 The negation can be expressed with the adverb *no*, but also with other negative adverbial and pronominal expressions, such as *nunca, jamás, tampoco, nada, nadie, ninguno*, etc. Furthermore, it can be modified with other words that reduce the factuality of the noun clause, such as *casi, (muy) poco, solo*, etc.

9) por supuesto, ninguno cree que seamos capaces de pasar de Santiago de Chile, con o sin moto. <CREA> [nobody believes that we may be able to get there from Santiago de Chile]

10) Escucho atento ese improvisado concierto y nunca pienso que eso pueda ser "ruido". <CREA> [I listen attentively to this improvised concert and I definitely don't think that this could be just 'noise'.]

11) De nuevo, estos son datos generacionales (. . .) y nada demuestra que vaya a seguir ocurriendo de esta forma. <CREA> [and nothing shows that this is going to continue like this]

12) Sin embargo, nadie dice que el amor no sepa navegar por internet. <CREA> [However, nobody says that love might not be able to navigate through the Internet.]

13) Si las comisiones parlamentarias claves quedan en manos demócratas, es casi seguro que las cosas se le compliquen gravemente a Colombia, . . . <CREA> [it is almost certain that things will be a lot more complicated for Colombia]

14) Sin embargo, muy pocos creen que el nivel futbolístico de Hernán Darío Gómez y sus dirigidos supere en resultados a Paraguay, Uruguay y Colombia. <CREA> [However, as far as results go, very few people believe that the level of soccer of Hernán Darío Gómez and his players exceeds those of Paraguay, Uruguay and Colombia.]

15) Solo tiene un amigo que sea verdaderamente inteligente.[8] <CREA> [S/he has only one friend who is really intelligent.]

16) En toda la historia de la cárcel una sola vez se dio el caso de que presos comunes participaran con la guarnición dando golpes a un grupo de los nuestros en la prisión de Guanajay. <CREA> [In the entire history of the jail there was only one case in which the common prisoners joined the garrison in hitting a group of ours]

§7 Other negative expressions in the main clause that can trigger the subjunctive are *no ser que, negarse a, ser/resultar difícil, absurdo, imposible, utópico, inconcebible*, etc. and have the same effect as a simple negation with *no*:[9]

17) El infiltrado me parece una novela muy restringida en términos históricos, y no es que crea que escribir sobre un determinado período sea un problema. (no es que crea = no creo)[10] <CREA> [not that I think that writing about a certain period may be a problem]

18) Bueno, Ofelia, lo siento, pero me niego a creer que a las mujeres lo que verdaderamente nos gustan sean los sinvergüenzas. <CREA> (me niego a creer = no creo que) [I'm sorry, but I refuse to believe that what woman really like are scoundrels]

19) Pero en esta ocasión, con las fuerzas tan parejas, es difícil pensar que haya cambios. <CREA> (es difícil pensar que = no pienso que) [it is difficult to think that there may be changes]

20) Hay una confusión, en algunas personas, . . . , que consideran que se pagó menos que el precio de mercado, lo cual es absurdo pensar que pueda ocurrir. <CREA> (es absurdo pensar que = no pienso que) [it is absurd to believe that this could happen]

21) resulta casi utópico pensar que nuestras administraciones puedan entender planteamientos de este tipo. <CREA> (resulta casi utópico

pensar = no pensamos que) [it is almost utopian to think that our administrations could understand this kind of proposal]

22) Llega a ser enteramente imposible, hasta inconcebible, pensar que hombres públicos, . . . , actúen aislados de la vida pública, que no tengan interés por los asuntos públicos de suma importancia como lo es la solución de la propiedad. <CREA> (llega a ser imposible = no pensar que) [It is completely impossible, even unimaginable, to think that a public person . . . could act independently from public life, and that s/he might not be interested in public affairs]

§8   Also the combination of the main predicate with *soler*[11] can enable the subjunctive:

23) Aunque también suele acontecer que por efectos de la prolongada hibernación del Poder parezca inerte y como obnubilado y que sus primeros pasos sean vacilantes y sin dirección como los de quien despierta de una larga pesadilla. <CREA> [due to the effects of prolonged hibernation of the POWER, it seems that its first steps are sometimes unsteady and aimless, like someone awakening from a long nightmare]

24) Además, suele suceder que hacia el atardecer o la noche se despierten llorando. <CREA> [it happens at nightfall or during the night that they wake up crying]

25) Ambas éticas, . . . , poseen su racionalidad respectiva, pero suele acaecer que sus representantes más militantes se la nieguen mutuamente. <CREA> [but it happens that both of its most militant representatives deny it]

§9   The negation can also be very indirect as in the following examples:

26) La Huerta de Juan Fernández tenía libre su acceso al pueblo de Madrid, que la había convertido en uno de sus predilectos lugares de esparcimiento, hasta que la Duquesa, reivindicando viejos derechos de propiedad, consiguió recuperarla y levantar en él su palacio de Buenavista. Esa actitud fue enormemente impopular y se dio el caso de que un personaje tan querido del pueblo madrileño como la Duquesa, viera de repente su nombre vituperado en pasquines que ni la Inquisición ni el Rey pudieron evitar se fijaran. <CREA> [This attitude was highly unpopular, and it happened that the Duchess, who was beloved by the people of Madrid, suddenly found her name mocked in little parodies that neither the Inquisition nor the King could stop from circulating.]

Here, the counterfacticity of *viera de repente su nombre vituperado* is the result of the fact that, otherwise, the duchess was a beloved person, with a good name, in the little village that would later become Madrid. This can also be observed in the next sample taken from Almudena Grandes, El lector de Julio Verne, Barcelona: Tusquets Editores, pages 362/63, and in similar cases that at first look seem to be clearly factual:

•   En el umbral de la puerta estaba mi hermana Dulce, y tenía los ojos llenos de lágrimas, aunque siempre nos hubiéramos llevado fatal. Al pasar a su lado, le cogí la mano y me la apretó [and her eyes were full or tears, although we probably never had gotten along well]

Here, again, the speaker says something which is not entirely true – and therefore s/he uses the subjunctive to express this, indirectly – because if it were true, the sister wouldn't have her eyes full of tears.

§10 The negation does not have the same effect on dependent clauses that would otherwise require the subjunctive:

- Quiero que venga. → No quiero que venga. (*No quiero que viene.)
- Es posible que haya venido. → Es imposible que haya venido. (*Es imposible que ha venido.)
- Me alegro que haya venido. → No me alegro que haya venido. (*No me alegro que ha venido.)
- Eso hace que venga mucha gente, . . . → Eso no hace que venga mucha gente, . . . (* Eso no hace que viene mucha gente, . . .)

§11 Exceptions are the already 'negative' verbs *dudar, poner en duda, negar, ignorar, desconocer, desmentir, objetar* and similar expressions. The negation can create the semantic conditions for the use of the indicative, the combination with something that is represented as a fact.

27) Para este banco empieza un tiempo nuevo. Y no dudo que será un tiempo de trabajo duro y de éxitos. <CREA> [I don't doubt that it will be a time of hard work and of success.]

§12 This, however doesn't happen automatically. The fact that the negation is not part of the nucleus of the main predicate offers the user the chance to consider it an independent and external modifier that doesn't modify, primarily, the meaning of the main predicate, but, secondarily, the combination of main and dependent predicate. In the following examples the subjunctive is used because it depends on the verb *dudo* and not on *no dudo*.

28) Desde luego, yo no dudo que al presidente de la república le preocupe la atención de los sectores más desfavorecidos de la población, ni de la voluntad política que lo condujo a establecer un programa piloto de atención integral – en materia de salud y educación – con el que se beneficiaría, llegando al año 2000, nada menos que a cuatro millones de las familias más pobres del país: algo así como a 20 millones de mexicanos. Tampoco dudo de que se distribuyan más de 2.5 millones de desayunos escolares por día, se apoye a cinco millones de niños para el consumo de leche, etc. Lo que yo creo – y de esto existen abundantes pruebas – es que la orientación, los alcances y la cobertura de la política social (de cuyos dos rubros fundamentales me he ocupado en estos comentarios) se encuentran en la actualidad severamente limitados por el contenido antipopular y leonino de la política económica de corte neoliberal, a la cual insiste en aferrarse la actual administración federal. [I personally don't doubt that the president of the republic is worried about the attention given to the most underprivileged sectors of the population . . . Neither do I doubt that everyday

more than 2.5 million breakfasts are distributed in schools, that 5 million
children get help to be able to drink milk, etc.]

29) Yo no dudo que en toda administración <u>haya necesidad</u> de racionalizar
el gasto. Creo que todos los gobiernos tienen como obligación y como
práctica ir cada vez más racionalizando el gasto, no al grado como ha
pasado en el Distrito Federal en donde hay más de dos mil millones de
pesos a diciembre no gastados y, sin embargo, hay aumentos de impuestos. En fin, esas cosas a veces uno no las comprende fácilmente, pero
debe haber alguna razón de que no se haya ejercido ese gasto autorizado
y que, a pesar de ello, se estén solicitando para el próximo año algo
más de siete mil quinientos millones de pesos en deuda tan solo para el
Distrito Federal. [I personally don't doubt that in every administration
there is a need to rationalize costs.]

Even though it is not difficult to find examples with *no dudar que* or *no poner en
duda* with the subjunctive in political speeches and literary texts, it must be said
that this use is rather unusual and stilted. The purpose is to achieve a rhetorical
effect. In example 28), the author answers a fictitious question, 'Duda Ud. que al
presidente de la república le <u>preocupe</u> la atención de los sectores más desfavorecidos de la población, . . . , <u>se distribuyan</u> más de 2.5 millones de desayunos escolares por día, <u>se apoye</u> a cinco millones de niños para el consumo de leche, etc.',
implying that there may be doubt. The reasons for that are given at the end of the
paragraph: 'el contenido antipopular y leonino de la política económica de corte
neoliberal'. By using the subjunctive, the writer creates an ambiguous message:
On one hand, s/he says 'I don't doubt all this', but on the other, s/he says that s/
he (or other people) still have doubts, and that there seems to be a contradiction.

9.1.1.2.2   THE ROLE OF INTERROGATION IN THE MAIN CLAUSE

§13   In practice, questions and question words rarely trigger the subjunctive in a
dependent clause. In combination with *creer, pensar* and similar verbs such
as *considerar*, the subjunctive marks the content of the dependent clause, the
question per se, as an option, a possibility. What we are asking is: Do you
believe in this possibility, why do you believe in it, what are the reasons, etc.?

30) Leroy, ¿tú crees que nos <u>ataquen</u> otra vez? <CREA> [Leroy, do YOU[12]
think that they might attack us again?]

31) ¿Por qué piensa que <u>sea</u> eso? <CREA> [Why do YOU think that it
might be this?]

32) J. R.- ¿Y a qué crees que <u>se deba</u>: el tener interés por trasmitir un mensaje concreto o simplemente que dominas más la escena? <CREA>
[And what do YOU think might be the reason: . . . ?]

§14   The subjunctive is more likely to be used in negative questions:

33) Pero ¿tú no consideras que para Bolivia, entonces, esa salida al mar <u>sea</u>
esencialmente <u>básica</u> para su desarrollo? <CREA> [But don't YOU

think that for Bolivia this access to the open sea might be basic to its development?]

34) ¿No crees que la composición te limite como cantante? <CREA> [Don't YOU think that the composition limits you as a singer?]

§15 Because the purpose of yes/no questions in general is to find out whether something is a fact/true or not, the indicative is much more frequent:

35) ¿Tú crees que te voy a esperar cada noche como tonta? <CREA> [Do you think I will wait every night like an idiot?]

36) Pero, ¿piensas que las creencias religiosas son necesarias? <CREA> [But do you think that religious beliefs are necessary?]

37) ¿Por qué crees que tiene tanto éxito en Venezuela? <CREA> [Why do you think s/he has so much success in Venezuela?]

38) ¿No crees que él lo mató? ¿Quizás accidentalmente? <CREA> [Don't you think that s/he killed him?]

§16 Therefore, the indicative is always used with *¿Sabes que . . .?*

39) ¿Y sabes que esta Adela y Pili hicieron un desfile de disfraces? <CREA> [Did you know that Adela and Pila were in a costume parade?]

§17 The same goes for the verb *parecer* with the meaning of *creer*.

40) ANA. – ¿Y a vos te parece que yo puedo estar tranquila? <CREA> [Do you think that I can be quiet?]

§18 If *parecer* is used with the subjunctive, it has the meaning of *querer*:

41) Vicente, ¿te parece que ahora entremos ya de lleno al tema del deporte? <CREA> [Vicente, should we already get completely into sports?]

42) Pero, en fin, ¿te parece que dejemos este tema? <CREA> [Do you think we should drop this topic?]

§19 After *quién dice que* both moods are used, but both cases are rhetorical questions.

43) Pero, ¿quién dice que esto deba (SUB) ser así? <CREA> [But who says that this should be like this?]

44) - ¿quién dice que se viste (IND) mal en Nueva York? <CREA> [Who says that people dress badly in New York?]

9.1.1.2.3 THE ROLE OF AUXILIARY VERBS

§20 The use of the modal verbs *poder* and *deber*, either in the main clause or dependent clause, can also trigger unexpected uses of the indicative or subjunctive:

45) ¿Y no crees que esa larga amnesia puede impedir que el público sitúe adecuadamente ese teatro? <CREA> (. . . esa larga amnesia impida que . . .) [And don't you think that this long amnesia can prevent the public from]

46) Por el contrario, él propone que a los niños se les debe dar la oportuni-
    dad de crecer en un ambiente sano. <CREA> (. . . él propone que a los
    niños se les dé la oportunidad de . . .) [he proposes giving the children
    the opportunity to grow up in a healthy environment]

47) Yo pienso que pueda hablar de mí mismo sin sentir ningún entusiasmo
    egotista, físico o intelectual. <CREA> (Yo pienso que habla de mí
    mismo . . .) [I think it is possible to talk about oneself without feeling]

48) Pero no sé que deba costar tanto este vencimiento al que se <CREA>
    (no sé que cuesta tanto . . .) [But I am not sure that this defeat should
    cost so much]

49) "Se puede pensar que Marivaux sueñe en poner fin, no tanto a la
    división de la sociedad en clases, antes bien a la infelicidad inherente
    a la injusticia social." <CREA> (Se piensa que Marivaux sueña en
    poner fin . . .) [One can think that Marivaux dreams about ending the
    unhappiness that is inherent to the social injustice.]

9.1.1.3 *Cause, explanation, justification, motif, origin, reason, consequence, tendency*

What distinguishes this group from 9.1.1.1 is that the main subject brings about, originates and produces the content of the dependent predicate without the contribution of the subject of the dependent clause. The main subject can be a person or a thing.

The use of the subjunctive here is mandatory in modern Spanish, comparable to the verbs and expressions in 9.1.1.1, because the embedded clauses are clearly dependent upon the effect or caused by the main subject.

The prototypical expressions of this group are **hacer que</I>**and **<I>causar que</I>**. Other expressions in this group are:

> (*considerar/ser/tener*) *la causa de que, conducir a que, conseguir que,* (*tener*) *la culpa de que, depender de que, explicar que,*[13] *la inclinación a que, justificar que, llevar a que, lograr que, dar lugar a que, ocasionar que,* (*ser*) (*el*) *origen de que, procurar que, producir que, provocar que, ser la razón de que, tender a que,* etc.[14]

- Son muchas las cosas que hacen que sea conmovedor estar aquí, delante de ustedes, en la institución más alta de vuestra democracia. <CREA> [There are many things that make it moving to be here before you]
- algunos tontos comenzaron a tirar objetos al terreno. Eso causó que se detuviera el partido <CREA> [this caused the match to be stopped]
- Creo que la personalidad de aquel hombre, su importancia y su grandeza, justifican que haga lo que voy a hacer. <CREA> [I think that the personality of this man, his importance and greatness, justify that I do what I will do.]

Ver and *mirar* can also be used like *causar* or *tratar de que*, but this is very rare:

• "Era la primera vez en mis 20 años de funcionaria que veía que se pagara por algo que no se hacía", indicó el alto cargo del Ministerio. <CREA> [It was the first time in my 20 years as a public servant that I witnessed that we paid for something that was not done.]

9.1.1.4 Intermediate and impersonal expressions of influence, preference, permission, concession, admission, possibility, necessity, frequency, etc.

The expressions in this group are treated as a separate category because they have an impersonal grammatical subject. Semantically, however, they are similar to the groups 9.1.1.1, 9.1.1.2 and 9.1.1.5, and therefore they are mostly used with the subjunctive. They mark the content of the dependent clause as a possibility, alternative and – indirectly – as the positive or negative intention and attitude of the speaker. Thus they occupy an intermediate position between personal and impersonal sentences.

Examples are:

acostumbrar que, estar acostumbrado a que, ser costumbre que, aceptar que, ser aconsejable que, admitir que, ser admisible que, existir la amenaza de que, ser banal que, bastar (con) que, estar bien que, ser bueno que, ser característico de que, ser una catástrofe que, ser chocante que, comprender que, ser comprensible que,[15] ser común que, ser contraproducente que, ser conveniente que, deber que, dejar que, ser una delicia que, depender de que, tener la desdicha de que, estar dispuesto a/de que, ser dudoso que, entender que, ser esencial que, ser espectacular que, ser estupendo que, ser extraordinario que, ser extraño que, ser fabuloso que, ser frecuente que, ser genial que, ser habitual que, ser hora de que, ser horroroso que, ser (un) horror que, dar igual que, ser imposible que, ser imprescindible que, improbable que, ser inadmisible que, ser increíble que, ser indiferente que, ser injusto que, ser ilógico que, ser inútil que, ser una injusticia que, ser innecesario que, ser inoportuno que, ser insuficiente que, ser insultante que, ser interesante que, ser justo que, ser (una) lástima que, ser una lata que, ser una locura que, ser lógico que, ser magnífico que, ser malo que, estar mal que, ser maravilloso que, ser una maravilla que, ser mejor que, ser un milagro que, dar lo mismo que, ser necesario que, ser normal que, la necesidad de que, ser ocioso que, ser oportuno que, ser peculiar que, ser peligroso que, existir el peligro de que, vale la pena que, ser peor que, ser perjudicial que, estar permitido que, ser posible que, dar(se)/existir/haber/la posibilidad de que, hacer posible que, ser preferible que, ser probable que, estar prohibido que, ser raro que, ser recomendable que, (con) la recomendación de que, ser ridículo que, existir el riesgo de que, ser sorprendente que, sorprender que, ser una suerte que, tener la suerte de que, ser suficiente que, ser terrible que, ser tiempo de que, ser una tontería que, ser triste que, ser urgente que, la urgencia de que, más vale que, ser una vergüenza que etc.

- Pero la verdad es que resulta indiferente que seamos o no favorables a la inmigración, porque el fenómeno está ahí y es ineludible. <CREA> [But the truth is that it is irrelevant whether or not we are in favour of immigration]
- Todo depende de que me renueven los papeles. <CREA> [Everything depends on whether or not they renew my papers.]

The adverb **tan** before an adjective to indicate that the quality described by the adjective is so relevant and extreme that it implies a certain consequence, that is also extreme,[16] can trigger the indicative:

- Era tan razonable que se me olvidó un detalle fundamental: Papandreu volvió a ganar después de presentarse y perder. <CREA> (= Era tan razonable y por eso se me olvidó . . .) [It was so reasonable that I forgot a basic detail]

The main clause is presented as the cause of the content of the subordinated clause. The conjunction *que* is equivalent to *y por eso* (→ 9.3.2.1 **Consecutive clauses**).

On the other hand, if *tan* only intensifies the adjective and has the meaning of *muy*, the subordinated clause is usually in subjunctive.

- Son chicos seleccionados de la cantera del Madrid y tienen clase. No es tan extraño que hayan llegado lejos en la Copa. <CREA> [It is not that strange that they have advanced so far in the run for the cup.]
- Es tan extraño que sea hoy, en esta tarde tan inhóspita, cuando estemos hablando de todo esto <CREA> [It is so strange that it is today . . . when we talk about all this]

In order for an impersonal expression to be used with the subjunctive, it must allow the dependent clause to be presented as something that is *not* generally known, accepted, believed or perceived as an independent fact. Therefore the following expressions are not used with the subjunctive: *ser cierto que, ser/estar claro que, estar demostrado que, ser evidente que, estar garantizado que, ser incuestionable que, ser indiscutible que, ser innegable que, ser obvio que, ser/estar seguro que, ser verdad que, etc.*:

- Quizá este aspecto se exagere, pero es seguro que atraerá mucha atención. <CREA> [Maybe this aspect is exaggerated, but it will definitely attract a lot of attention.]
- El dirigente ahora piensa en Destroyers y está seguro que su equipo saldrá adelante. <CREA> [Now the leader . . . is sure his team will go on.]
- También es la primera vez que recibe el premio si bien es cierto que concursa por segunda vez. <CREA> [It is also the first time that s/he is getting the prize, even if it is certain that s/he is competing for the second time.]

The negation usually triggers the subjunctive:

- Muchos conductores pasan toda la noche en la cola para ser los primeros en abastecerse cuando abra. No es seguro que lo consigan. <CREA> [Many drivers spend the night in line hoping to be the first ones to fill up when it opens. It is not certain that they'll be successful.]
- El parlamentario también dejó en claro que no está seguro que exista financiamiento para este crédito ya que no sabe de dónde saldrán los recursos. <CREA> [The member of Parliament made it clear that he is not certain that financing for this credit exists.]
- Tampoco es cierto que "se vaya a lavar dinero ahí". <CREA> [It is also not certain that money is being laundered here.]

In this group we also find value judgements introduced by the neuter article *lo*, such as *lo mejor/normal/peor/malo/importante/lógico es que* . . . [the best/normal/ worse/bad/important/logical (thing) is that . . .], which are usually followed by a verb in subjunctive:

- En nuestro país, lo habitual es que en todo asunto en que una persona pobre reclama de algún abuso . . . termine con problemas mayores que aquellos por los cuales reclama (La Época, Ch.) [In our country, it is usual that in any matter in which poor people complain about some abuse, they end up with worse problems than the ones they are complaining about][17]

Butt/Benjamin point out that "if the main verb is timeless, habitual or in the past, the verb is usually in the indicative, also the subjunctive is also possible, in which case the event seems more doubtfull" (2013: 256).

9.1.1.5 *Feelings and emotions*

The prototypical expressions of this group are **sentir que, alegrarse (de) que** and **temer que**.

- Se ha señalado, con ironía, que los paleontólogos serían los únicos científicos que se alegran de que falten (SUB) datos <CREA> [It has been pointed out, with certain irony, that palaeontologists would be the only scientists happy with a lack of data]
- Los abogados del zoológico temen que la empresa propietaria de los terrenos tenga (SUB) nuevos intereses urbanísticos en ese suelo <CREA> [The zoo's lawyers are afraid that the company that owns the plot may have new interests to develop this land]

However, expressions of feelings are not always used with the subjunctive; for example, the most general meaning of the verb *sentir* ('to feel') itself.

1) "Todo el paquete es atractivo: las fotos, la música, las composiciones. Siento que todo es (IND) un conjunto armonioso." <CREA> ["The entire package is attractive: .... I feel it's a harmonious ensemble."]

When *sentir* is used with the subjunctive, which is not all too often, it has the meaning of 'to be sorry':

2) pero escucha lo que digo: aquí me quedo yo y aquí me tienes, y la verdad, lo siento, lo reconozco que lo siento que te vayas (SUB): me había hecho a la idea de que ya no ibas a irte <CREA> [I am sorry that you are leaving: I really thought you wouldn't leave]

In 1), the speaker is only confirming the fact that everything is a harmonious ensemble and that s/he agrees with it. In 2), on the other hand, the speaker is not only confirming a fact. Rather, by stating a negative feeling, s/he expresses the wish for the other person not to leave. This makes *sentir* very similar to the expressions in group 9.1.1.2, which manifest the negative intention of the speaker, and, indeed, there are many transitions between the two groups. Another example would be the verb *gustar*, which is listed under 9.1.1.1, as a wish, but could also be categorized as expressing a positive emotion:

- "A mí me gustaría que me nombraran (SUB) presidente honorario del Ateneo", afirma Lara. <CREA> [I would like them to name me honorary president of the Ateneo.] (= Quiero/Quisiera que me nombren presidente honorario del Ateneo.)

If we look closely, we could divide the entire group of expressions and emotions into two subgroups: positive and negative emotions or intentions:

positive emotions (= quiero)	*negative emotions (= no quiero)*
adorar que	*aburrir que*
ser adecuado que	*apenar que*
agradar, estar agradecido de que, (ser) de agrado que	*alarmar que, ser alarmante que*
alegrar que, (sentir) alegría de que, llenar de alegría que	*asustar que, estar asustado que*
amar que	*cansar que, estar cansado que*
ser apropiado que	*desesperar que*
ser bueno que	*detestar que*
complacer que	*disgustar que*
congratular que	*doler que*
estar contento con/de que, hacer contento que	*enfadar que*
convenir que, ser conveniente que	*entristecer que*

positive emotions (= quiero)	negative emotions (= no quiero)
ser una delicia que	dar/producir envidia que
divertir que, ser divertido que	extrañar que, ser extraño que, producir extrañeza que
emocionar que, ser emocionante que	fastidiar que
encantar que, estar encantado de que	frustrar que
entusiasmar que	estar harto de que
ser estupendo que	ser inadecuado que
ser fabuloso que	ser inapropiado que
fascinar que	indignar que
dar/entrar ganas que	ser inconveniente que
dar/producir/entrar gracia que	ser injusto que
gustar que	ser inoportuno que
importar, ser importante que	llenar de inquietud que
interesar que, ser interesante que	ser inútil que
ser lógico que	irritar que, ser irritante que
ser magnífico que	ser inútil que
ser oportuno que	lamentar que, lamentarse de que
estar orgulloso de que, llenar de orgullo que	dar/entrar miedo que
estar satisfecho de que, dar satisfacción que	molestar que
etc.	dar lástima que
	odiar que
	dar pena que
	preocupar que
	proceder que
	dar rabia que
	dar reparo que
	repeler que
	ser malo que
	sentir que ('to be sorry')
	sorprender que, estar sorprendido que, ser sorprendente que
	temer(se) ('to be afraid') que,[18] causar/dar/entrar/producir temor de que
	ser terrible que
	estar/ser triste que
	dar/llenar de vergüenza que
	etc.

Many of these expressions can also be categorized as indicating will, wish, influence, preference, necessity and order, etc. What distinguishes them is that they can NOT ONLY introduce intentions and wishes 1), BUT ALSO comment on existing facts 2):

1) Sería interesante saber por qué ha tenido tanto éxito en Francia y me gustaría que suceda (SUB) lo mismo aquí. <CREA> [It would be interesting to know why s/he had so much success in France, and I want the same to happen here.]
2) Me gusta que esté (SUB) limpia mi casa. <CREA> [I like the house to be clean.]

In both examples the noun clause is not presented as a fact, but as a wish or an intention. It doesn't matter if the house is indeed clean. This cannot be expressed by the subjunctive, because the subjunctive NEVER REFERS TO FACTS. Certain people who confuse language with reality, and see the indicative as the mood of reality and the subjunctive as unreality or virtuality, like to show examples such as the following and argue that the subjunctive can very well be used to refer to something existing or factual:

• Se dirigieron a la casa de Jonás Viricochea, pues Calixto había traído un obsequio para su amigo y salvador. Encontraron al flaco en sus quehaceres cotidianos; pues entraron de rondón. -Cuánto me alegro que hayas venido (SUB)! Ayer supe de tu llegada y me extrañaba [I am so happy that you came.]

Here the speaker (Jonás Viricochea) doesn't refer to the fact, which is obvious, but indirectly to his wish for the friend (Calixto) to come. Indirectly Jonás criticizes Calixto for not coming earlier. Here is another example: When I am hosting a party and greet a person with *me alegro que (usted) haya venido*, I am manifesting my joy and my intention for the person to come to the party. I am not pointing out a fact.

Because of their potential to comment on facts, which means on events that are going on or have already happened at the time of utterance, there is the possibility to use the objects of expressions of emotions also with the indicative.[19] In this case the speaker is stating his feelings and declaring something that is represented as a fact:

• Me alegro mucho de que es (IND) así. (Example from Bolinger, 1956) [I am glad it is like this.]
• ¡Lástima que se acaba (IND) ya! (Example from Bolinger, 1956) [What a pity that it already ends!]
• Temo que no lo puedo hacer (IND). (Example from Bolinger, 1956) [I am afraid I can't do it.]
• Estoy muy satisfecha de que supo terminarlo (IND) él solo. (Example from Lope Blanch, 1958) [I am very happy that s/he was able to finish it by himself.]
• Tengo miedo de que tu hermano fue (IND) él que se lo dio. (Example from Lope Blanch, 1958) [I am afraid that it was your brother who gave it to him/her.]

- No lo puedo remediar: me da coraje que lo hizo (IND) sin mi permiso. (Example from Lope Blanch, 1958) [I can't help it: it upsets me that s/he did it without my authorization.]

The subjunctive offers the advantage that the speaker doesn't have to specify whether the event about which s/he comments is a fact or not or should be considered as such. With the subjunctive the speaker only expresses his/her positive or negative attitude, and at the same time, his/her intention for the event to happen, to have happened or not.

- Me alegro que vengas (SUB) a mi fiesta este fin de semana. = Quiero que vengas a mi fiesta este fin de semana. [I am glad that you are coming to my party this weekend. = I want you to come to my party this weekend.]
- No se trata de eso, es que me molesta que jueguen (SUB) con Ramón. <CREA> [it bothers me that they play with Ramón.] = Quiero que no jueguen con Ramón. [I don't want you to play with Ramón.]

In examples with the indicative, the conjunction *de que* often is equivalent to *porque* and describes the real cause of something, such as after *alegrarse de que* or *quejarse de que*:

- En primer lugar, se alegra sobremanera cuando estalla la guerra y ellos se encuentran "milagrosamente" fuera de España. En la carta fechada el 20 de julio de 1936 dice: "¡Cómo me alegro de que estás (IND) en Francia! <CREA> [In a letter from July 20, 1936 he says: "I am so happy that you are in France!"] (= . . . porque estás en Francia) [= because you are in France]

Butt/Benjamin (2013: 255) write, "when the verb is followed by *de que* the indicative mood is sometimes heard in relaxed speech when the verb is in the present or past" and give a series of examples.

9.2 Adjective or relative clauses

Relative clauses are dependent upon a noun – and occasionally a clause – that they modify. This noun or clause, which is also called ANTECEDENT, can stand directly before the relative clause (the first of the following two examples) or refer to something outside of the sentence (the second of the following two examples):

- Busco un amigo que no me mienta. [I am looking for a friend who doesn't lie to me.][20]
- El que diga lo contrario, no sabe nada. (The relative pronoun *el que* refers to 'the person that')

Relative clauses are introduced by relative pronouns, adverbs or other relative words. The relative pronouns in Spanish are **que**, **quien/quienes**, **el que/la que/**

los que/las que, el cual/la cual/los cuales/las cuales and **cuanto/cuanta/cuantos/cuantas**. The possessive adjectives **cuyo/cuya/cuyos/cuyas** and the adverbs **donde, adonde, como** and **cuando** are also used as relatives. All of these words are markers of syntactic subordination. The predicate of a relative clause can be in indicative or in subjunctive. The subjunctive characterizes the antecedent as non-existent or only potentially existent at the time specified by the main predicate:

- Tengo un libro que <u>explica</u> el uso del subjuntivo de forma sencilla y lógica. [I have a book that explains the use of the subjunctive in an easy and logical way.] (**IND** = existent)
- Busco un libro que <u>explique</u> el uso del subjuntivo de forma sencilla y lógica. [I am looking for a book that explains the use of the subjunctive in an easy and logical way.] (**SUB** = potentially existent)

Relative clauses with an antecedent in the sentence have the same function as other elements that modify nouns, particularly adjectives. Therefore, they are also called adjective clauses. See the following example:

- <u>Busco</u> un libro <u>que explique el uso del subjuntivo de forma sencilla y lógica</u>. (What kind of book?) Busco un libro **sencillo y lógico**. (What kind of book?)

Adjectives provide additional information, but are not necessary for a sentence to be considered complete:

- Busco un libro.

Even though the adjective clause depends syntactically on the noun *libro*, semantically it depends on the entire main predicate and the verb *busco*, because if we replace *busco* by *tengo*, the dependent clause will be in indicative:

- <u>Tengo</u> un libro <u>que explica el uso del subjuntivo de forma sencilla y lógica</u>. [I have a book]

Relative clauses can be divided into defining and non-defining clauses.[21] Defining clauses provide information that is necessary for the meaning of the sentence. They are never separated from the antecedent by a comma. Non-defining clauses provide additional information about the antecedent and are always preceded and followed by a comma in Spanish:[22]

- <u>Los alumnos</u> que se prepararon bien sacaron buenas notas en el examen. (Only those students, who were well prepared, got good grades on the exam. = Defining)
- <u>Los alumnos</u>, que se prepararon bien, sacaron buenas notas en el examen. (All the students were well prepared and got good grades on the exam. = Non-defining)

The subjunctive can only be used in defining relative clauses:[23]

- Busco un guitarrista al que le guste tocar en una banda reggae. [I am looking for a guitarist who likes to play in a reggae band.]

Even though a relative or adjective clause has a different grammatical function in a sentence, the semantic criteria for the use of the indicative or the subjunctive in it are the same as in noun clauses. The subjunctive characterizes the content of the adjective clause as dependent upon the **intention or influence** of the speaker or sentence subject, **NOT** as an independent **fact**:

- Busco un libro que me ayude a comprender el uso del subjuntivo.
- He encontrado un libro que me ayuda a comprender el uso del subjuntivo. [I found a book that]

Syntactically and semantically, the adjective clause modifies the noun, in this case *un libro*, and specifies its characteristics. The subjunctive in the relative clause characterizes the object of *buscar* as non-existent (not known) from the perspective of the speaker and sentence subject. If I am looking for something, it is my intention to find it. This characterizes it as an intention/wish, which is expressed with the subjunctive:

- Quiero encontrar un libro que me ayude a comprender el subjuntivo.[24] [I want to find a book that helps me to understand the subjunctive.]

Other verbs that require or enable the subjunctive in adjective clauses are:

acometer, aconsejar, ambicionar, anhelar, ansiar, aspirar a, autorizar, confiar en, conseguir, contentarse con, decidir, demandar, depender de, desear, disponer, elegir, empeñarse en, encantar, esforzarse por, esperar, examinar, exigir, faltar, hacer falta, gustar, ilusionar, insistir en, intentar, lograr, luchar por, ser menester, necesitar, negar, oponerse a, optar por, ordenar, pedir, permitir, perseguir, precisar, preferir, pretender, dar/otorgar prioridad a, probar, proponer, querer, rechazar, reclamar, recomendar, reivindicar, requerir, rogar, seleccionar, solicitar, sugerir, tratar, urgir, etc.

- sino que reclama acciones que favorezcan el fin de este derramamiento de sangre <CREA> [but rather he requires actions that favour ending this bloodshed]
- Aseguró que García niega el derecho de que la asociación funcione en instalaciones del Batallón <CREA> [He says that García denies the right of the association to work in the facilities of the Batallón]

- Jorge Briz Abularach, resaltó que dicha entidad rechaza cualquier medida que impida el libre comercio, como es el caso de la Ley Helms Burton. <CREA> [the aforementioned entity rejects any measure that interferes with free commerce]
- Pero, en fin, le diré que todo depende del esfuerzo que uno desarrolle. <CREA> [I will tell him that everything depends on the effort one gives.]
- A nuestro modo de ver, si bien la autorización de que una misma empresa maneje ambos servicios podría justificarse desde el punto de vista de las economías de escala y de la rebaja de costos, ella no resulta apropiada <CREA> [even though authorization that the same company be allowed to handle both services could be justified from an economic point of view]
- comentaristas y oyentes compartían la confianza de que la revuelta represente el primer paso en el desenlace que anhelan desde hace décadas. <CREA> [commentators and listeners shared the confidence that the riot could be the first step towards the solution they have been desiring for decades.]

Because of the common element <Intention>, it is not surprising to find here many verbs and expressions that require or allow the subjunctive in noun clauses as well. Even though noun and relative clauses have different functions, they can contribute to the same sentence meaning:

- Pero, en fin, le diré que todo depende del esfuerzo que uno desarrolle. <CREA> (≈Pero, en fin, le diré que todo depende de que uno se esfuerce.) [I will tell him that everything depends on the effort one makes.]
- Ahora, el futuro de Iberia depende de que la Unión Europea apruebe la reestructuración financiera que prevé una ampliación de capital de 130.000 millones de pesetas. <CREA> (≈Ahora, el futuro de Iberia depende del hecho[25] que la Unión Europea apruebe la reestructuración financiera que prevé una ampliación de capital de 130.000 millones de pesetas. [Now the future of Iberia depends on the fact that the European Union approves the financial restructuration that foresees a capital increase of]
- Aseguró que García niega el derecho de que la asociación funcione en instalaciones del Batallón <CREA> (≈Aseguró que García niega que la asociación tenga el derecho de funcionar en instalaciones del Batallón) [He says that García denies the right of the association to work in the facilities of the Batallón]

The future tense and commands in the main clause can be indicators of the intentional character of the relative clause:

- Localice un archivo que tenga como extensión (las tres últimas letras, que aparecen detrás de un punto) SYS, . . . o algún nombre similar. <CREA> [Find a file that has the extension . . . SYS]
- El Paciente Interactivo sirve para entrenar al médico en la tarea de asesorar a un paciente que tenga dolores abdominales <CREA> [The interactive patient trains the doctor to assist a patient who might have abdominal pains]

Still, it is not the element <Intention> alone that triggers the subjunctive in the relative clause. Because relative clauses don't have the status of arguments, but as free modifiers, **it is the combination of both, the element <Intention> AND the subjunctive in the relative clause that characterize the object of the main predicate as intentional, not known or non-existent.** This is the reason why the subjunctive and the indicative can often alternate in relative clauses:

- Busco el libro que (siempre) está en este estante.
  [I am looking for the book that always is on this shelf.]
- Busco un libro que (siempre) está en este estante.
  [I am looking for a book that is always on this shelf.]
- Quiero leer el libro que me regaló Juan.
  [I want to read the book that Juan gave me.]

Even if the governing predicate doesn't contain any of these verbs or expressions of <Intention>,[26] the subjunctive in the relative clause can **characterize the antecedent as not being a fact**, such as **something or someone non-existent or not known.**

- Pero estar al acecho y entre los primeros, con dos semanas de Tour en las piernas, tres jornadas de Pirineos y dos de Alpes, no es algo que esté al alcance de cualquiera. <CREA> [But ... it is not something that anyone can do.]
- es importantísimo que la persona que esté a cargo de una empresa demuestre su aprecio por cualquier innovación provechosa. <CREA> [it is very important that the person who might be in charge of the business shows his appreciation]
- Pero no hay nada que el Gobierno japonés pueda hacer. <CREA> [But there is nothing that the Japanese government could do.]
- Pero entonces, ¿hay algo que podamos conocer directamente gracias a nuestro aparato perceptivo? <CREA> [Is there anything we could learn through our own perception?]
- Pero como la vivienda es chica y las viviendas del campamento están así lado a lado, no hay un lugar donde vayan a jugar los chiquitos; <CREA> [there isn't a place where the little ones could go to play]
- dime lo que sepas, porque quiero saber quién es, no para denunciarla, sino para agradecérselo; <CREA> [tell me whatever you may know]

The examples show that negative expressions, questions and even commands with the indefinite pronouns and expressions *alguien, algo, alguna cosa, alguna persona*, etc., also enable the subjunctive in relative clauses, if they characterize the antecedent as not existing or if they question its existence. The same goes for words that reduce the factuality of the noun clause, such as *casi, (muy) poco, solo*, etc.

- somos una generación jodida, "hay pocos que se encuentren bien, ya sabes, parecen trivialidades, pero una se pregunta muchas veces qué sentido tiene todo esto <CREA> [only a few find themselves well]

The meaning here is basically 'there isn't practically anyone who is well off'. If, on the other hand, there are really a few people (=fact), then the indicative is used:

- Si la riqueza de un país está mal distribuida y hay pocos que tienen mucho y muchos que tienen poco, eso seguirá igual aún cuando la población no aumente. <CREA> [If the riches of a country are distributed unevenly and if there are some who have a lot and many who have very little]

Also in comparisons, especially the past subjunctive is sometimes used to express that something or someone resembles another thing or person without actually being that thing or person. This concept can also be expressed with the verbs *parecer que, (a)semejar(se) (a)* or the expression *(es) como si*:

- el hemisferio trágico de Agatón y el hemisferio alegre de Aristófanes, y esquizofrénico como un hombre que estuviera simultáneamente en Londres y en la ciudad de México y tuviera que manejar por el carril de la derecha y por el carril de la izquierda al mismo tiempo <CREA> [and schizophrenic, like a man who would be simultaneously in London and Mexico City and had to drive on the right and left side of the road at the same time]
- Le recuerdo muy rubito, aunque aquí en la foto parece que tenga el pelo más oscuro. <CREA> [I remember him being very blond, even if in the photo it looks like he had darker hair.]
- y nunca experimentó un miedo tan sin cuerpo, puesto que aquella impenetrable calima más semejaba un sudario que envolviese al universo, que un mero fenómeno atmosférico <CREA> [because this impenetrable haze resembled more a shroud that covers the universe than a simple atmospheric phenomenon]
- Pasamos por Las meninas, donde la gente baja la voz como si estuviera en la iglesia. <CREA> [where people lower their voice as if they were in a church]

Especially in written Spanish, superlatives are used with the subjunctive. In this case, the speaker somehow evaluates, positively or negatively, the quality of something or someone. This is similar to the expression of feelings and emotions in noun clauses.

- "Puede llegar a ser el mejor nadador que hayamos tenido y puede que el mejor que haya visto el mundo." <CREA> [He can become the best swimmer that we have ever had ...]

Of course, superlatives can also be used with the indicative to simply state facts.

- "Sigo creyendo que el mejor homenaje que le podemos hacer a estos bravos luchadores del 7 de marzo es estar bien parados en la realidad en que vivimos. <CREA> [I keep thinking that the best tribute that we can pay those brave fighters]

The use of the subjunctive is much more frequent if the antecedent is used with an indefinite article, but ultimately what matters is whether the antecedent and its characteristics are presented as facts, if something or someone is existent/known, or not. The definite article can be used, for example, in generic contexts:

- El Partido Popular Democrático de Afganistán. "El PDPA sólo quiere una representación proporcional a la función que quiera otorgarle la sociedad afgana." <CREA> ["The PDPA only wants a proportional representation according to what the Afghan society wants to grant her."]
- En aquellos tiempos hacíamos a veces servicios de una semana entera, noche y día, buscando al que fuera. Y no parábamos hasta que lo cazábamos, costara lo que costara. <CREA> [looking for whoever it was]

Even though the semantic criteria for the use of the indicative or the subjunctive in relative clauses are the same as in noun clauses, there is one important difference between them: **Noun clauses are arguments of the main predicate and therefore necessary to complete its meaning. Relative clauses only modify and specify this argument. Therefore, the relationship between both is much looser.** Both are relatively independent and therefore, in many cases, the indicative and the subjunctive can produce grammatically correct sentences:[27]

- Pero, en fin, le diré que todo depende del esfuerzo que uno desarrolle/desarrolla.
- Pero estar al acecho y entre los primeros, con dos semanas de Tour en las piernas, tres jornadas de Pirineos y dos de Alpes, no es algo que esté/está al alcance de cualquiera.
- . . . , es importantísimo que la persona que esté a cargo/está a cargo de una empresa demuestre su aprecio por cualquier innovación provechosa.
- Pero como la vivienda es chica y las viviendas del campamento están así lado a lado, no hay un lugar donde vayan a jugar/pueden jugar los chiquitos;
- . . . , dime lo que sepas/sabes, porque quiero saber quién es, no para denunciarla, sino para agradecérselo;
- . . . , y nunca experimentó un miedo tan sin cuerpo, puesto que aquella impenetrable calima más semejaba un sudario que envolviese/envuelve al universo, que un mero fenómeno atmosférico, . . .
- "Puede llegar a ser el mejor nadador que hayamos tenido/hemos tenido y puede que el mejor que haya visto/ha visto el mundo."

Although *buscar algo que* is generally followed by the subjunctive, there are also situations that call for the indicative:

- Yo busco algo que no existe en la cooperativa: transparencia. <CREA> [I am looking for something that doesn't exist in the cooperative: transparency.]
- Yo aproveché, agarré el diario, busqué las páginas que correspondían a aquellos días. <CREA> [I looked for the pages that matched those dates]

In relative clauses, the subjunctive is not automatic or a direct reflex of the main predicate; it always characterizes its antecedent as NOT being an independent FACT.

9.3 Adverb or circumstantial clauses

Adverbial or circumstantial clauses are the third and last type of dependent and subordinate clauses. They modify the main predicate and specify the circumstances in which it unfolds. The conjunctions that connect the main clauses and the adverbial or circumstantial clauses predetermine the mood choice in the latter.

Adverbial or circumstantial clauses modify the main predicate, just like simple adverbs or circumstantial non-predicative expressions:

- Juan camina <u>allá/poco/solo/lentamente</u>, <u>rápidamente/cuidadosamente/con cuidado</u>. . . [Juan walks over there/little/alone/slowly/quickly/carefully/ . . .]
- María vendrá <u>mañana/en tres horas/un poco más tarde</u>/ . . . [Maria will come tomorrow/in three hours/a little later/ . . .]

Adverb and circumstantial clauses, however, can go beyond the basic circumstances of time, place, and general manner to indicate more complex conceptual associations between two events, such as final, concessive, conditional or causal relations between main and subordinate clause.[28] This relationship is determined by a connector, an adverbial conjunction or relative adverb, such as **para que, aunque, antes de que, después de que, sin que, cuando, como**, etc. Some of them are only used with the subjunctive, but most with both moods:

- Te lo digo <u>para que</u> lo <u>sepas</u>. [I am telling you so that you know.] (PURPOSE OF TELLING IT)
- Solís, no puedo fiarme de usted, <u>aunque sabe</u> bien que le aprecio. <CREA> [Solís, I cannot trust you, though you very well know that I do appreciate you.] (CONCESSION)
- ya no quiere más que tener la razón, <u>aunque sepa</u> que no la tiene <CREA> [all he wants is to be right, even though he may know that he is not] (CONCESSION)

The relationship between the two events can also be very loose and free. The listener might have to fill in missing, but implied, information:

- ¡Mi mujer y yo vamos a separarnos, <u>para que</u> lo <u>sepas</u>! <CREA> [So that you know, my wife and I are separating!] (The purpose of TELLING YOU IS for you to know).

Circumstantial clauses of time, place and general manner are often used similarly to relative clauses because relative adverbs can also function as relative pronouns without an explicit antecedent and introduce adverb as well as adjective clauses:

- se tienen que probar dos cosas: la propiedad del objeto y el hecho de que ese objeto estaba en el lugar donde se produjo el robo. <CREA> [we have to check out two things: the characteristics of the object and the fact that this object was in the place where the robbery took place.] (Here *donde se produjo el robo* syntactically depends on the explicit antecedent *lugar*. Therefore, syntactically, it is an adjective clause.)

9.3.1 Conjunctions and expressions that always require the subjunctive

There is no sanctioned classification of conjunctions, and there is a grey zone between conjunctions, prepositions and relative adverbs that can also introduce circumstantial clauses. There is a limited number of pure conjunctions and there are many expressions that can assume the function of conjunctions.

Subordinating conjunctions have two functions. First, they provide a necessary transition between two ideas in a sentence. Second, the subordinating conjunctions reduce the importance of one clause so that the reader understands which of the two ideas is more important. The more important idea belongs in the main clause, the less important in the clause introduced by the subordinate conjunction.

A few conjunctions – and some of the most common ones – are always followed by the subjunctive.

para que	in order that, so that
antes de que	before
a menos que	unless
a no ser que	unless
de no ser que	unless
con tal de que	provided that, as long as, so that
siempre y cuando	provided that, as long as
en caso de que	in case (that)
sin que	without

9.3.1.1 Para que

Para que is one of the final conjunctions and expressions that introduce subordinated final clauses and are always followed by the SUBJUNCTIVE. Final clauses are non-factual and specify intentions or consequences, possibilities or purposes.

- Nosotros somos dueños del diario *La Prensa de Lima*, para que sepas. <CREA> [So that you know, we are the owners of the newspaper *La Prensa de Lima*.]
- Los niños deben acudir al dentista para que sepan cómo cepillarse y se familiaricen con el especialista. <CREA> [The children must go to the dentist so they learn how to brush their teeth and get accustomed to the specialist.]

The element <Intention> is a powerful trigger for the subjunctive, as we have already seen in the chapter about the subjunctive in noun clauses. It is especially prevalent after *querer que*, which is always followed by the subjunctive, but also after many other expressions that contain the element <Intention>.[29]

- Queremos que sepas que nosotros somos dueños del diario *La Prensa de Lima*.
- Los niños deben acudir al dentista porque se quiere /es necesario/es importante/es bueno/es oportuno/conviene/lleva a/conduce a/. . . que sepan cómo cepillarse y se familiaricen con el especialista.

In order to clarify the type of <Intention>, final clauses can also be connected to the main clause with

---

a efectos de que, a fin de que, con el fin de que, con la finalidad de que, con (la) intención de que, con (la) idea de que, con motivo de que, con (el) propósito de que, con (el) objeto de que, al objeto de que, en orden a que, con pretexto de que, con vistas a que, por que, a que, justo que, etc.

If the subject of a main and dependent clause is the same, *que* is omitted and the infinitive is used.

- IU ha exigido que el Congreso abra una investigación para saber quién envió desde un ordenador del recinto y por correo a su grupo . . . un video <CREA> (el Congreso abre la investigación y el Congreso quiere saber quién envió el video) [IU has demanded that Congress open an investigation in order to find out who sent . . . the video]
- es que este Gobierno es el primero que ha dado pasos muy importantes, . . . , en orden a defender la cooficialidad de las lenguas cooficiales y su uso en la UE. <CREA> [this government is the first one that has taken important steps. . . . . to defend the co-official status of the co-official languages and their use in the EU.]

The same happens when there is an impersonal subject in the main clause. It is also true for other final expressions.

- Habrá que esperar a la autopsia para saber si hubo o no agresión sexual. <CREA> [One has to wait for the autopsy to know whether or not there was a sexual assault.]
- Del Castillo explicó que todavía es pronto para saber cómo ha incidido este Plan <CREA> [Del Castillo explained that it is still too early to know the impact of this Plan]
- Y ello a pesar del deseo mayoritario de olvidarlo a fin de mantener la imagen de unidad, muy propia del estilo de este foro internacional. <CREA> [And

this, despite the wish of the majority to forget it in order to maintain the appearance of unity]

9.3.1.2 *Antes de que*

Antes de que is very similar to *para que* in that it marks the content of the dependent adverbial clause as happening after the time defined by the main clause. What distinguishes both is that *para que* introduces a purpose, and that *antes de que* indicates non-existence at the time specified in the main clause.

- Pero el que es sagaz los [refers to 'estorninos', starlings] ahuyenta a petardadas o cosecha <u>antes de que</u> <u>lleguen</u> los depredadores y lleva las olivas a la almazara inmediatamente después de la recolecta. <CREA> [But if you are clever, you use firecrackers to chase them away or harvest before the predators arrive]
- El propio Friedman, sin embargo, dice que habrá que esperar varios años <u>antes de que</u> <u>llegue</u> al mercado un posible remedio milagroso <CREA> [However, Friedman himself says that we will have to wait several years before a potential miracle remedy comes on the market]

The starlings may still show up and the remedy may become available, but in both cases, this is presented as a possibility. In the next example, the sequence of events and the content of the main clause, *la enfermedad es eliminada*, present the content of the adverbial clause, getting into the food distribution chain, as something impossible. Still it is marked not as an independent fact, but dependent on an earlier event.

- El consejero castellano-leonés defendió las medidas . . . para controlar la enfermedad porque aseguran que la carne de vacuno en España es segura porque la enferma es eliminada <u>antes de que</u> <u>llegue</u> a las cadenas de distribución de los alimentos. <CREA> [they assure that beef in Spain is safe, because the sick animal is eliminated before it enters the food distribution chain]

In the following example, the outcome of the event in the adverbial clause is unknown. The loss of contact with the spaceship makes it impossible to know if it will actually come close to Mars. The subjunctive here refers to an intended event ('debe llegar').

- WASHINGTON. – Los técnicos de la NASA han perdido comunicación con la nave espacial Mars Observer, tres días <u>antes de que</u> <u>llegue</u> a las proximidades del planeta Marte <CREA> [The NASA technicians have lost contact with the spaceship Mars Observer three days before arriving in the proximity of Mars]

The past subjunctive, with reference to the past, follows the same logic: the content of the adverbial clause is always posterior to that of the main clause and presented as a possibility.

- los misiles fueron disparados contra el puente <u>antes de que</u> <u>llegara</u> el tren. <CREA> [the missiles were launched against the bridge before the train arrived.]

Antes de que is always used with the subjunctive, even though the event is in the past. The reason for this is that *antes de que* is equivalent to a negative expression and introduces something non-existent at the TIME OF REFERENCE, which is represented by the main predicate.

- Es más – agregó – yo lo sabía <u>antes de que</u> <u>se diera a conocer</u> públicamente. (Todavía no se había dado a conocer cuando ya lo sabía.) <CREA> [I knew it before it was publicly announced.]
- Los servicios médicos de la cárcel practicaron al preso maniobras de reanimación <u>antes de que</u> <u>fuera trasladado</u> al hospital Torrecárdenas, de Almería <CREA> [The medical team of the penitentiary applied reanimation manoeuvres to the prisoner before he was moved to the hospital of Torrecárdenas] (Todavía no había sido trasladado al hospital. . .)

If the subject of the main and dependent clause is the same, *que* can be omitted and the infinitive is used.

- Concejal, de 31 años, murió <u>antes de</u> <u>llegar</u> al hospital de la población. <CREA> [The 31-year-old Concejal died before arriving at the hospital. . . .] (Concejal murió y Concejal no llegó al hospital.)

The same happens when there is an impersonal subject in the main clause.

- Sin embargo, la primera estación de esta línea que conecta con otras de mayor intensidad, según el actual diseño de la red de Metro, es la de Cartagena, pero hay al menos siete paradas <u>antes de</u> <u>llegar</u>. [. . . the first one is the Cartagena station, but there are at least seven stops before arrival.]

9.3.1.3 A menos que, a no ser que, siempre y cuando, en caso de que, and con tal de que

A menos que, a no ser que, siempre y cuando, en caso de que and **con tal de que** are conditional conjunctions. Conditions are always possibilities. Conditional clauses are similar to logical equations: <if A, then B>. But not all of them are used with the subjunctive; for example, *si* is never used with the present subjunctive. It's the meaning of the conjunction that is decisive. Conditional clauses are similar to noun clauses. They express the intention of the speaker or the main subject to manipulate someone or something (e.g. the media in the following example):

- el gobierno dio a conocer un anteproyecto de Ley de Secretos Oficiales, en el cual se establece la posibilidad de multar a los medios de información <u>en caso</u>

de que divulguen secretos oficiales. <CREA> [the government announced a draft of law regarding the Official Secrets Act, which opens the possibility of fining mass media, if for some reason they divulge official secrets.] (= . . . porque no quiere que divulguen secretos oficiales.)

The same goes for *a menos que* and *a no ser que* with the exception that they specify negative conditions: <if not A, then (not) B>.

- "No podemos hacer nada a menos que varíe la Ley y eso no es asunto del gobierno o mío, debe hacerlo la Asamblea Nacional", expresó el titular de ENITEL[30] <CREA> [There is nothing we can do unless the Law changes, and this is not up to the government or to me]
- Por otra parte, algunos economistas consideran que a partir de 1992 Yugoslavia quedará marginada, a menos que reestructure rápidamente su economía. <CREA> [from 1992 on, Yugoslavia will be marginalized, unless it quickly restructures its economy]

All five conjunctions can be used with the present or past subjunctive according to the tense of the main clause and meaning of the main clause. The imperfect subjunctive is mostly used with the conditional in the main clause, similar to the conditional clauses with *si*.

- el Banco Mundial dejó establecido que no entregaría más dineros para centrales hidroeléctricas en el Biobío, a menos que se realizara un estudio de impacto ambiental acumulativo. <CREA> [the World Bank made it clear that it would not invest more money in hydroelectric power stations unless a study about its cumulative environmental impact was carried out.] (= si no se realizara un estudio . . .)

Con tal de que can be used as a conditional conjunction, such as *siempre* and *cuando*:

- crece mi confianza en que también Cuba evolucionará hacia una democracia, con tal de que no se siga excluyendo a ese Estado insular. <CREA> [I am getting more confident that Cuba as well will evolve into a democracy, so that it isn't excluded from] (≈ . . . siempre y cuando no se siga excluyendo . . . or . . . si no se sigue excluyendo . . .)

However, many times **con tal de que** is used as a final conjunction, with the meaning of *para que*:

- Y yo, con tal de que se alegrara un poco le dije que sí, que allá van todas las cosas cuando se mueren <CREA> [And I, in order to cheer him up a little bit, I said 'yes'] (=para que se alegrara)

Sometimes only the larger context can help us decide whether **con tal de que** is used as a conditional or as a final conjunction:

- La familia de Dardana J. Monge está dispuesta a llegar a las últimas consecuencias <u>con tal de que</u> la Fiscalía <u>investigue</u> al ex novio de su hija, a quien señalan como responsable de la tragedia vial en la Zona Rosa. <CREA> [The family . . . . is prepared to go all the way so that the prosecution investigates the daughter's ex-boyfriend] (. . . si la Fiscalía investiga al ex novio . . . or . . . para que la Fiscalía investigue al ex novio . . .)

Especially **con tal de que** shows the similarities between noun versus adjective and adverb clauses.

- La familia de Dardana J. Monge está dispuesta a llegar a las últimas consecuencias bajo la condición de que la Fiscalía investigue al ex novio de su hija, a quien señalan como responsable de la tragedia vial en la Zona Rosa. (adjective clause)
- La familia de Dardana J. Monge está dispuesta a llegar a las últimas consecuencias, pero quiere que la Fiscalía investigue al ex novio de su hija, a quien señalan como responsable de la tragedia vial en la Zona Rosa. (noun clause)

9.3.1.4   Sin que

Sin que is a compound conjunction formed with the preposition *sin* and the conjunction *que*. It specifies the manner in which the main predicate unfolds, but in a negative way, by indicating what did NOT happen.

- A las urnas acuden más votantes que nunca, <u>sin que</u> <u>se produzca</u> el menor incidente. <CREA> [More voters than ever participated in the elections, without there being even a minor incident.]

The preposition *sin* can also be followed by a noun and, in this case, *que* would be a relative pronoun introducing an adjective clause:

- Arcadi Espada decía, en un artículo reciente, que <u>sin personas</u> que <u>revelaran</u> secretos, . . . , no habría periodismo <CREA> [Arcadi Espada said, ... that without people revealing secrets, ... there wouldn't be journalism]

If the subject of the main and dependent clause is the same, *que* is omitted and the infinitive is used:

- Ahora estoy trabajando la técnica de carrera . . . , pero en lo que pienso es en trabajar a fondo, hacer las cosas bien <u>sin</u> <u>pensar</u> en cuándo volveré a jugar. <CREA> [but what I want is to do things well without thinking about when I will play again]

9.3.2 Conjunctions and adverbial expressions that are used with the indicative and the subjunctive

The mood in the following adverbial clauses is determined by the same principle that was applied earlier. The indicative is used if its content is represented as an independent fact (which means as true, generally accepted and real), otherwise the subjunctive is used. Semantically, but also syntactically, the indicative makes the conjunction a coordinating conjunction.

If you want to see examples for a specific conjunction or expression, you can find them at the end of the book in the alphabetic appendix. The following are key considerations regarding mood use in the different types of adverbial clauses, as well as exemplary descriptions.

Adverbial clauses can be divided into the following groups:

a.   consecutive clauses
b.   causal clauses
c.   concessive clauses
d.   conditional clauses
e.   circumstantial clauses of time, place and manner

All the clauses under a. though d. are somehow united by the semantic notions of cause and effect. From the perspective of the cause, the source that triggers an action, we can group together b., c., and d. Consecutive clauses are related to the final clauses that were discussed in the previous chapter and are always used with the subjunctive. These relationships can exist within a complex sentence, a main and a dependent clause or can be divided among different sentences within one paragraph.

9.3.2.1   Consecutive clauses

Consecutive clauses express the consequence of a fact that is stated in a main clause. Most of them are independent, syntactically and melodically, from the main clause and separated by a period, semicolon, comma, the coordinating conjunction **y** and connectors such as *así que, conque, por consiguiente, por (lo) tanto, por lo que, de modo/manera/forma/suerte que,* and *de ahí que.* The majority of them are used with the indicative. Only *de ahí/aquí que* has some idiosyncrasies. A typical example, on the other hand, is *así que.*

• A petición de la Asociación de Grandes Maestros, la FIDE amplió a 3 años el ciclo del Campeonato Mundial, <u>así que</u> solo en 1990 <u>se repetirá</u> ese encuentro. <CREA> [... the FIDE expanded the cycle of the World Championship to three years, so this encounter will only repeat itself in 1990.]

The majority of coordinating expressions can start an independent sentence:[31]

• Sí tenemos presidente hasta la tercera semana de enero. <u>Así que</u> <u>tenemos</u> mucho tiempo de acá a eso. <CREA> [We will have a president until the third week of January. Therefore, we will have a lot of time until then.]

If the consecutive clause is needed to complete the meaning and structure of the main clause,[32] it is subordinated and forms part of the main clause. In this case, the subjunctive is used and there is no comma or pause between the two clauses:[33]

- Por este motivo, el anuncio debe ser diseñado de forma que sea capaz de transmitir con velocidad la esencia del mensaje.[34] <CREA> [For this reason, the announcement must be designed in a way that enables the essence of the message to be transmitted rapidly.]

Nevertheless, in this case, the adverb clause expresses a wish or purpose and not a fact, and therefore this kind of clause has more of a final, rather than a consecutive, meaning. The non-factual content of the main clause is expressed with the future tense, *ir + a + infinitive*, the conditional, the subjunctive, imperatives, expression of will, necessity or purpose (for example impersonal expressions and modal verbs), expressions of hope (such as *ojalá*), etc.:

- se va a proponer a la junta la modificación de los estatutos sociales de forma que sea la junta de accionistas la que fije el importe máximo de la retribución de los consejeros. <CREA> [they will propose a modification of the social statutes to the board, so that it will be the assembly of shareholders that establishes the payment limit of consultants]
- En opinión del catedrático, . . . , esta técnica se podría perfeccionar de forma que sea posible reconocer otros compuestos químicos. <CREA> [this technique could be perfected so that it is possible to examine other chemical components]
- Una vez obtenida esta información es necesario analizarla de forma que las decisiones . . . , sean las más adecuadas a la realidad. <CREA> [Once this information is obtained, it is necessary to analyze it so that the decisions are as realistic as possible.]
- Hazlo de modo que sea bien legible, pero que quepa en un bolsillo pequeño. <CREA> [Make it so that it is clearly readable, but that it fits in a small pocket.]
- Las puertas y sus marcos han de concebirse de forma que sea mínimo el riesgo de que puedan quedar prendidas las ropas. <CREA> [The doors and their frames have to be designed in such a way that the risk of clothes getting caught is minimal.]

The subjunctive is also used in subordinated consecutive clauses, if the main clause contains something non-existing that can be expressed with negative expressions.

- La respuesta a la pregunta anterior no es clara, si "la convención usada" para evitar el uso de paréntesis no se ha hecho de forma que no deje lugar a interpretaciones <CREA> [The answer to the previous question is clear if 'the convention used' to avoid the use of parenthesis is not done in a way that it doesn't leave room for interpretation]

The connector *de ahí/aquí que* coordinates two apparently independent sentences, but it is mostly followed by the SUBJUNCTIVE. This conjunction is always separated from the main clause that it refers to by a period, semicolon, comma and/or the coordinating conjunction *y*:[35]

- Al comienzo, la mayoría de los productos son demasiado costosos y difíciles de manejar. De ahí que solo escasas personas los utilicen. <CREA> [At the beginning the majority of products are too expensive and difficult to use. Therefore, only a few people use them.]
- Cristina Mendoza, . . . , ha incluido en el catálogo la reproducción no sólo de lo expuesto, sino también de todas las obras hasta ahora conocidas; de ahí que el total ascienda a 328 dibujos. <CREA> [Cristina Mendoza, . . . , has not only included in the catalogue what is on display, but also all the works known until now; therefore, the total is 328 drawings.]
- pero él pocas veces se ha sentido deseado, de ahí que en su literatura no haya amor <CREA> [but only rarely has he felt desired; therefore there is no love in his literary work]
- Asimismo, explica Vega que el nivel de los técnicos de su país es excelente y de ahí que algunas cinematografías latinoamericanas se trasladen a Cuba para producir películas. <CREA> [Vega explains that the quality of the technicians in this country is excellent and therefore some Latin American cinematographers have moved to Cuba in order to produce movies.]

This expression is different in many respects from other consecutive conjunctions, such as *de modo que* or *así que*. It not only allows the very general verb *ser* before *que*, such as the *así (es) que*, but also more specific verbs such as *proceder*, *resultar*, *derivarse*, etc. These verbs pass on their own semantic and morphologic characteristics, as well as other kinds of adverbial expressions. This is an indicator that *de ahí/aquí que* in reality consists of an implicit predicate plus a circumstantial adverb and a subordinate clause with the function of lexical subject introduced by the conjunction *que*. The consecutive value stems from the capacity of *ahí* and *aquí* to refer back to the origin of a deduction that is presented as just one possible outcome or consequence. In any case, the part introduced by *de ahí/aquí que* is not represented as an independent fact, but becomes dependent on something.

De ahí que is used with the INDICATIVE if the content of the proposition is presented as an independent fact that is based on another fact. It equals *por eso*, which is always used with the indicative.

- Ambos impuestos (IRPF e IVA) son la columna vertebral del sistema impositivo español y de ahí que no parece factible que un hipotético gobierno del PP se aventure a introducir modificaciones que puedan poner en peligro la capacidad recaudatoria de ambos tributos. <CREA> [Both taxes . . . are the pillars of the Spanish tax system and therefore it doesn't seem doable for a hypothetical Partido Popular government to introduce changes]

→ **You can find examples with the other consecutive connectors in the alphabetic list of conjunctions at the end of the book.**

9.3.2.2   *Causal clauses*

The most common causal conjunction is *porque*. Other causal connectors are:

> *por causa de que, a causa de que, por razón de que, debido a que, gracias a que, merced a que, por culpa de que, por aquello de que, puesto que, dado que, en vista de que, a la vista de que, cuando, si, ahora que, como, ya que, supuesto que, just que*, etc.

Porque introduces a specific cause, reason or the motivation for the content of another clause. The use of the INDICATIVE characterizes the content of that other clause as a fact and the link between them as real and effective, no matter what. This is the case in typical causal clauses.

- Y en sueños Simón suda, porque vuelven a su mente los traumáticos hechos de su infancia. <CREA> [And in his dreams, Simón sweats, because the traumatic events from his childhood haunt him.] (CAUSE/REASON/ MOTIVATION)

Syntactically, causal clauses can be very independent and separated from the predicate that they refer to:

- **Nosotros no tenemos ninguna opción para volver.** Aunque no pudimos evitar la tentación de inscribirnos en la "lista de espera". No es sólo por el dinero, **porque vivir en el centro de Europa es un privilegio incluso para nuestros hijos.** ¿Dónde encontraríamos un trabajo parecido en Chile? <CREA> [We can't possibly go back. ... It is not only for the money, because living in the centre of Europe is also a privilege for our children. Where would we find a similar job in Chile?]

With the subjunctive we question the effectiveness, validity and exclusivity of the causal relationship. This can be the case if there is a negation – *no, tampoco, ni*, etc. – involved.[36] Then this clause mentions something that is NOT the cause. The real cause can be referenced later, for example with the help of *sino*, or not at all. The negation can precede *porque* or be part of the higher clause.

- El partido será histórico. No porque sea el primer enfrentamiento entre ambas, que no lo es. Sino porque es la primera vez en la historia de los torneos del Grand Slam que dos españolas disputarán una semifinal de tan alto nivel. <CREA> [The match will be historic. Not for being the first confrontation between both players, which is not the case, but because it is the first time in the history of the Grand Slam tournament that two Spaniards will play against each other in the semi-finals.]

- Y los clientes no son más o menos <u>porque sea</u> época decembrina, de enamorados o de días especiales. Su número es estable durante todo el año. <CREA> [And there are not more or less clients because we are in December, the time for lovers and special occasions. The number is consistent throughout the year.]

The adverb *solo* before *porque* indicates that the cause is not sufficient or enough to justify something:

- Lo que duele no es ser homosexual; lo que duele es que lo echen en cara como si fuese la peste. Hace falta tener mucha ponzoña en el alma para lanzar los cuchillos sobre una persona, sólo <u>porque sea</u> de tal o cual modo. <CREA> [What hurts is not the fact that a person is homosexual . . . . How poisoned must your soul be to throw knives at a person for being one way or the other?]

In a similar way, adverbial expressions, such as *tal vez*, *quizá*, *posiblemente*, *probablemente*, etc., can make the cause just a possible cause.

- El Romanticismo artístico es un movimiento difícil de definir tal vez <u>porque sea</u> más un movimiento social y espiritual, "un modo de sentir" que un estilo en el más estricto sentido del término. <CREA> [Artistic Romanticism is a movement hard to define, partly because it is more a social and spiritual movement, 'a way of feeling', rather than a style in a narrower sense of the expression.]

The subjunctive can also be triggered by a command or wish in the main clause, which obviously presents it as not being a fact.

- Si bebéis, hacedlo <u>porque sea</u> vuestro libre deseo, no por otros y, en cualquier caso, valga la frase de Chesterton: "Bebed <u>porque seáis felices</u>, pero nunca <u>porque seáis desgraciados</u>." <CREA> [If you drink, do it of your own free will . . . "Drink because you are happy, but never because you are in despair."]

Even the mention of an emotion can present the cause just to be a personal opinion or wish and reduce its factuality. The causal conjunction *porque* is now similar to the generic *que*.

- He oído que Melchor Rodríguez, el viejo anarquista de la guerra civil, que anda por ahí contando los días que le quedan a Franco, y es tan viejo como él, está indignado <u>porque sea</u> marqués el secretario general de la Organización Sindical. <CREA> [I have heard that Melchor Rodríguez, ... is outraged because the general secretary of the Union is a marquis.]

Every time there is more than one reason – *ya . . . ya, o . . . o, bien . . . bien*, etc. – the subjunctive is used:

- las Inspecciones Provinciales de Trabajo pueden autorizar la realización de algunas de estas actividades si queda garantizada la salud y seguridad de la mujer o del menor, bien <u>porque haya realizado</u> un aprendizaje, bien <u>porque sea</u> una actividad adecuada a sus condiciones. <CREA> [<u>can authorize the execution of some of these activities if the health and safety of the woman or minor is guaranteed, either because they have completed an apprenticeship or the activity is suitable to their condition.</u>]

In some cases, *porque* is also used with the subjunctive if it has a final meaning, similar to *para que* or *que*:

- De manera que, todavía, los exámenes médicos pueden ayudar a que el juez se pierda por los vericuetos político-jurídicos, que ahora discuten si su demencia es leve o moderada. En Chile, políticos y militares coinciden en que es moderada, lo que mitigaría el efecto de la Justicia. Hasta la familia – un poco tarde – pugna <u>porque sea declarado loco</u> de remate. El médico canadiense, Luis Fornazzari, rector de la Universidad de Toronto, se negó a firmar el informe final, que habrían alterado sus colegas haciendo desaparecer la palabra leve. <CREA> [<u>Even the family . . . . insists that he be declared completely insane.</u>]

Questions can be used with either mood, whether we are asking for facts (INDIC-ATIVE) or alternatives (SUBJUNCTIVE).

- ¿Por qué nos atacan? – pregunta – ¿Será <u>porque vamos a perder</u>? ¡Nos atacan porque nos temen y porque saben que vamos a ganar! <CREA> [<u>Could it be that maybe we are going to lose?</u>]
- Es muy bueno el Pepe. – ¿Dejará de ser sargento <u>porque sea bueno</u>? <CREA> [<u>Will he stop being a sergeant, because he may be good?</u>]

Como, as a causal conjunction, is used with the indicative.

- <u>Como</u> no <u>quiero</u> ser dogmático, al final del libro transcribo su receta. <CREA> [<u>Because I don't want to be dogmatic, I will transcribe the recipe at the end of the book.</u>]

What distinguishes it from other causal connectors is that here the cause always precedes the consequence or effect.

In narrations, sometimes the past subjunctive is used after the causal *como*. These cases are limited to a certain written register and can be explained with the existence of a negative expression, either *nadie* or *no*. They could make the cause none existent. There could also be diachronic reasons.[37] In the latter case, the imperfect subjunctive could be used instead of the imperfect indicative. It would be always correct to use the imperfect here:

- <u>Como</u> no <u>tuviera</u> respuesta, se inclinó hacia él y observó con ansiedad el color cadavérico del rostro del Joselito <CREA> [As he didn't have an answer, he bent over him and observed anxiously the deathly paler of Joselito's face.] (= Como no <u>tenía</u> respuesta, ...)
- <u>Como</u> no <u>respondiese</u> a sus nuevos llamados, se propuso subir a ayudarle. <CREA> [As he didn't respond to his latest call, he proceeded to go up to help him.] (=Como no *respondía* a sus nuevos llamados, . . .)

→ **You can find examples with the other causal connectors in the alphabetic list of conjunctions at the end of the book.**

9.3.2.3   *Concessive and adversative clauses*

Adversative and concessive clauses are similar in many respects.[38] The most popular adversative conjunctions are *pero* and *sino*. Other adverbial expressions (such as *empero*, *sin embargo*, *no obstante* and *con todo*) also introduce adversative clauses. They always express that two concepts, that are coordinated, are in opposition. *Pero* only introduces restrictions and *sino* indicates incompatibility. Adversative clauses are always in indicative:

- Para Andrews "se trata de una operación compleja que requiere una coordinación muy profesional, <u>pero</u> <u>creemos</u> que no habrá ningún problema." <CREA> [For Andrews "it's about a complex operation that requires a very professional coordination, but we think that there will be no problems".]
- una infinidad de pueblos y paisajes históricos están aproximadamente en la misma latitud, alrededor de los 410 Norte, y <u>sin embargo</u> <u>creemos</u> que poseen calidades luminosas propias. <CREA> [An infinite number of people and historic landscapes are approximately the same latitude, ... but nevertheless we think that they have their own luminous qualities.]

Concessive clauses express the opposite of conditional clauses. A conditional clause would be:

- Si Juan está cansado, no debe conducir.
  [If Juan is tired, he should not drive.]

There is a condition – *si Juan está cansado*- and if this condition is met, then there is a specific consequence – *no debe conducir*. In concessive clauses we are saying: Even though the condition is not met, the consequence is the same, for reasons that don't have to be explained.

- <u>Aunque</u> Juan no está cansado, no debe conducir.
  [Even though Juan is not tired, he shouldn't drive.]

In other words, the conclusion is different from what one would expect or has no direct connection with it. The content of the concessive clause is inoperative or irrelevant with respect to the main clause. This means that here *aunque* is used as a coordinating adversative conjunction, similar to *pero, sin embargo, no obstante*, etc.:

- Juan no está cansado, <u>pero</u> no debe conducir.
  [Juan is not tired, but he should not drive.]

The most prototypical concessive conjunction is **aunque**. Even though it is used mostly with the indicative, as a coordinating adversative conjunction, it can also be combined with the subjunctive, just like **a pesar de que, por más que, aun cuando, por mucho que** and **por muy que**.

If the concessive clause is in indicative, *aunque* can be replaced by the adversative conjunctions *pero, sin embargo, no obstante*, etc. The content introduced by *aunque* is presented as a fact.[39]

- <u>Aunque</u> <u>es</u> conservador, su candidatura es considerada multipartidista. (=Su candidatura es considerada multipartidista; no<u>obstante, es</u>conservador.) <CREA> [Even though he is conservative, his candidacy is considered party independent.]

If *aunque* is followed by the subjunctive instead of the indicative, it is used as a real concessive and subordinating conjunction. The speaker signals that the content of the concessive clause should not be considered a(n) (absolute) fact, but just a possibility or alternative and even a doubt, mild opposition or protest. In the following examples, the subjunctive could be translated with 'Some/everybody may think/talk . . . '; It is possible that some/everybody may think/talk . . . '; etc.:[40]

- <u>Aunque</u> algunos <u>crean</u> que se las saben todas, la mayoría de los ahorradores no conoce sus propias necesidades financieras, y mucho menos las opciones de inversión que existen en el mercado. <CREA> [Even though some may think that they know it all, the majority of savers don't know their own financial needs]
- Poco se sabe de Oklahoma en los mismos Estados Unidos. Pocos la han visitado antes, <u>aunque</u> ahora todos <u>hablen</u> como expertos. <CREA> [Few have visited it (Oklahoma) before, even though now they all talk as if they were experts.]

The idea of possibility can also be expressed with the future tense – or the conditional – because this can be a secondary (con)textual effect of the original meaning of these verb forms. Nevertheless, only the subjunctive can block a factual interpretation:

- VOZ DE CINZIA: ¿Cuál será entonces su próxima película? VOZ DE GLORIA: Sigue siendo mi mayor secreto, <u>aunque</u> ya <u>se estará imaginando</u> que le hablo de un papel extraordinario <CREA> [VOICE OF CINZIA: Which will be your next movie? VOICE OF GLORIA: This remains my biggest secret, even if you already imagine that I am talking about an extraordinary role]

The idea of possibility is also the reason for the use of the subjunctive in contexts that do not seem compatible with its general meaning,[41] such as in the following example.

- [THE FATHER IS TALKING] "Créeme, hija, tu padre está desesperado: son las cuatro de la madrugada y hasta ahora no ha podido dormir." . . . "Por favor, no le digas nada a tía Emma, ya sabes que, <u>aunque</u> <u>sea</u> mi hermana, para estas cosas es como una piedra." <CREA> ["Believe me, child, your father is desperate: it is already four o'clock in the morning and until now I have not been able to sleep." . . . "Please, don't say anything to Aunt Emma. You know that even though she is my sister, in these matters she is like a stone."]

In English we can say: 'she MAY well be my sister' or 'even though she MAY be my sister, but . . .'. Although this is not the most common wording, it can serve as an example to show how modality can be expressed in English, with the same meaning as in Spanish. By presenting something as a possibility instead of as a fact it actually is, we are saying that, in this context, it doesn't matter whether she is the person's sister or not, because in those things she is like a stone. The meaning of *aunque* here could be paraphrased with *no importa que*, which is always used with the subjunctive. Used with the indicative, however, *aunque* would become an adversative conjunction, but repeating the obvious fact that Aunt Emma is the father's sister, especially after 'ya sabes' (you know), the indicative wouldn't make any sense here:

- *"Por favor, no le digas nada a tía Emma, ya sabes que, <u>aunque</u> <u>es</u> mi hermana, para estas cosas es como una piedra." (= ya sabes que es mi hermana, <u>pero</u> para estas cosas es como una piedra.)

Here is another example with *aunque* plus subjunctive:

- "Sería justo que a un entrenador gallego que hemos contratado con mucha ilusión se le reconociese su trabajo. Es un hombre que sabe lo que hace, pero hay que tener en cuenta la dificultad de esta categoría. Espero que en Balaídos la gente entienda que, <u>aunque</u> <u>sea</u> (SUB) gallego, está capacitado. <CREA> [It would be fair to recognize the work of a Galician coach that we have hired with high hopes. It's a man that knows what he is doing, but you have to consider the difficulties at that level. I hope that in Balaídos people will understand that even though he is Galician, he is qualified for the job.]

Aunque sea gallego is not a statement, because it had already been stated in the sentence before with *un entrenador gallego que hemos contratado*, and means even though he is only from Galicia or even though he is not a world-renowned coach.

The imperfect subjunctive, referring to an event in the present or future, expresses counterfactuality.

- Pero te juro por lo más sagrado que, <u>aunque</u> me <u>ofrecieras</u> el plato entero, lo <u>rechazaría</u>. <CREA> [But I swear by everything that is sacred to me that even if you offered me the entire plate, I would reject it.]

In the previous example, *aunque* is used similarly to *si* (if) or *aun si* (even if), but again, the content of the main clause is always contrary to the content of the adverb clause. It would be impossible to say:

- *Pero te juro por lo más sagrado que, <u>aunque</u> me <u>ofrecieras</u> el plato entero, NO lo <u>rechazaría</u>.

The mood does not affect the concessive relationship between the two clauses. *Aun si* cannot be followed by the present subjunctive:

- Pero <u>aun si</u> <u>hemos perdido</u>, nadie osará echarte la culpa. <CREA> [But even though we have lost, nobody will dare to blame you.] (*Pero aun si háyamos perdido, nadie osará echarte la culpa.)

Aunque, on the other hand, can be used with both moods, even in present:

- Pero <u>aunque</u> <u>hemos perdido/háyamos perdido</u>, nadie osará echarte la culpa.

The past subjunctive, referring to an event in the past, always expresses counter-facticity, which is inferable from the context. The interpretation of the following example is: 'Even though I was there in front of him, and **not** Luisa, it was Luisa to whom he talked' or 'fue como si yo NO estuviera delante sino Luisa', or 'en realidad yo no estaba delante sino Luisa':

- Pero en aquella ocasión su manera de hablar sí fue extraordinaria y distinta, como si la presencia de Luisa hubiera adquirido ya tanto peso como para que prevalecieran el tono y la complacencia seguramente empleados con ella a solas, sobre el tan antiguo tono, más irónico, que había usado siempre conmigo, en la infancia como en la edad adulta. Y cuando Luisa salió de la habitación un rato para hablar por teléfono, la manera de comentar y contar de mi padre cambió, o mejor dicho se interrumpió. Como si cayera en la cuenta de que yo estaba allí, empezó a hacerme preguntas sobre Nueva York que ya me había hecho inmediatamente después del regreso. . . y cuyas respuestas ya conocía o no le interesaban. <u>Aunque</u> yo <u>estuviera delante</u>, era a Luisa a quien se dirigía, y en cuanto ella volvió reanudó sus comentarios con una vivacidad insólita <CREA> [Even though I was in front of him, it was Luisa who he was talking to, and as soon as she was back, he resumed his commentary with incredible vigour]

This can also be seen in the following example, where, in the same sentence, *aunque* is followed first by the subjunctive and then by the indicative. The subjunctive points out the contradiction between *la música superior. . . la batería. . . las trompetas y los clarinetes. . . un piano y un saxofón. . . sonidos metálicos. . . un sonido contagioso y rápido* and Amanda being quiet. In reality, Amanda WAS NOT quiet. The indicative in *veía la Alameda*, on the other hand, is strictly factual and straight forward.

- A solas, . . . , Amanda sólo pensaba en lo que había visto; . . . , ella misma sentía ganas de recrear algunas escenas de la película con cantantes y bailarines espléndidos. De pronto . . . la música era superior a cualquier otra: la batería le contestaba a los instrumentos de cuerda y las trompetas y los clarinetes dialogaban con un piano y un saxofón. Parecía que los zapatos se movían con sonidos metálicos en la punta y en los tacones; era un sonido contagioso y rápido. Aunque Amanda estuviera quieta, aunque sólo veía la Alameda como si nada estuviera pasando, en su mente las cosas eran muy distintas; <CREA> [Even though Amanda was quiet and even though she only saw the Alameda as if nothing was happening, in her mind things were very different]

A riesgo de que, which is very similar to *aunque*, introduces a negative possibility or alternative and should only be used with the subjunctive.

- De todos modos, y a riesgo de que me interpretes mal, aprovecharé la ocasión. <CREA> [In any case, and even at the risk that you may misunderstand me, I will cease the opportunity.]

Con (todo) lo que, *con lo* + adjetivo/adverbio *que*, *eso que* can be used with the indicative to refer to (absolute) facts, or the subjunctive to mention possibilities or alternatives:

- Ello implicaría renunciar a estar presente en la unión monetaria prevista para comienzos de 1999 con todo lo que ello supone. <CREA> [This would mean refusing to be present in the monetary union which is expected at the beginning of 1999, with everything that this implies.]
- la tendencia mundial de los medios de comunicación, . . . , es la de mantener entretenido al televidente. Entretenerlo con noticias, con música, con dramatizados, con concursos, con todo lo que se venga a la cabeza, pero entretenerlo. <CREA> [the worldwide trend in mass media, . . . , is to keep the viewer entertained; to entertain him with news, with music, with dramas, with game shows, and whatever else one can think of, as long as it entertains him.]

A sabiendas de que (= knowing that) is only used with the indicative.

- ¡No! -exclamó en español aun a sabiendas que no podían entenderle. ['No!' he shouted in Spanish, still knowing they couldn't understand him.]

The subjunctive is also used in more or less idiomatic formulas such as *llegue o no*, *cueste lo que cueste*, *haga lo que haga*, *vaya adonde vaya*, etc.

→ **You can find examples with the other concessive connectors in the alphabetic list of conjunctions at the end of the book.**

9.3.2.4 *Conditional clauses*

There are all kinds of conditional clauses, real ones and pseudo-conditional clauses. Real conditional clauses are by nature the domain of the subjunctive. Conditions are choices or possibilities that trigger specific consequences or effects. Pure conditional conjunctions or expressions can only be used with the subjunctive. There are, however, several conjunctions that only function as conditional conjunctions when they are used with the subjunctive.

- la decisión de adquirir un perro debe ser consensuada entre todos los miembros de la familia. "En el caso de que se trate de un regalo, tiene que estar muy claro que la persona que lo va a recibir lo quiere." <CREA> [the decision to acquire a dog should be an agreement between all the family members. "In case it is a gift, it must be very clear that the person who gets it wants it."]

The subjunctive presents the condition as one of several possibilities. In the previous example, the dog could also not be a gift, but a purchase for the entire family.

The present subjunctive specifies the conditions as open-ended, potential events or options that still exist (possibility). The present perfect subjunctive characterizes them as consumed possibilities, the imperfect as unlikely possibilities and the past perfect subjunctive as unlikely and consumed possibilities. The tense in the main clause must reflect that the effects are either coexistent with or following the conditions. The conditional as a relative tense, marks the content of the main clause as a possibility as well and indicates that the outcome of the main clause is tied to the one in the conditional clause. The future, present and imperfect indicative anticipate one specific outcome, as if the possibility in the conditional clause were already a fact. They seem to be very close to pseudo-conditional if-clauses with the indicative (in parenthesis below).

- En el caso de que no se cubra la vacante de Narcís Serra, las tareas de la vicepresidencia quedarían diluidas entre varios ministerios. <CREA> [In case the vacancy of Narcís Serra is not filled, the function of the vice-presidency would be absorbed by various ministries.]
- En el caso de que [la lavandina, hipoclorito de sodio] haya sido mezclada con otras sustancias limpiadoras y existan síntomas respiratorios, el manejo de los mismos se hace en forma sintomática <CREA> [In case it has been mixed with other cleaners and other respiratory symptoms exist, it is treated in a symptomatic way] (= Si ha sido mezclada . . . , el manejo se hace de forma sintomática.)
- En el caso de que se procediera a la elección de un nuevo presidente, éste sería el número diecinueve de los que ha tenido la veterana entidad desde

1932. <CREA> [In case it came to the election of a new president, it would be the nineteenth that the veteran organization has had since 1932.]

- Además de las penas de prisión, el fallo establece que los acusados devuelvan a las diecinueve mujeres el dinero incautado en el registro del local (cerca de cinco millones de pesetas), al estimar que les pertenece. En el caso de que no se pudiera devolver a las afectadas, este dinero se ingresará en la cuenta del Tesoro Público. <CREA> [In case it could not be returned to the people affected, this money will be deposited in the Public Treasury account.] (Si no se pudo devolver . . . , este dinero se ingresará en la cuenta . . .)
- En el caso de que los abstencionistas encuestados hubieran decidido votar en las europeas, un 16 por ciento lo habría hecho por el PSOE, un 10 por ciento por IU y un 9,7% por el PP. <CREA> [In case the abstainers that participated in the survey had decided to vote in the European elections, 16 percent would have voted for the PSOE, 10 percent for IU and 9.7 for PP.]
- En el caso de que la tripulación del "Challenger" hubiera sobrevivido a la explosión, no disponían de un método seguro para salir de la nave y utilizar paracaídas. <CREA> [In case the 'Challenger' crew had survived the explosion, they would not have had a safe method to leave the ship and to use parachutes.] (Si la tripulación . . . sobrevivió, no disponía de un método seguro . . .)

Pure conditional conjunctions and expressions are *en (el) caso de que, a condición de que, en el supuesto de que, con tal de que, con que*. . . There are also a series of expressions that can serve as conditional conjunctions when they are used with the subjunctive, such as, the very popular *si*, but also *cuando, mientras, siempre que, a menos que, salvo que, excepto que, a no ser que*, and *como*.

By far the most frequent conjunction in conditional clauses is *si*.[42] It can only be followed by the past and past perfect subjunctive and correlated with the conditional and the conditional perfect in the main clause:

- Y conozco el árabe, pero si tuviera que hacer una frase no podría.[43] <CREA> [I know Arabic, but if I had to create a phrase, I couldn't.]
- José Luis me ha asegurado que si tuviese que hacerlo por obligación o por imposición se negaría. <CREA> [José Luis assured me that if he had to do it by obligation or imposition, he would refuse.]
- ya que él habría hecho lo mismo si hubiera tenido ocasión.[44] <CREA> [because he would have done the same, if he had had the occasion.]
- y si hubiese aniquilado a los Titanes y a todo el pueblo egeo lo único que habría logrado sería acabar consigo mismo pues recordemos que los dioses griegos requerían de un pueblo que los reconociese y adorase. <CREA> [and if he had annihilated the Titans and the entire Aegean people, the only thing that he would have managed to do would have been to finish himself off]

Conditional *si*-clauses must be distinguished from *si*-clauses that state facts.[45] Here main and if- clauses have the status of two independent statements that are united by an equal sign: A = B. This makes this kind of sentence different from real conditional clauses and constructions, where the if-clause expresses a wish or an assumption that could or could not become a reality. They are used with any indicative tense, but not with the future and conditional. Otherwise, the use of tenses is relatively free and determined by the context:

- Si algo tiene este chico es ternura. <CREA> [If this boy has something, it is tenderness.] (El chico tiene algo. This 'algo' equals 'ternura'.)
- Si tiene dinero, podrá preguntar y cogerá a uno que haya hecho prácticas, pero si carece de dinero, no hay elección y le pueden poner, para un asunto difícil, un abogado inexperto, que hará los imposibles, se entregará, pero no habrá hecho prácticas y esto es peligrosísimo. <CREA> [If he has money, he will be able to ask and he will find someone who has practical experience, but if he lacks money, he doesn't have a choice, and they can give him an inexperienced lawyer for this difficult problem]
- Si aún tiene dudas llame a la Línea T: 410 37 37 <CREA> [If you still have doubts, call Line T: 410 37 37]
- "Si ella tiene razón, sería realmente una exclusiva, e iría contra más de 2.000 años de tradición y contra todos los testimonios de los historiadores antiguos", afirmó. <CREA> [He said: "If she is right, it would be a real sensation and would go against 2,000 years of tradition and against all the testimony of ancient historians."]
- Si tuvieron un desacuerdo tan grave, debió estar motivado por una causa lo suficientemente importante. <CREA> [If they had such a big disagreement, it must have been motivated by very important reasons.]
- "Era necesario un pacto. Si tenían cuentas pendientes estas no podían resolverse en la Cárcel. <CREA> [If they had unfinished business, it could not be settled in jail.]

The conjunction *si* has yet another function. It introduces a noun clause as an argument to complete the meaning of a verb (for example, *depender de si*, *(no) saber si*, etc.). It can be used with the imperfect and past perfect subjunctive, but not with the present subjunctive, and all tenses, including the future. With the indicative we present facts and with the subjunctive possibilities:

- La policía practicó diversas detenciones en Rentería y Hernani entre marzo y noviembre de 1982, pero al no constar ningún nombre en el texto no se puede saber si tuvieron relación con el mismo. <CREA> [but since there was no name in the text, it was impossible to know if they had contact with him]
- La situación deportiva ya es de por sí atípica para el Real Zaragoza, que no sabe si se salvará antes de que comience el partido de mañana en el Manzanares <CREA> [for Real Zaragoza, who doesn't know if it will save itself before the match in Manzanares starts]
- "Uno no sabe si hubiera sido mejor no haberlos capturado", sostuvo. <CREA> [He maintained: "One doesn't know if it would have been better had they not been captured."]

- Quién sabe si quisieran operarlo. <CREA> [Who knows if they want to operate on him.]

Como has different uses. It can be a causal, modal or conditional conjunction, as well as a relative or comparative adverb. As a conditional conjunction it is always followed by the subjunctive:

- Como no te comportes, te quito el nombre y te llamo otra cosa cualquiera <CREA> [If you don't behave, I am taking away your name and I'll call you something else]
- Como no nos carguemos al duque, a sus enanos y a sus guardias, el duque nos mata a los dos. <CREA> [If we don't kill the duke and his midgets and guards, the duke will kill both of us.]
- Como no fuera en sentido figurado, ya nadie podría hablar de Imperio. <CREA> [If it were not in a figurative sense, nobody could talk about an Empire anymore.]

Cuando can have the meaning of a conditional conjunction, similar to *si*, in generic contexts. In this case, it is used with the indicative:

- Cuando un maestro habla o escribe en código elaborado se podría valorar como "rebuscado", incomprensible o complicado. <CREA> [When a teacher speaks or writes using elaborate language, it could be judged as 'stilted', incomprehensible or complicated.]

→ **You can find examples with the other conditional connectors in the alphabetic list of conjunctions at the end of the book.**

9.3.2.5 *Adverbial clauses of time*

Conjunctions or adverbial expressions of time are:

> *a que, a medida (de) que, al (mismo) tiempo que, al poco tiempo que, antes de que,[46] apenas, así que, cada vez que, conforme, cuando, desde que, después (de) que, en cuanto, en tanto que, entre tanto que, hasta que, luego (de) que, mientras (que), no bien, según, siempre que, tan pronto (como), una vez (que),* etc.

One of their functions is to define the time frame for the main clause and the chronology of events. In this case, the indicative is used. The chronology of events stems from the meaning of the adverbial expression and the tenses used in the main and dependent clause. The dependent clause helps to contextualize the main clause. If the event in the dependent clause is presented as a fact that already happened, is/was happening, happens habitually or is a recurrent event, then the indicative is used:

- <u>Mientras</u> <u>pasaban</u> la calle . . . , muy cerca de allí, un taxi Mazda, . . . había arrollado a un motociclista y acelerado la marcha para emprender la fuga (The event in the main clause happens simultaneously with the event in the adverbial clause.) <CREA> [While crossing the street, . . . very close to here, a Mazda taxi . . . had run over a motor biker]
- <u>Cuando</u> caminaba por la intersección de Alameda con Ricardo Cuming, repentinamente sufrió un colapso. (The event in the main clause happens simultaneously with the event in the adverbial clause.) <CREA> [While walking through the intersection of Alameda and Ricardo Cuming, he suddenly collapsed.]
- Pero <u>siempre que</u> <u>llueve</u>, escampa <CREA> [But whenever it rains, it stops again]
- <u>Desde que</u> la persona <u>nace</u>, el cobre se empieza a acumular. (The event in the main clause begins at the moment specified in the adverbial clause.) <CREA> [From the moment a person is born, copper starts accumulating.]

If the event in the dependent clause has not happened yet by the time specified in the main clause, and therefore is hypothetical, the subjunctive is used:

- <u>Cuando</u> <u>regrese</u> ya no estaré aquí. <CREA> [When he comes back, I will not be here anymore.]

Many adverbial expressions of time (for example *cuando, mientras (que), siempre que, una vez que, tan pronto como*, etc.) can also be used as conditional conjunctions, such as *en (el) caso de que* or *si*. Here, the concept of time is less important. In this case, both the indicative and the subjunctive are found. The clauses in indicative are similar to pseudo-conditional clauses with *si*:

- En el resto de las naciones, <u>cuando</u> una persona <u>necesita</u> sangre tiene que acudir a familiares o donantes pagados <CREA> [In other countries, when a person needs blood, s/he has to rely on relatives or paid donors] (≈ . . . si una persona necesita sangre tiene que acudir . . .)
- Y, por lo demás, <u>mientras</u> la persona no <u>es sentenciada</u>, se presume inocente. <CREA> [while a person is not sentenced, s/he is presumed innocent.] (≈ . . . si la persona no es sentenciada, se presume . . .)
- Y eso que, <u>siempre que</u> <u>se tomaron</u> estas medidas, la opinión estaba mayoritariamente en contra. <CREA> [Whenever these measures were taken, opinion was mainly against them.] (≈ . . . , si se tomaron estas medidas, la opinión estaba . . . en contra.)

The clauses in subjunctive are more or less equivalent with real conditional clauses with *en (el) caso de que*. The subjunctive presents the condition as one of several possibilities.

- Se trata de un servicio especial de Diners Club. <u>Cuando</u> el socio <u>necesite</u> más información sobre los servicios y beneficios que ofrece Diners Club, puede utilizar la línea 9800–13611, si se encuentra fuera de Bogotá. <CREA> [When a member needs more information about the services and benefits offered by Diners Club, he can call 9800–13611] (≈ En caso de que el socio necesite . . .)
- ¿Usted era consciente de que <u>cuando</u> <u>llegara</u> el momento había una consigna para terminar primero con usted? <CREA> [Were you aware that when the moment would come, there were instructions to finish with you first?] (≈ . . . en caso de que llegara . . .)
- A su juicio son necesarios 13.000 millones de pesetas para emprender una primera acción correctora eficaz, pero esos préstamos no pueden alcanzarse <u>mientras</u> Bilbao no <u>sea declarada</u> "zona de atmósfera contaminada." <CREA> [but these credits are not available as long as Bilbao is not declared an 'atmospherically contaminated zone'] (≈ . . . a no ser que Bilbao sea declarada . . .)
- Según Alvarez, si no se detectan lesiones, el ex jugador podría recuperarse, <u>siempre que</u> <u>tome</u> la decisión de seguir un tratamiento y <u>logre</u> abandonar la adicción a las drogas. <CREA> [the ex-player could recuperate as long as he made the decision to follow treatment and manages to quit his drug addiction] (≈ . . . en caso de que tome . . . y logre . . .)
- Vencerlos entonces, era una fuente de honor <u>siempre que</u> <u>se respetaran</u> los derechos del vencido. <CREA> [Being victorious was a source of honour as long as the rights of the loser were respected.] (≈ . . . en caso de que se respetaran . . .)

Other adverbial expressions, for example *después de que* and *antes de que*, pretty much maintain their reference to chronology, but the subjunctive ties the content of the main clause to a condition, possibility or alternative:

- El agrio de naranja se le pone a última hora al sancocho, <u>después de que</u> <u>estén</u> todos los ingredientes cocidos. <CREA> [The sour orange is added to the soup last, after all the ingredients are cooked.]
- Si este porcentaje se alcanzara <u>antes de que</u> <u>estén en funcionamiento</u> las nuevas presas habría que tomar medidas restrictivas. <CREA> [If this percentage is reached before the new dams are functioning, restrictive measures would have to be taken.]

Antes de que is ALWAYS used with the subjunctive, even if the event is in the past. This is because 'antes de que' is equivalent to a negative expression and introduces something non-existent at the time of reference, which is represented by the main predicate.

- "Es más – agregó – yo lo sabía <u>antes de que</u> <u>se diera a conocer</u> públicamente. <CREA> [I knew it before it was made public.] (Todavía no se había dado a conocer cuando ya lo sabía.)

Después de que[47] can be used with the indicative (for facts) or the subjunctive (for possibilities or alternatives). The question is why is it used with the past subjunctive when the content of the adverbial clause seems to be clearly factual, which can be seen in the possibility to use a past indicative tense (the preterit and the past perfect) in the same context:[48]

- Durante el pasado fin de semana, "La Lola" ya no hizo su habitual salida al portal del edificio, lo que extrañó a sus vecinas. Después de que varias de ellas llamaran a la puerta de la casa, fue el dueño de un ultramarino cercano quien logró entrar en la casa y encontró a la mujer tendida en las escaleras. <CREA> [After a number of them knocked at the door of the house, it was the owner of a nearby convenience store who managed to enter the house] (≈Después de que varias de ellas llamaron a la puerta de la casa, . . .)

This 'anomaly' can also be seen with other adverbial expressions (for example *desde que*, causal *como*, modal *tal como*, etc.) and is often attributed to a certain kind of prose used, particularly in journalism, as a way to provide additional or background information.[49] Still, there must be a basic characteristic of the subjunctive that enables a writer to use this mood in such a way. The reason is that the subjunctive as a marker of subordination converts clauses with *después de que* into subordinate clauses. The subordinating conjunction describes the order of events, and the subjunctive reduces the importance of the adverb clause so that a reader understands which of the two ideas is the main idea and which one is the supporting idea. The past subjunctive situates the event only very generically in the past, because it lacks the richness – but also the rigidity – of the past indicative tense system. In this respect it is very similar to the conditional that can also refer to an event in the past, but happens after the main event.

- Te dije que vendrías a verme. [I told you to come see me.]

With the indicative form, the events are represented in a strictly chronological order. The adverb clause is only syntactically dependent, but semantically coordinated:

- Después de que se firmó el tratado, los Estados Unidos pasaron una legislación mediante la cual los contribuyentes norteamericanos no cubren para nada el traspaso del Canal. <CREA> [After the agreement had been signed, the United States passed a law based on which the US American taxpayers wouldn't pay anything for the transfer of the Canal.] (= Primero se firmó el tratado y después los Estados Unidos pasaron una legislación.)

This is not necessarily the case in the following example where the chronology seems less important. The adverb clause here is more similar to an adversative or conditional clause.[50]

- El agrio de naranja se le puso a última hora al sancocho, <u>después de que</u> <u>estuvieran</u> todos los ingredientes cocidos. <CREA> [<u>The sour orange was added to the soup last, after all the ingredients were cooked.</u>]

Here the adverb clause is not presented as a fact, but as a possibility, or one possible condition, which we know was met, because the preterit 'puso' indicates that the event was completed in the past, and the main clause as a consequence. In English we could translate the adverb clause with 'after WHENEVER all the ingredients were cooked'. In this context, *después de que* can be replaced with **cuando**:

- El agrio de naranja se le puso a última hora al sancocho, **cuando** estuvieran todos los ingredientes cocidos.

Here, the subjunctive has a similar function as in a relative clause:

- El agrio de naranja se le puso a última hora al sancocho, <u>en el momento</u> **en que**/**cuando, después de que** estuvieran todos los ingredientes cocidos.

The use of the past subjunctive in this context is often polemic and can mean 'whenever you said this' or 'when you may have said this':

- Ayer, cuando dijiste/dijeras eso, tendrías haber pensado en las consecuencias. [Yesterday, when you said this, you should have thought about the consequences.][51]

Cuando can even be used with the indicative when the event in the adverb clause has not happened yet to refer to a specific rather than a hypothetic, not specified or possible time or moment:

- Me pongo a pensar. Luego te diré <u>cuando</u> <u>empiezo</u> a tener pavor. <CREA> [<u>I'm thinking about it. Later I will tell you when I start panicking.</u>]

→ **You can find examples with the other connectors of time in the alphabetic list of conjunctions at the end of the book.**

Notes

1 Adapted from NGLE (Manual) (2010: 477–478).
2 *Admitir* is mostly used in indicative.
3 Something similar happens with the expression of will such as *querer, tener (la) intención (de), desear*, etc., under 9.1.1.1:

- "Lo único que le digo a mi hijo es que hago todo esto por ayudar a salvar su vida y porque <u>no quiero que</u> mi familia <u>sufra</u>. (= . . . porque <u>quiero que</u> mi familia <u>no</u> <u>sufra</u>.)

4 As an exception the NGLE mentions situations where the subordinating verb is already in subjunctive. In this case, the indicative would be the most natural choice:

> Pero me callo bien la boca, para que no piense que me he convertido en una de esas "personas mayores" que yo aborrecía con tanta violencia cuando era chica.

5 The NGLE (2009: 1910), points out that in Spain and some Central American countries, it is more common to find 'creerse' + indicative than 'creer' + indicative in a negated context. At the same time, they note that the use of the indicative with negated 'creer', 'creerse' or 'parecer' is rather unusual because it creates the impression that there is a contradiction between the negative meaning in the main and the affirmative meaning in the subordinate clause.

6 The NGLE (2009: 1909), states that the subjunctive is the only option in *No sabemos que tenga problemas económicos* or in *No veo que te quede grande la camisa*. The authors believe that the indicative would lead to a logical contradiction because one cannot affirm in the subordinate clause what is represented as false in the main clause. This is not correct because, first, not knowing or not seeing something is not the same as saying that it is false and, second, there are plenty of examples that prove the validity of the indicative:

> El escritor ejemplifica con los volcanes, y dice que "hay dos posiciones al juzgarlos": "Una es la tradición de todas las culturas antiguas de considerarlos como seres vivos y la otra es la posición racionalista, materialista de tomarlos como cosas inertes. Es justo ésta posición la que ha llevado a la destrucción del medio ambiente, porque como no sabemos que están vivos, ignoramos que los podemos matar".

7 Notice that *ninguna* becomes *alguna* because now that dependent verb has lost its negative/indefinite meaning.
8 Example taken from NGLE (2009: 1908).
9 The NGLE (2009: 1871), even quotes an example where 'llorar al pensar que' that could be paraphrased with 'no querer pensar que' can trigger the subjunctive in the noun clause: *Lloro al pensar que pueda ser cierto* (Somoza, Caverna)
10 Because *no creer que* can also be followed by the indicative, this would be possible here as well:

> Porque no es que crean de verdad que el señor González no tiene la culpa

11 *Soler* has the meaning 'ocurrir ordinariamente, normalmente, frecuentemente', etc. Therefore 'suele acontecer/suceder/acaecer/ . . . que' could be paraphrased with the impersonal expressions 'es normal/frecuente/natural/ . . . que' that are usually followed by the subjunctive.
12 The writing with uppercase letters indicates that the speaker stresses YOU.
13 Only if the meaning of the verb is 'being the cause or reason of something'.
14 If the meaning is 'to be based upon something' (for example in *proceder de que*, *debido a que* or *gracias a que*), the indicative is used:

> Seguramente el error procede de que Guinaco empleaba en sus trámites el castellano, que sigue siendo lengua comercial en Guinea Ecuatorial.
>   Esa retirada provocó muchas airadas protestas debido a que se comentaba que esto era una medida que fomentaba el transporte privado y no el público.
>   Y gracias a que se conocen, gracias a que se producen esos efectos digo, gracias a esas causas, resulta que un espermatozoide y un óvulo pues naces tú.

15 Even though *comprender* and *ser comprensible* are normally used to refer to facts, they can also introduce a supposition, expectation or speculation of the speaker,

comparable to *deber que, ser (muy) probable que, ser posible que, ser lógico que*. The same goes for *admitir, entender, especular, justificar, suponer*, etc.:

> Entiendo y comprendo que estén enfadados porque el Gobierno del Partido Popular ha puesto en marcha en dos años actuaciones paralizadas por gobiernos anteriores.

16 NGLE (Manual) (2010: 874, § 45.6.1a).
17 This example is taken from Butt/ Benjamin (2013: 256).
18 *Temer* and especially *temerse* can also have the meaning of *sospechar* or *creer*. In this case the indicative is used:

> La verdad es que me temo que no seremos capaces de cumplir nuestra parte de los compromisos ya que la reducción tendría que ser mucho mayor de lo que es hoy.

19 This has been documented and commented for example in Bolinger (1956), Butt/ Benjamin (2013: 255), Hunnius (1976), Lope Blanch (1958), etc. Referring to the observation that in Old Spanish verbs of emotions were used with the indicative and the fact that the object clause was not fully subordinated to the governing verb and had rather the status of a causal clause (*He was glad that it happened.* = 'He was glad that it happened.'), Bolinger concludes that in modern Spanish 'the indicative probably went underground, but never disappeared in familiar speech' (1956: 460) This might also be the reason for the higher frequency of the indicative in Latin American Spanish that often conserved forms that are extinct or considered archaic in Spain. Lope Blanch shows that the use of the indicative is not only limited to Latin America (Mexico), but that it can also be found in modern Spanish literature. He also points out that the indicative can only be used with events that already happened or are still going on.
20 The antecedent is underlined twice.
21 This terminology is adopted from Chiquito (2012: 118). In Spanish, for example in the NGLE (2009: 1921), they are called 'especificativas'/'restrictivas' or 'explicativas'/'apositivas'.
22 Quoted from Chiquito (2012: 118).
23 *Mi madre, que en paz descanse, acudió a mi auxilio* is not an exception. The desiderative and other independent uses of the subjunctive are discussed in chapter **7.4**.
24 Because the object is characterized as not known, the indefinite article is used. The definite article could also be used here, but it would have a generic meaning: *Busco el libro que me ayude a comprender el uso del subjuntivo*. Here is another example: Desde entonces he andado muchos caminos, pero no todos, y aún me busco el rostro que sea semilla, tallo, hoja, flor y fruto de la palabra.
25 The word *hecho* in *el hecho de que* has nothing to do with the original meaning of this word anymore. In this context it is completely grammaticalized and is synonymous with the relative pronoun *el que*. As a pronoun it refers to a noun or noun clause, in this case *la aprobación* or *que la Unión Europea apruebe* . . . which, with the subjunctive, is presented only as a possibility.
26 The NGLE (Manual) (2010: 485), also sees the conditional as a subjunctive indicator: *Muy pronto encontraría una bocacalle que me devolviera al punto de partida* (Muñoz Molina, Beltenebros).
27 Native speakers usually find the indicative strange in contexts where the main predicate is clearly desiderative (expresses that the antecedent is not a fact but a desideratum) and where the antecedent is marked as indefinite or non-existent.
28 There is an ongoing discussion about the nature and status of adverb clauses in the contemporary literature. The NGLE, for example, doesn't have a separate chapter about modality in adverb clauses and treats them under the heading 'Elección del

modo con las partículas – Elección del modo con las conjunciones subordinantes' (NGLE [Manual], 2009: 487).

29 The connection between final clauses and noun clauses expressing intention, intended consequence, outcome or purpose has been pointed out by many authors, for example Ahern (2008: 68–69), Pérez Saldanya (1999: 3308–3309) and Rivero (1972).

30 *A menos que* and *a no ser que* are mostly – but not exclusively – used in combination with a negation or negative expression in the main clause: "No podemos hacer nada a menos que varíe".

31 The following example with the subjunctive is no exeption, because 'pasemos' is an imperative and is independent from the main clause:

   • *Más arriba, hemos hablado ya del objeto de estudio, así que pasemos ahora a exponer a qué tipo de objetivos de investigación nos estamos refiriendo* (= Más arriba, hemos hablado ya del objeto de estudio. Así que pasemos ahora a exponer a qué tipo de objetivos de investigación nos estamos refiriendo)

32 If the adverb clause is not necessary to complete the meaning and structure of the main clause, both clauses are separated by a comma:

   • Lo primero que se hizo fue definir la nueva distribución, de forma que se adaptara a las necesidades de su actual propietario.

33 The following example is not an exception, because what comes after the comma is not necessary to complete the main clause. It has already been completed with 'de forma limpia y sin obstáculos'. Without it, there is no reason for a comma.

   • El objetivo es que tanto la bajada como la subida se hagan de forma limpia y sin obstáculos, de forma que sea posible una utilización más cómoda de la nueva carretera. (= El objetivo es que tanto la bajada como la subida se hagan de forma que sea posible una utilización más cómoda de la nueva carretera.)

34 The expressions *de modo/manera/forma que*, with the quantifier *tal* should not be included among the consecutive conjunctions because here the dependent clause functions as a relative clause that modifies the nouns modo/manera/forma:

   • De todas maneras, me gusta vestirme de tal forma que es muy difícil encontrar las cosas.
   • La prevención y el control del tabaquismo se inscribe en este contexto; es necesario insistir en la aplicación de una estrategia integral. . . , de tal forma que sea posible frenar el inmenso poder que tiene la mercadotecnia de la industria tabacalera.

35 There are many theories about why consecutive clauses are followed by the subjunctive. Ahern (2008: 66–67), Borrego et al. (2003: 59–60), Pérez Saldanya (1999: 3297–3299) and Schifko (1967: 44) see the reason in the thematic nature of the consecutive clause. This may be a pragmatic, but not a semantic reason.

36 This does not mean that a negation always triggers the subjunctive, as can be seen in the previous example.

37 Again some authors, for example Pérez Saldanya (1999: 3293–3295), argue that the use of the imperfect subjunctive is triggered by the fact that *como* introduces old, known, shared and information that is easily deductible from the context. In this case I am wondering why the use of the subjunctive in this context is so rare, and why most of the time the indicative is used. Furthermore, in the few examples that I could find,

it is not at all the case that the subjunctive refers to known information, as can be seen in the following example:

- Una tarde, en un tranvía repleto de gente, dos ojos femeninos me miraron expresivos y hechiceros. La presión de aquella masa humana compacta me obligaba a ir apretado contra esa joven. Gracias a esta circunstancia me fue muy fácil rozar su mano. Como no la retirara, me atreví a cogerla y apretarla. Me miró con expresión bovina. Le dije: . . .

38 *Pero* and *aunque*, the most important concessive conjunction, have a very similar meaning and function in the following examples:

- Él está convencido de que no son sus amigos, aunque todavía no sabe que le han engañado.
- Él está convencido de que no son sus amigos, pero todavía no sabe que le han engañado.

One difference, however, is that *pero* must always stand after the clause that it restricts:

- Aunque todavía no sabe que le han engañado, él está convencido de que no son sus amigos.
- *Pero todavía no sabe que le han engañado, él está convencido de que no son sus amigos.

39 The NGLE (2009: 1945) considers this an adversative clause.
40 As with other uses of the subjunctive, many authors – for example Ahern (2008), Flamenco García (1999) and Pérez Saldanya (1999) – defend the idea of a 'thematic' subjunctive, that indicates that the information expressed in the concessive clause is known and therefore 'factual'. They try to prove this especially with little dialogs in which one speaker responds to an argument of the other speaker, almost literally repeating the argument, but now using the subjunctive instead of the indicative. This is their explanation why the subjunctive is used to refer to 'factual' information. Here is one example from Flamenco García (1999: 3830):

- A: No, no debería salir la niña, estos días ha estado muy enferma. B: Ya, pero aunque haya estado muy enferma, ¿no crees que le conviene moverse un poco?

As I have claimed earlier, there is no doubt that the subjunctive, thanks to its function within the system of the Spanish language, can be used for fore- or backgrounding of information, but this is just one of the many (con)textual realizations or effects of the meaning of the subjunctive as a grammatical paradigm. In other words: Only the specific context can help decide whether the content of the concessive clause contains old or new information. What is invariable is that the subjunctive ALWAYS represents the events as possibilities, not as specific facts, but potential events. In this specific example, speaker B doesn't represent the past state of the girl ('muy enferma') as a fact, but as a possibility, because basically everything that you have not lived – seen and felt – personally, always remains abstract, questionable, not officially vetted, confirmed, and just reported. This might also be the main reason why the subjunctive in German is used mostly to indicate indirect speech, which means to report what another person said, to indicate that this is not your opinion and that you cannot vouch for its truth. German also uses a past subjunctive if the speaker thinks that what the other person said is not true. Also, 'enfermo' and even 'muy' are very general concepts. By using 'haber estado enfermo' with the subjunctive, we open up all kind of possibilities, for example: "Yeah, right, she has been very sick. She went out every night" or "Yes, but I think you cannot be so sick that you can't move around a little bit. You need some exercise." This means speaker B makes the absolute statement 'ella ha estado enferma' into a relative statement that can be interpreted as doubt about the entire or parts of the original statement, inability or unwillingness to confirm it, impartiality, etc.

41 There has been a lot of discussion about the so-called rhetorical use of the subjunctive after 'aunque', such as in the example *lo desheredo aunque sea mi hijo* found in Trujillo (1996: 37–39), which for many people, again, serves as an example that the subjunctive can very well refer to facts, because, obviously, the person referred to actually is the son of whoever utters this sentence. The question then is why the speaker didn't say 'lo desheredo aunque es mi hijo'? Again, many experts would call this a thematic use of the subjunctive, to render information that is not new and already known. Trujillo (1996) calls it a metaphorical use of the subjunctive. With that he means that the speaker goes beyond the simple fact and refers to the abstract or hypothetical situation of disinheriting a son.

42 The problem with *si* is that it doesn't only serve as a conditional conjunction and connect possible causes to certain effects, but also to correlate two facts or introduce a noun clause.

43 In some places in Latin America and in northern Spain you will hear the conditional instead of the past subjunctive: *Si tendría que hacerlo, lo haría*. In colloquial Spanish you can also hear the imperfect indicative instead of the past subjunctive (imperfect subjunctive): 'Si tenía que casarme, lo haría con uno de los hombres . . .'. This language use, however, is not generally accepted and is considered incorrect by the Spanish Language Academy.

44 In colloquial Spanish, other verb forms can be used to express the idea of irreality, for example the imperfect and present indicative instead of the conditional perfect. Here the listener must rely on the context to interpret the intended content. The following examples are from the NGLE/Manual (2010: 912):

- Si se lo hubiera contado a alguien, seguro que se reía de mí.
- ¿Qué hubiera pasado si Martín no llega a tiempo?

45 There are all kinds of if-clauses that can be used with the indicative. They all have in common that the if-clause is only pseudo-conditional because, first, it is presented as a fact and, second, because the condition is not necessary for the conclusion. Often cause and effect can be inverted:

- Por ejemplo si llueve muy fuerte la televisión satelital tiene problemas de interferencia. OR Por ejemplo si la televisión satelital tiene problemas de interferencia llueve muy fuerte.

According to their content, there are clauses that have been called epistemic conditional clauses because they reflect what we know about how things work in this world, just like in the previous example, illocutionary conditional clauses that don't really express a condition but that are common expressions to show courtesy or to organize the discourse:

- Porque, si no estoy equivocado, eso es lo que has hecho durante este tiempo.
- Ahora, si no le importa, tendrán que salir del cuarto.
- pero si me permite haré tres o cuatro comentarios muy rápidos.

You can find more information about the different kinds of conditional clauses in the NGLE/Manual (2010: 897–922), in the NGLE (2009) and the *Gramática descriptiva de la lengua española* (1999: 3643–3878)

46 *Antes de que* was previously discussed in the section: **Conjunctions and expressions that always require the subjunctive**.

47 See also Alcoba Rueda (1991).

48 There are many theories about the use of the past subjunctive after 'después de que'. Again, in recent years, it has been attributed to the thematic nature of the subjunctive, to provide previously known information or background information, and also to historic reasons, to analogy, etc. Borrego et al. (2003: 18), for example, describe that, due to its etymology, the forms ending in -ra, are still used in some literary documents or in some regions instead of the past perfect indicative:

- Nombraron, por fin, ministro al general que años antes <u>fuera propuesto</u> para ese cargo. (= había sido propuesto)

They also point out and criticize the use of the past subjunctive forms in -ra instead of the preterit, especially in the media:

- La noticia que diera ese diario no ha tenido confirmación oficial. (= dio)

For this and other theories, see Pérez Saldanya (1999: 3314–3316). It is also interesting to know that in modern French we can see a similar tendency to use 'après que' (after) with the subjunctive instead of the indicative as well. See Kronning (1999) and Molitor (2000)

49 The NGLE (2009: 1954), points out a preference for the subjunctive in European and of the indicative in Latin American Spanish.

50 The loss of their original reference to time and the similarity with conditional conjunctions can also be seen in *mientras, siempre que* and *siempre y cuando*:

- Dijo que la licencia es similar a la que se otorga a los bancos, con carácter indefinido <u>mientras</u> <u>cumplan</u> con las disposiciones legales y que puede ser revocada en caso de infracciones. (. . . en caso de que cumplan . . .)

51 This example is taken from the Borrego et al. (2003: 140).

10 The communicative potential of the subjunctive

Some people who confuse language with logic and think that linguistic signs directly describe reality like to show examples such as the following and argue that the subjunctive can very well be used to refer to facts:

- Juan, me alegro que <u>hayas venido</u> a verme.

They ask: How is it possible that the subjunctive is used in propositions that are clearly facts?[1] The reason is that there is a difference between stating something as an independent fact, which is only possible with the indicative, and which would be very awkward and superfluous if Juan were standing in front of the speaker. We must never forget that language – words, grammatical structures, intonation, etc. – is not only a tool to inform about the existence of something, but also a very powerful device to manipulate people and reality. Here lies the real function and potential of the subjunctive. With the indicative we express directly what we want to say, but with the subjunctive we do it indirectly by referring to sets of alternative possible worlds. In this specific case, what the speaker really wanted to say could be:

- Pensaba que no querías venir. [I thought you wouldn't come.]
- Pensaba que no tenías tiempo. [I thought you didn't have time.]
- Hace tiempo que no viniste a verme. [It has been a while since you last visited.]
- etc.

The communicative potential of the subjunctive and the indicative lies in the general grammatical meaning of moods, which are used to mark propositions as absolute or relative statements. With the indicative we have a set of verb endings to indicate that what is said should be interpreted as a direct statement or a declaration about something that exists, is going on, is considered or represented as a fact, happens, happened, will happen, etc. The subjunctive, on the other hand, can only be defined in negative terms, by the absence of the meaning that characterizes the indicative. Other than the indicative, the subjunctive doesn't make direct reference but refers to a contextual alternative or the contrary of what is expressed with the indicative; or just as an intention.

Example	*Reference (that which we are referring to)*	*Alternative/the contrary*
Me alegro que Juan haya venido. [I am glad that Juan came.]	Juan came to the party even though he had told me before that he wouldn't come.	Juan no ha venido a la fiesta. [Juan didn't come to the party.]
No creo que Paraguay sea el único país sin acceso al mar. [I don't think that Paraguay is the only country without access to the sea.]	Someone told me that Paraguay is the only country without access to the sea.	(Sé que) Paraguay no es el único país porque Bolivia tampoco tiene acceso directo. [I know that Paraguay is not the only country because Bolivia doesn't have access either.
Quiero que María aprenda español. [I want Maria to learn Spanish.]	Maria doesn't learn Spanish.	María aprende español. [Maria learns Spanish.]
Busco un compañero de cuarto que no fume. [I am looking for a flatmate that doesn't smoke.]	I don't have a flatmate or one that smokes.	Tengo un compañero de cuarto que no fuma. [I have a flatmate that doesn't smoke.]
No veo que ahora la gente esté mejor. [I don't see that people live better today.]	Today people live better.	Ahora la gente no está mejor. [Today people are not living better.]
Me inclino a que se respete la voluntad popular. I am inclined to think that the will of the people should be respected.]	The will of the people should be respected.	No se respeta la voluntad popular. [The will of the people is not respected.]

In other words, the subjunctive is a signal for the reader or listener to not interpret an utterance literally but to look for clues in the surrounding and situational context in order to figure out what the speaker really wants to say. In the previous examples, this context is very obvious, especially in those cases where the use of the subjunctive is almost mandatory (for example, after *querer que, hacer que, dudar que, alegrarse (de) que, para que, antes de que*, etc.). Here the subjunctive is required because the meaning of the indicative is incompatible with the lexical meaning of the context (wish, cause, doubt, emotion, purpose, non-existence, etc.). However, many lexical items are polysemous, which means that they have slightly different meaning in different contexts (for example, *decir* and other communication verbs that can also be used to formulate wishes and commands). Here the subjunctive accesses the meaning 'wish/command'.

The economy of language reserves the subjunctive for those situations that require additional steps to interpret the message and have a variety of communicative functions. It allows us to contradict someone without being impolite, to express doubt, polite rebuttal, negation, critique, disapproval etc. even if we don't know exactly or don't want to say why we are against it. It allows us to be vague and non-committal and to be polite in general. In other words, sometimes it is not so important what we say, but how we say it, and how we organize speech acts.

This is also true for those uses of the subjunctive that sometimes are called rhetorical or metaphorical, or categorized as exceptions, such as after *aunque* when referring to something that is clearly a fact.[2]

With the subjunctive we always invite the listener or reader to think and to go beyond what is said or written. By the same token, the use of the subjunctive also opens the door to deception, purposely nebulous messages, distraction, unexpected turns in the argument structure, manipulation, etc., as has been shown by Lavandera (1983, 1990). The subjunctive creates a fictitious, alternative world and signals that the dependent predicate must be interpreted according to the context and not taken as a literal statement. With the subjunctive we don't refer to something that IS (exists, is going on, is considered a fact, happens, happened, will happen, etc.), but something that MAY BE (= is possible, hypothetical, fictitious, intended) or MAY NOT BE (= is the opposite, inexistent, impossible).

Notes

1 It has been pointed out that the subjunctive is also used to provide background or shared information, which would make sense in this example because both the speaker and especially Juan know that he has come. Still, this argument transfers the question what the subjunctive means from the level of the language system to the level of (con)text. And even if the subjunctive could only be explained at the (con)textual level, we must first define its abstract, systemic value.
2 See chapter 9.3.2.3.

11 Mood variation throughout the Spanish speaking world

Very often you hear people saying that there is a tendency for the Spanish subjunctive to be used less or disappear, especially in Latin American varieties. Is this really true or is it based on a lack of understanding of the place of the subjunctive within the Spanish language system and its meaning? Is it the result of the myth that the subjunctive doesn't mean anything? Is this evaluation based on sufficient evidence or only the product of personal, sporadic and episodic experiences? Does this claim refer to all uses and forms or only to some of them? Finally, if the subjunctive verb forms were indeed disappearing, what is occupying their place? The purpose of this section is to find out if there is valid empirical data to back up the claim that the subjunctive is disappearing.

The majority of studies arguing that the subjunctive is disappearing were done in places where Spanish is in contact with other languages that don't use the subjunctive, particularly indigenous languages and English, such as in Puerto Rico and the United States.[1] Others think that there is "very little variation in the use of the subjunctive in educated circles throughout the Spanish speaking world" (Butt/Benjamin, 2013: 245). They only point out "a strong tendency in familiar speech to use the conditional instead of the imperfect subjunctive", the use of "the indicative after subordinators of time that point to the future, e.g.' se lo diré cuando viene", and "the popular Latin-American use of the future indicative after phrases such as *es posible que*" (2013: 245).

11.1 The studies by De Sterck, and Lastra and Butragueño

The lack of empirical studies prompted De Sterck (2000) to conduct an exhaustive and systematic analysis of subjunctive/indicative variation after negative or negated perception and communication verbs (e.g. *no creo que, no digo que*), as well as in questions (e.g. *¿crees que?, ¿dices que?*) in a large corpus of non-literary texts, essays, opinion articles, conferences, treaties about general topics, etc. of well-known Spanish and Spanish American writers compiled by De Kock et al. (1991, 1996), as well as additional texts[2] and nine corpora of spoken Spanish from the 'Proyecto de estudio coordinado de la norma lingüística culta del español hablado de la principales ciudades de Iberoamérica y de la Península Ibérica' (PILEI). The material was recorded in Madrid, Sevilla, Buenos Aires, Bogotá,

Caracas, Lima, Ciudad de México, Santiago de Chile and San Juan (Puerto Rico) at the end of the 1970s and beginning of the 1980s. The primary goal of the analysis was to find out if there are regional and text type specific differences in the use of the subjunctive and the indicative after perception and communication verbs.

As a conceptual and methodological starting point, the author uses the famous classification by Borrego et al. (1985: 1st ed.), specifically part 2: The subjunctive alternates with the indicative, the contexts R. 40, 41, 42 and 43. As Borrego et al. point out, under R. 38 and 39, perception and communication verbs are usually followed by the indicative because with this mood, the speaker communicates to the listener specific information and commits to its truth (2003: 9th ed., 86). If they are negative, negated or used in questions, however, often both moods can produce grammatically correct and meaningful sentences, and the subjunctive is the natural first choice, because the speaker doesn't commit to the truth of the dependent proposition and doesn't say if it is true or not (2003: 86).

Borrego et al. show convincingly that mood use is not dictated unilaterally by certain verbs in the main clause, but that one has to consider the meaning of the entire main clause and that there is interplay between its meaning and the meaning of the two moods which contribute to the overall meaning of a sentence.

The data analyzed by De Sterck shows clearly that mood variation in the kind of noun clauses that she studied is subject to the same semantic and pragmatic mechanisms in all varieties of Spanish (at least the ones considered in this study) (2000: 89). This means, on both sides of the Atlantic, speakers make use of the subjunctive to signal semantic and pragmatic subordination of the dependent noun clause under the meaning of the main clause. The frequency of the subjunctive in the entire corpus was the highest (77.32%) after negated perception verbs in first person (*no creo que*), followed with 58.14% by negated communication verbs (*no dice que*) and negated communication verbs in first person (*no digo que*) (56.70%). Also perception verbs with a negative meaning (*dudar/negar/ignorar/ . . . que*) are followed a little bit more often by the subjunctive than by the indicative. In questions, perception and communication verbs are predominantly used with the indicative (9.86% and 6.25%) (2000: 84).

The author found quantitative differences in the use of subjunctive and indicative in certain geographical areas. However, they are not as pronounced as the differences between written and spoken Spanish, which were also more significant in America than in Spain. In America, the author could attest to the coexistence of three tendencies: The spoken language in Mexico City was very similar to the spoken and written language in Madrid and Seville. Knauer (1998) came to the same conclusion after analyzing the Corpus del Español de México (CEMC). The speakers in Caracas, San Juan (Puerto Rico) and Lima used the indicative more than the average Spanish speaker. The corpora of Bogotá, Buenos Aires and Santiago de Chile occupy an intermediate position between the two extremes (2000: 86).

A more recent study about the vitality of the subjunctive in the Spanish of Mexico City and alternations with the indicative, in 2012, by Lastra and Butragueño, who are the coordinators of the Sociolinguistic Corpus of Mexico City, the largest urban area in the Spanish speaking world, with around 20 million inhabitants, confirms the results obtained by De Sterck.[3] The study is based on 1164 samples of subjunctive forms in 18 speakers from this corpus and "reaffirms the full vitality of the subjunctive (especially in people with more education, youth and women)" (102).

The study and the data of De Sterck largely focused on *no creer* (and also on *no decir*). There was very little data and space dedicated to mood choices in questions (*¿(no) creer que?*). In the overwhelming majority of the few examples that they found, perception verbs in questions were followed by the indicative (90.14%) (69). In the few contexts where the subjunctive was used, the perception verb was almost exclusively *creer*. This suggests that *creer* is more likely to be used with the subjunctive than other perception verbs. There was no significant geographic mood variation between Spain and Latin America, even though the subjunctive was used more often in Caracas, whereas in other areas there was a clear preference for the indicative.

11.2 The studies by Fukushima and Miyashita

A similar study was conducted by Fukushima (2013: 67-80). As a starting point, Fukushima took a study by Miyashita (2008) about mood use after *(no) creer que* in questions, who had registered in a more or less random computation in Mexican web pages a very high percentage of subjunctives, 37 indicative forms and 66 subjunctive forms in yes/no questions of the type *¿Crees que en Chiapas se [sic] suceda el mismo conflicto electoral que en las del 2 de julio?* (MSN: 22-VII-2006), and 29 indicative versus 86 subjunctive forms in information questions of the type *¿Quién crees que gane las elecciones presidenciales en EU?* (MSN: 1-XI-2004). Fukushima searched the entire Corpus de Referencia del Español Actual (CREA) for the sequence *¿crees que?* (and *¿Crees que?*) and came up with a total of 1356 examples in indicative (99.5%) and 7 in subjunctive for Spain and 807 examples in indicative (87.6%) and 114 (12.4%) in subjunctive for Latin America. This result doesn't corroborate the high frequency of the subjunctive in the study of Miyashita. Nevertheless, it shows a relatively high percentage of subjunctive use in this context in Latin America compared to Spain. Fukushima then showed some of the subjunctive examples that he had found to a random group of educated adult speakers from Spain, Peru and Chile and confirmed the findings. The speaker from Spain wanted to use the indicative in all the examples. The speaker from Chile accepted both the indicative and the subjunctive and the speaker from Peru wanted to use the subjunctive, with the exception of two examples in which she was split between the indicative and the subjunctive. In order to add a diachronic perspective, Fukushima also searched the entire Corpus Diacrónico del Español (CORDE) for the same word and came up with very similar results: Spain = 250 examples with indicative (95.1%) and 13 with subjunctive (4.9%); Latin America = 48 examples with indicative (87.3%) and 7 (12.7%) with subjunctive. The findings not only contradict the claim that the subjunctive is disappearing in Latin America or that there is a preference for the indicative, but also the hypothesis of the archaic character of Latin American Spanish; that is, that it conserves characteristics of prior states of language.

11.3 The VARIGRAMA project

In 2001, a research project with the title 'Encuesta sobre problemas sintácticos de la lengua española', that in 2004 was re-baptized Project VARIGRAMA (Variación Gramatical del Español en el Mundo), was started by Tagagaki, Ueda, Miyamoto, Fukushima and Ruiz Tinoco (2004). Its objective was the study of the diatopic (geographical) variation of certain syntactic structures of the Spanish language. It is based on a questionnaire of 105 sentences, all of which contain one syntactic structure that differs in the Spanish speaking world. Later six more sentences were added. This list was sent to 207 informants in 10 Spanish cities (Oviedo, Pamplona, Alcalá de Henares, Madrid, Barcelona, Salamanca, Sevilla, Huelva, Tenerife, Las Palmas) and 301 people in Latin American universities (Ciudad de México, (México), San José (Costa Rica), La Habana (Cuba), San Juan (Puerto Rico), Caracas (Venezuela), Bogotá (Colombia), Quito (Ecuador), Lima (Perú), La Paz y El Alto 4 (Bolivia), Asunción (Paraguay), Santiago (Chile), Montevideo (Uruguay) and Buenos Aires (Argentina)). The informants had to decide: (A) 'I would say that'; (B) 'I wouldn't say that but I have heard it'; and (C) 'I wouldn't say that and I have not heard other people saying it'. The syntactic structures compared in the survey were verb moods, personal pronouns, reflexive structures, relative pronouns, reference, agreement, prepositions, etc. The following are the questions of the survey about verb moods that were sent to speakers from all over Spain (Oviedo, Pamplona, Alcalá de Henares, Madrid, Barcelona, Sevilla, Huelva, Tenerife, and Las Palmas) in 2004:

[1]   Es probable que los precios allí <u>serán</u> (IND) más bajos. [It is likely that the prices there will be lower.]

[2]   Es una lástima que no <u>hizo</u> (IND) sol ayer. [It is a pity that the sun was not shining yesterday.]

[3]   Es interesante que usted <u>sigue</u> (IND) con el mismo trabajo. [It is interesting that you still have the same job.]

[4]   Es bueno que <u>tenemos</u> (IND) tiempo para visitar a Juan también. [It is good that we have time to visit Juan as well.]

[5]   Me alegro de que te <u>has mejorado</u> (IND). [I am glad that you are feeling better.]

[6]   Digo yo, que qué carajo nos importa lo que pase en el Golfo ese, yo ni siquiera sé dónde está. El hecho de que no <u>sabes</u> (IND) dónde está, no quiere decir que no exista. [The fact that you don't know where it is doesn't mean that it doesn't exist.]

[7]   Quisiera llamar la atención sobre el hecho de que en Finlandia la libertad de prensa <u>está garantizada</u> (IND) en la legislación. [I want to call attention to the fact that in Finland free speech is guaranteed by law.]

[8]   No hay duda de que ya lo <u>ha logrado</u> (IND). [There is no doubt that s/he has already achieved it.]

[9]   Claro que soy español, pero, aunque <u>sea</u> (SUB) español, no me gustan los toros. [Of course I am a Spaniard, but even though I am a Spaniard, I don't like bullfighting.]

[10] Claro que soy español, pero, aunque <u>soy</u> (IND) español, no me gustan los toros. [Of course I am a Spaniard, but even though I am a Spaniard, I don't like bullfighting.]

The results of the survey were tabled together with information about the speakers (location, sex, education, occupation and age) and are presented in Table 11.1 as follows:

Table 11.1

# of question	Would say that	Wouldn't say that but have heard it	Wouldn't say that and have not heard it	Total
1 Es probable que + IND	13 (7%)	64 (35%)	105 (58%)	182
2 Es una lástima que + IND	34 (18.4%)	106 (57%)	45 (24.3%)	185
3 Es interesante que + IND	8 (4%)	53 (28%)	125 (67.2%)	186
4 Es bueno que + IND	7 (4%)	77 (42%)	99 (54.1%)	183
5 Me alegro de que + IND	1 (0.5%)	64 (35%)	119 (64.7%)	184
6 El hecho de que no sabes . . . + IND	28 (15%)	107 (58%)	51 (27%)	186
7 el hecho de que + IND	142 (75.5%)	37 (20%)	9 (5%)	188
8 No hay duda de que + IND	166 (88.8%)	17 (9%)	4 (2%)	187
9 Claro que soy español, pero aunque sea español . . .	170 (91%)	15 (8%)	2 (1%)	187
10 Claro que soy español, pero aunque soy español . . .	89 (48.4%)	80 (43%)	15 (8%)	184

A second questionnaire was sent to Mexico in 2008. Unfortunately, the numbering was a little different compared with 2004. Still it is possible to compare most of the answers, as seen in Table 11.2:

Table 11.2

# of question	Would say that	Wouldn't say that but have heard it	Wouldn't say that and have not heard it	Total
1 Es probable que + IND	Question was different			
2 Es una lástima que + IND	47 (43.1%)	45 (41%)	17 (15.5%)	109
3 Es interesante que + IND	23 (21.3%)	48 (44%)	37 (34.3%)	108
4 Es bueno que + IND	74 (67.9%)	27 (25%)	8 (7%)	109
5 Me alegro de que + IND	17 (16%)	60 (57%)	29 (27.4%)	106

(Continued)

Table 11.2 Continued

# of question	Would say that	Wouldn't say that but have heard it	Wouldn't say that and have not heard it	Total
6 El hecho de que no sabes . . . + IND	Question was different			
7 el hecho de que + IND	88 (81.5%)	16 (15%)	4 (3%)	108
8 No hay duda de que + IND	73 (67.6%)	30 (28%)	5 (5%)	108
9 Aunque soy mexicano, no me gusta el mole.	56 (50.5%)	44 (40%)	11 (10%)	111
10 Aunque sea mexicano, no me gusta el mole.	93 (83.8%)	13 (12%)	5 (4.5%)	111

A third questionnaire – which was sent to Costa Rica (San José) (Table 11.3), Venezuela (Caracas) (Table 11.4), Ecuador (Quito) (Table 11.5), Perú (Lima) (Table 11.6), Bolivia (La Paz and El Alto) (Table 11.7) and Uruguay (Table 11.8) – is dated 2010:

Table 11.3 Costa Rica

# of question	Would say that	Wouldn't say that but have heard it	Wouldn't say that and have not heard it	Total
1 Es probable que + IND	Question was different			
2 Es una lástima que + IND	22 (96%)	1 (4%)	0 (0%)	23
3 Es interesante que + IND	3 (13%)	15 (65%)	5 (21.7%)	23
4 Es bueno que + IND	20 (87%)	2 (9%)	1 (4.3%)	23
5 Me alegro de que + IND	3 (13%)	5 (22%)	15 (65.2%)	23
6 El hecho de que no sabes . . . + IND	Question was different			
7 el hecho de que + IND	23 (100%)	0 (0%)	0 (0%)	23
8 No hay duda de que + IND	15 (65.2%)	3 (13%)	5 (21.7%)	23
9 Aunque soy costarricense, no me gusta el "casado"	23 (100%)	0 (0%)	0 (0%)	23
10 Aunque sea costarricense, no me gusta el "casado".	13 (56.5%)	8 (35%)	2 (8%)	23

Table 11.4 Venezuela

# of question	Would say that	Wouldn't say that but have heard it	Wouldn't say that and have not heard it	Total
1 Es probable que + IND	Question was different			
2 Es una lástima que + IND	19 (76%)	5 (20%)	1 (4%)	25
3 Es interesante que + IND	1 (4%)	12 (48%)	12 (48%)	25
4 Es bueno que + IND	21 (84%)	4 (16%)	0 (0%)	25
5 Me alegro de que + IND	1 (4%)	15 (60%)	9 (36%)	25
6 El hecho de que no sabes . . . + IND	Question was different			
7 el hecho de que + IND	22 (88%)	3 (12%)	0 (0%)	25
8 No hay duda de que + IND	17 (74%)	7 (28%)	1 (4%)	25
9 Aunque soy venezolano, no me gusta la hallaca.	24 (96%)	1 (4%)	0 (0%)	25
10 Aunque sea venezolano, no me gusta la hallaca.	9 (36%)	13 (52%)	3 (12%)	25

Table 11.5 Ecuador

# of question	Would say that	Wouldn't say that but have heard it	Wouldn't say that and have not heard it	Total
1 Es probable que + IND	Question was different			
2 Es una lástima que + IND	12 (52%)	8 (35%)	3 (13%)	23
3 Es interesante que + IND	4 (17.4%)	7 (30%)	12 (52%)	23
4 Es bueno que + IND	18 (78.3%)	3 (13%)	2 (8.7%)	23
5 Me alegro de que + IND	5 (22.7%)	11 (48%)	6 (27.3%)	22
6 El hecho de que no sabes . . . + IND	Question was different			
7 el hecho de que + IND	21 (91.3%)	1 (4%)	1 (4.3%)	23
8 No hay duda de que + IND	19 (82.6%)	3 (13%)	1 (4.3%)	23
9 Aunque soy ecuatoriano, no me gusta el llapingacho.	22 (96%)	1 (4%)	0 (0%)	23
10 Aunque sea ecuatoriano, no me gusta el llapingacho.	13 (56.5%)	5 (22%)	5 (21.7%)	23

Table 11.6 Perú

# of question	Would say that	Wouldn't say that but have heard it	Wouldn't say that and have not heard it	Total
1 Es probable que + IND	Question was different			
2 Es una lástima que + IND	12 (52%)	8 (35%)	3 (13%)	23
3 Es interesante que + IND	3 (13%)	14 (61%)	6 (26%)	23
4 Es bueno que + IND	15 (65.2%)	8 (35%)	0 (0%)	23
5 Me alegro de que + IND	6 (26%)	12 (52%)	4 (17.4%)	22
6 El hecho de que no sabes . . . + IND	Question was different			
7 el hecho de que + IND	21 (91.3%)	1 (4%)	0 (0%)	22
8 No hay duda de que + IND	22 (96%)	1 (4%)	0 (0%)	23
9 Aunque soy peruano, no me gusta el cebiche (ceviche).	17 (74%)	6 (26%)	0 (0%)	23
10 Aunque sea peruano, no me gusta el cebiche (ceviche).	7 (30.4%)	13 (57%)	2 (8.6%)	22

Table 11.7 Bolivia

# of question	Would say that	Wouldn't say that but have heard it	Wouldn't say that and have not heard it	Total
1 Es probable que + IND	Question was different			
2 Es una lástima que + IND	12 (31.6%)	21 (55%)	5 (13%)	38
3 Es interesante que + IND	10 (25.6%)	22 (56%)	7 (18%)	39
4 Es bueno que + IND	16 (40%)	16 (40%)	8 (20%)	40
5 Me alegro de que + IND	11 (27.5%)	23 (57.5%)	6 (15%)	40
6 El hecho de que no sabes . . . + IND	Question was different			
7 el hecho de que + IND	30 (75%)	5 (12.5)	5 (13%)	40
8 No hay duda de que + IND	26 (65%)	11 (27.5%)	3 (7.5%)	40
9 Aunque soy boliviano, no me gusta el chairo.	26 (65%)	13 (32.5%)	1 (2.5%)	40
10 Aunque sea boliviano, no me gusta el chairo.	15 (37.5%)	18 (45%)	7 (17.5%)	40

Table 11.8 Uruguay

# of question	Would say that	Wouldn't say that but have heard it	Wouldn't say that and have not heard it	Total
1 Es probable que + IND	Question was different			
2 Es una lástima que + IND	9 (45%)	9 (45%)	2 (10%)	20
3 Es interesante que + IND	1 (5%)	9 (45%)	10 (50%)	20
4 Es bueno que + IND	12 (63%)	6 (32%)	1 (5.2%)	19
5 Me alegro de que + IND	2 (10%)	10 (53%)	7 (37%)	19
6 El hecho de que no sabes . . . + IND	Question was different			
7 el hecho de que + IND	18 (90%)	2 (10%)	0 (0%)	20
8 No hay duda de que + IND	18 (90%)	1 (5%)	1 (10%)	20
9 Aunque soy uruguayo, no me gusta la carne.	18 (90%)	2 (10%)	0 (0%)	20
10 Aunque sea uruguayo, no me gusta la carne.	15 (79%)	3 (16%)	1 (5.2%)	19

The fourth questionnaire, which was sent to Spain (Salamanca), Cuba and Puerto, is dated 2014. I have only listed here the results for Cuba and Puerto Rico, as seen in Tables 11.9 and 11.10, respectively:

Table 11.9 Cuba

# of question	Would say that	Wouldn't say that but have heard it	Wouldn't say that and have not heard it	Total
1 Es probable que + IND	Question was different			
2 Es una lástima que + IND	8 (48.6%)	8 (44%)	2 (11%)	18
3 Es interesante que + IND	4 (21%)	10 (53%)	5 (26.3%)	19
4 Es bueno que + IND	Question was different			
5 Me alegro de que + IND	5 (29.4%)	7 (41%)	5 (26.3%)	17
6 El hecho de que no sabes . . . + IND	Question was different			
7 el hecho de que + IND	15 (83.3%)	1 (6%)	2 (11%)	18
8 No hay duda de que + IND	12 (66.6%)	5 (28%)	1 (5.5%)	18
9 Aunque soy cubano, no me gusta la pelota.	18 (100%)	0 (0%)	0 (0%)	18
10 Aunque sea cubano, no me gusta la pelota.	8 (48.6%)	8 (44%)	2 (11%)	18

Table 11.10 Puerto Rico

# of question	Would say that	Wouldn't say that but have heard it	Wouldn't say that and have not heard it	Total
1 Es probable que + IND				
2 Es una lástima que + IND	11 (50%)	10 (45%)	1 (4.5%)	22
3 Es interesante que + IND	11 (50%)	10 (45%)	1 (4.5%)	22
4 Es bueno que + IND	Question was different			
5 Me alegro de que + IND	3 (13.6%)	15 (68%)	4 (18.1%)	22
6 El hecho de que no sabes . . . + IND				
7 el hecho de que + IND	20 (90.9%)	2 (9%)	0 (0%)	22
8 No hay duda de que + IND	13 (59%)	7 (32%)	1 (4.5%)	22
9 Aunque soy puertorriqueño, no me gusta la pelota.	13 (59%)	8 (36%)	1 (4.5%)	22
10 Aunque sea puertorriqueño, no me gusta la pelota.	14 (63.5%)	6 (27%)	2 (9%)	22

As far as I know, the results for the subjunctive that appear in the tables have not been analyzed yet. The survey shows that on both sides of the ocean there are speakers who think that both the indicative and the subjunctive make sense in the sentences given to them, because the content of the subordinated clause could either be interpreted as a relatively independent fact, but also the dependent content of the speaker's judgement or opinion. Not even in Spain was the indicative rejected completely in any of the examples. However, there is a very clear overall preference in Spain for the subjunctive in the examples 2, 3, 4 and 5, in which the main predicate expresses emotions, feelings and judgements.

11.3.1 Es probable que + IND, es una lástima que + IND, es interesante que + IND, es bueno que + IND, me alegro de que + IND

2 Es una lástima que no hizo sol ayer.	Would say that
Spain	18.40%
Bolivia	31.60%
Mexico	43.10%
Uruguay	45.00%
Cuba	48.60%
Puerto Rico	50.00%
Ecuador	52.00%
Peru	52.00%
Venezuela	76.00%
Costa Rica	96.00%

3 Es interesante que Ud. sigue con el mismo trabajo.

Spain	4.00%
Venezuela	4.00%
Uruguay	5.00%
Costa Rica	13.00%
Peru	13.00%
Ecuador	17.40%
Cuba	21.00%
Mexico	21.30%
Bolivia	25.60%
Puerto Rico	50.00%

4 Es bueno que tenemos tiempo para visitar a Juan también.

Spain	4.00%
Bolivia	40.00%
Uruguay	63.00%
Peru	65.20%
Mexico	67.90%
Ecuador	78.30%
Venezuela	84.00%
Costa Rica	87.00%
Cuba	Question different
Puerto Rico	Question different

5 Me alegro de que has mejorado.

Spain	0.50%
Venezuela	4.00%
Uruguay	10.00%
Costa Rica	13.00%
Puerto Rico	13.60%
Mexico	16.00%
Ecuador	22.70%
Peru	26.00%
Bolivia	27.50%
Cuba	29.40%
	16.27%

In example 5, after *me alegro de que*, only one out of 184 speakers from Spain opted for the indicative, and nowhere in Latin America more than 30% of the participants chose the indicative, even though the tense in the dependent clause (present perfect) could suggest that its content referred to a fact. The only clear difference between the examples 2, 3, 4 and 5 is the meaning of the main sub-ject and that the subject of the main clause is the speaker himself, while in the examples 2–4 we have an impersonal subject. In example 2 (*es una lástima que*) there was a much stronger occurrence of the indicative, which went up to 96% in Costa Rica. And even in Spain, 18.4% of the participants would have used the indicative personally and 57.3% claim that they have heard other people use the indicative in this context. (However, in the comments that the participants could include, the majority expressed a preference for *hiciera* o *hiciese*.) The results for example 3 (*es interesante que*) are somehow comparable with example 5 (*me alegro de que*). Only in Puerto Rico (50%) the indicative made up for half of the answers. The indicative use in Venezuela and Uruguay, on the other side, is comparable to the one in Spain. In example 4, again, there is a strong difference between Spain and Latin America when it comes to the use of the indicative, which is very rare in this context in Spain (4%) and over 50% in the Latin American countries, with the exception of Bolivia (40%). It is very clear that after all the expressions that somehow express the positive or negative attitude of the speaker towards the content of a dependent clause, the use of the indicative is relatively rare in Spain, but that percentage can go up to 96% in Latin America.

11.3.2   El hecho de que + IND

A lot of ink has been spilled over *el hecho (de) que* and why the subjunctive is used in examples that are clearly seen as facts, such as in Delbecque/Lamiroy (1999), Demonte (1977), Fukushima (2008), Keenan (1971), Kiparsky/ Kiparsky (1971), Krakusin (1992) and Rivero (1970). Fukushima tries to summarize the different hypothesis. He distinguishes the representatives of what he calls the 'subordination theory' that claim that *el hecho (de) que* should always be followed by the subjunc-tive, which is clearly not the case taking into consideration the many documented cases of mood variation in this context. In second place he lists authors that accord-ing to him represent the so-called neutralization theory, such as Butt/Benjamin (2013) and Porto Dapena (1991). Generally speaking, these authors think that the semantic mood difference here is obscured. More specifically, Butt/Benjamin write:

> The subjunctive is used whenever any kind of value judgement or emotional reaction is involved, or whenever any idea of cause or influence is involved . . . The indicative is required when the main verb is a verb of knowing or perceiv-ing (e.g. *enterarse de* 'to find out', *darse cuenta de* 'to realize'). When *el hecho de que* is preceded by a preposition it almost always takes the indicative . . . In some cases, the subjunctive and indicative appear to be interchangeable.
>
> (2013: 260)

In third place Fukushima lists the 'original function theory' where the

core meaning of the two moods are maintained in the construction in ques-tion. If the subjunctive is used, there is a shade of doubt with respect to the realization of the matter expressed by the *hecho* clause, and if the indicative is selected, there is no such hypothetical nuance.

(2008: 5)

In fourth place, Fukushima describes what he calls the 'predicate theory' according to which the "mood of the subordinate verb is determined by the meaning of the predicate verb, adjective or noun, neglecting the influence of the head of the clause *hecho*, due to its poor meaning substance" (2008: 5). As representatives he mentions Leonetti (1999) and Woehr (1975). Finally, Fukushima describes the 'information theory', which he represents himself, together with Ahern (2008), Hummel (2001), Matte Bon (1992), Pérez Saldanya (1999), Wasa (2006) and many other authors. According to this theory, the subjunctive after *el hecho (de) que* is explained with the function of the subjunctive to refer to already known, old or less important information. Fukushima establishes the following hypothesis:

> a. If the subjunctive is used in the appositive clause preceded by *el hecho de que* 'the fact that', this clause carries just the background information which helps to express other more important information. Such clauses often function as the subject of the sentence, and precede the main clause. b. If the indicative is used in this type of clause, the clause bears the main information of the sentence. Such clauses are usually located after the main clause, as the object of a verb or a preposition.

(2008: 7)

Based on a very detailed analysis, Pérez/Süss conclude that *el hecho de que* is followed by the subjunctive when the speaker draws a personal or subjective conclusion or when s/he deduces a consequence. On the other hand, s/he uses the indicative when s/he makes an objective assertion. They also found that when the clause with *el hecho de que* has the function of a subject, usually at the beginning of the sentence, the verb is systematically in subjunctive, no matter whether the event or situation is real, hypothetical or imaginary or whether the verb is used affirmatively or negated. When the clause with *el hecho de que* is used as an indirect or prepositional object, the verb is generally in indicative. Exceptions are when the expression or verb that precedes *el hecho de que* is negated, when the speaker questions something or expresses his/her surprise about something or when *el hecho de que* is used in combination with expressions that require the subjunctive; for example, *Estoy orgulloso del hecho de que* mi nombre *sea* (SUB) *sinónimo de un hombre que ha mantenido su palabra y complido su promesa.* [I am proud that my name is synonymous with that of a man that has kept his word and his promise.] Used as a direct object it can be replaced by *que* and followed either by the subjunctive or indicative. Finally, combined with *ser* and *estar* (for example *está/es el hecho de que . . .*), the expression is followed by the indicative (2009: 85–86).

This survey shows that probably in the entire Spanish speaking world, even in Spain (75.5%), the majority of speakers favour the indicative after *el hecho de que* in this specific context. Only in Bolivia (75%) was it used a little less than in Spain. My own research supports the observations by Pérez/Süss and Fukushima that used as a sentence subject – often, but not always, at the beginning of a sentence – *el hecho de que* is mostly followed by the subjunctive. However, used as a direct or circumstantial object, it is followed predominantly by the indicative, which would be the case in example 7. A search of the entire CORPES on August 8, 2015, for *sobre el hecho de que* yielded a total of 164 examples from Spain and Latin America, only 30 (18.3%) of which were followed by the subjunctive. With the indicative, *hecho* really means an 'absolute, (relatively) independent and (generally) established fact' as in the following example:

- Y llamaron la atención sobre el hecho de que no existen programas universitarios en ese campo. [And they called attention to the fact that there aren't any college programmes in this field.] (= No existen programas universitarios en ese campo.)

  <CORPES, August 8, 2015>

With the subjunctive, it has lost its original lexical meaning and just functions as part of a compound relative pronoun, similar to *el que*. It is used as a determiner to modify the epistemic value of the subordinated clause. Instead of presenting the content of the subordinated clause as a process and event, it is presented as a result or already established fact, 'algo previo a la enunciación del verbo principal', according to Delbecque/Lamiroy (1999: 1999). Here *hecho* stands for 'possibility' or whatever meaning it is getting from context, particularly the linguistic elements in the main clause. Often the predicate of the subordinated clause is modified by adverbs, such as *quizá(s)*, *frecuentemente*, *a veces* and similar adverbs that underline the idea of possibility or alternative. Only if the dependent clause should be marked as a possibility, alternative, one element among others or intention instead as a specific and definite fact, then the subjunctive is used. Here is an example:

- Tengo un hombro más alto que el otro. También la caracola de la oreja. El fisioterapeuta me llama la atención sobre el hecho de que QUIZÁ mi marido no me quiera lo suficiente, porque nunca se ha fijado en el detalle de que un hombro, una oreja, se sitúan por encima de la otra oreja, del otro hombro.

  <CORPES, August 8, 2015>

- [One of my shoulders is higher than the other. The same goes for my ear. The physical therapist calls my attention to the fact that maybe my husband doesn't love me enough, because s/he has never noticed this detail . . .]

  (. . . QUIZÁ mi marido no me quiera → POSSIBILITY, SPECULATION)

El hecho de que cannot be used with prospective predicates, which include causative (*hacer*) and desiderative predicates (*querer*, *desear*, *esperar*), but also other expressions that are semantically not compatible with *el hecho*, such as *saber*: *Sé el hecho que está enfermo* and perception predicates (*Vi el hecho que Juan está *enfermo*). The reason for this is probably that *saber* and *ver* already contain 'hecho' in their meaning, which is repeated again with the indicative in the noun clause that also contains the idea of 'hecho'. *Saber* was used by Delbecque and Lamiroy to claim that *el hecho de que* is not compatible with asserted contents. However, there are many examples that contradict this hypothesis.

El hecho (de) que is not compatible with predicates of doubt or negation, because here the speaker contradicts the idea that the content of the noun clause is some established fact (**Dudo el hecho (de) que Juan esté enfermo.*) Only if 'duda' is negated is it possible to use *el hecho (de) que* (*No dudo el hecho (de) que Juan esté enfermo.*)

The analysis shows that before we can analyze mood variation after *el hecho de que*, we have to distinguish the syntactic and semantic function of the dependent clause in which it occurs and the meaning of the dependent predicate. However, it seems that on both sides of the Atlantic speakers use the two moods to emphasize the same semantic differences.

11.3.3 *No hay duda de que* + IND

The results of question 8 are surprising, because I would have expected a higher incidence of the indicative throughout the entire Spanish speaking world for the simple reason that when negating a doubt, we are saying that we are not doubting anymore. This means the conditions for the use of the subjunctive no longer exist. As the survey shows, however, this doesn't necessarily mean that you always want to represent the content of the subordinated clause as an absolute, (relatively) independent and (generally) established fact. The NGLE (1912, 25.7n.), for example, writes that when verbs of doubt are negated, the semantic conditions CAN arise for the use of the indicative. Yet, they continue, there are also examples with the subjunctive in this context, especially when information is presented that the speaker accepts and then adds an objection of major argumentative weight (1912, 25.7n.). In order to justify unexpected uses of the subjunctive, the NGLE also operates with the problematic concept of 'low informational value' (1913, 25.7ñ.). Only in Uruguay (90%) and Peru (96%), more speakers chose the indicative than in Spain (88.8%). In all the other countries the percentage was lower. The country with the lowest incidence of the indicative, Puerto Rico (59%), is the country where, according to some researchers, the subjunctive is on its way out because of the influence of English.

11.3.4 *Aunque*

The use of the subjunctive after *aunque* in contexts that clearly seem to refer to facts is another litmus test that shows the validity of the concept that one has of the subjunctive.[4] Here again, the NGLE makes use of the 'informational value' of the subordinated clause (2009: 25.13.i.). If this rule were true, then Cubans (100%) and Costa Ricans (100%) had the best grip of the subjunctive, followed by Ecuadorians (96%), Venezuelans (96%), Spaniards (91%) and Uruguayans (90%). Mexicans, on the other hand, were rather undecided when it came to the use of the subjunctive (50.5%) and even leaned heavily towards the indicative (83%). One would also expect a correlation between the percentages in examples 9 (in indicative) and 10 (in subjunctive). Ideally the sum of the two percentages should be 100%. Bolivians and Peruvians seem to be the most consequent, with 102.5% and 104.4% respectively. The most undecided here were the Uruguayans, with 169%. All these numbers suggest that the rule formulated in the NGLE is not correct and that there are other reasons for the use of the subjunctive in this context. Neither does the idea of a 'polemical subjunctive' apply here, which according to the NGLE is used to contradict, dismiss or reject a previous assertion (2009: 25.13.i.). It is not difficult to find examples that clearly show that the subjunctive doesn't have anything to do with 'low informational value', as in the following:

- Mucho me ha servido también la experiencia de estar entre los campesinos. Porque, aunque mis padres sean (SUB) de extracción campesina, toda mi formación la tuve entre los mineros. En Los Yungas, por primera vez me pude dar cuenta, personalmente, de otra realidad que se vive en mi país y que es la realidad del campo. [The experience of living among farmers has served me well. Because, even though my parents were originally farmers, I grew up among miners.]

<CREA, August 7, 2015>

Aunque can be used as a concessive or an adversative conjunction. Most of the time, it is used with the indicative, as a coordinating adversative conjunction. If the clause is in indicative, *aunque* can be replaced by the adversative conjunctions *pero, sin embargo, no obstante*, etc. The content introduced by *aunque* is presented as a fact.

If *aunque* is used with the subjunctive instead of the indicative, it is used as a real concessive and subordinating conjunction just like *a pesar de que, por más que, aun cuando, por mucho que* and *por muy que*. The speaker signals that the content of the concessive clause should not be considered a(n) (absolute) fact, but just a possibility or alternative and even a doubt, mild opposition or protest. In the following examples, the subjunctive could be translated with 'Some/everybody may think/talk . . . '; It is possible that some/everybody may think/talk . . . '; etc:

- Aunque algunos crean (SUB) que se las saben todas, la mayoría de los ahorradores no conoce sus propias necesidades financieras, y mucho menos las opciones de inversión que existen en el mercado. [Even though some may think that they know it all, the majority of savers don't know their own financial needs]

<CREA, August 7, 2015>

11.3.5 *The studies by DeMello*

In an article from 1995, which is one of a series that uses the material of the 'Proyecto de estudio coordinado de la norma lingüística culta de la principales cuidades de

Hispanoamérica' (PNCH), DeMello also analyzes mood variation within the Spanish speaking world. This project was started by Juan M. Lope Blanch in 1964[5] with the purpose of determining what distinguishes and unites the Spanish spoken by educated speakers in each and every national/regional dialect of Spanish.

In his article, DeMello (1995a) compares the use of the indicative and the subjunctive in predicates that depend upon *probablemente/posiblemente, a lo mejor/ seguramente, ser posible/probable que, acaso/quizá(s)/tal vez,* and *puede/pueda (ser) que* in sentences uttered by educated speakers. The empirical material is taken from the samples of speakers in 12 cities collected between the end of the 1960s and the beginning of the 1980s from the corpus mentioned. The results are as follows:

11.3.6   *Probablemente and posiblemente*

According to the study, with both adverbs, speakers mostly used the indicative; for *posiblemente,* 73% used the indicative and 27% the subjunctive; with *probablemente,* 75% used the indicative and 25% the subjunctive. This confirms the assessment by the NGLE (2009: 1955) that the indicative is the standard mood in this context, but that the subjunctive can also be found.[6]

If the average use of the indicative in the 12 capitals was 73%, in the case of *posiblemente,* Madrid and Bogotá (57%) were below average. This means that, in these cities speakers used the subjunctive more often. In all other Latin American cities, the indicative was used more often: Buenos Aires = 79%, Caracas = 69%, La Habana = 100%, La Paz = 90%, Lima = 67%, Mexico City = 83%, San José = 86%, San Juan = 67%, Santiago = 64%.

If the average use of the indicative in the 12 capitals was 75%, in the case of *probablemente,* Madrid (100%), Sevilla (100%), Lima (100%), San José (100%) and Bogotá (57%) were above average. In these cities, speakers used the indicative exclusively or more often. In all other Latin American cities, the indicative was used less: Buenos Aires = 50%, La Paz = 50%, Mexico City = 64%, San Juan = 60%, Santiago = 64%.

11.3.7   *Poder ser que*

DeMello finds that in educated speech, *pueda (ser) que* is used very little instead of *puede (ser) que.* He mostly confirms the observation of Butt/ Benjamin (2013: 16.3.1) that *puede/pueda (ser) que* are always followed by the subjunctive. He only found 3 instances with the indicative (3% of the 157 examples he found), all of which are from Latin America (Caracas and San Juan).

In the entire CORPES (08/10/2015), I only found 18 examples with *pueda ser que*; only one from Spain and the rest from Latin America. For *puede ser que* I found 1222 cases; 1159 were followed by the subjunctive (95%) and 63 by the indicative (5%); 15 (24%) examples with the subjunctive were from Spain and 48 (76%) from Latin America. The results from the CORPES confirm that *pueda (ser) que* is rarely used, especially in Spain. However, it contradicts the statement by Butt/ Benjamin (2013: 16.3.1) that *puede ser que* is always followed by the subjunctive because I found 63 examples with the indicative, a fourth from Spain and the majority from Latin America.

11.3.8   *Tal vez*

The general opinion in literature is that there is a clear preference for the subjunctive after *tal vez*.[7] Anadón (1979: 38–39) found a preference for the indicative among Latin American college students.[8] This study was confirmed by DeMello, who found that in his corpus there was only a preference for the subjunctive in Spain and Mexico. In the rest of Latin America, he found a predominance of the indicative. In Spain, 73% of the examples were in subjunctive and, in Latin America (except Mexico), 72% were in indicative.

I compared DeMello's results with a spot check in the CORPES. Because there were 26,761 cases of *tal vez* in 7,865 documents, I restricted the search to written examples with *Tal vez* at the beginning of the sentence in the areas of non-fiction, press, actuality/leisure and daily life. With these search criteria, I found 94 examples from Spain, 35 of which were in indicative (37%); 31 from Mexico, 16 of which were in indicative (52%); 21 from Colombia, 9 of which were in indicative (43%); 9 from Cuba, 3 of which were in indicative (33%). Because I could only find very few examples in this specific area for Cuba, I extended the search to all the occurrences of *Tal vez* at the beginning of the sentence in the areas of non-fiction and press. Here I found 91 cases, 35 of which were in indicative (38%).

My spot check didn't validate all of DeMello's results. I couldn't find a clear preference for the indicative in either Spain or in Latin America (even though in Mexico the percentage exceeded 50% by a little bit).

11.3.9   *Quizá(s)*[9]

First of all, DeMello tries to find out which adverb is more frequent. He compares his corpus with Woehr (1972) who had found 121 (69%) instances of *quizá* in his corpus and only 55 (31%) of *quizás*, and comes up with exactly the opposite, *quizá* = 31% and *quizás* = 69%.

A search in the CORPES among all occurrences of *quizá* (24.024 = 57%) and *quizás* (17.900 = 43%) reveals a preference of *quizá*, which confirms Woehr's findings. If we compare the regional use of the two adverbs, we see the following distribution, as shown in Table 11.11:

Table 11.11

	Total	Spain	Latin America
quizá	24.024 = 57%	12.119 = 50.5%	11.905 = 49.5%
quizás	17.900 = 43%	5.004 = 28%	12.896 = 72%
Total	**41.924**	**17.123 = 41%**	**24.801 = 59%**

Quizá is used pretty much as often in Spain as in Latin America; *quizás* is used three times more often in Latin America than in Spain.

As far as mood distinction goes, DeMello claims that the indicative dominates over the subjunctive for both, *quizá* and *quizás* (70% and 61%). Again, I have searched the CORPES for written examples with *Quizá* at the beginning of the sentence in the areas of non-fiction, press, actuality/leisure and daily life. Table 11.12 shows some of the results:

Table 11.12

	Total cases	Indicative
Spain	190	94 (49.5%)
Colombia	10	8 (80%)
Venezuela	11	5 (45%)
Argentina	41	27 (66%)
Mexico	43	33 (77%)

These findings only partly validate DeMello's claim that the indicative dominates in some Latin American countries, because in Venezuela it doesn't.

According to the authors of the NGLE, the tense of the dependent predicate has an influence on the mood choice as well. They think that the adverb *quizá(s)* is incompatible with the present indicative when referring to the future (§ 23.6n-p). Woehr (1972) came to a similar result and concluded that the subjunctive is more common when the sentence refers to the future or present and much less common with a past temporal reference. To a lesser degree, Renaldi's data (1977) coincided with this conclusion.

Unfortunately, a study by García (2011) about the differences in use of *quizá* and *quizás*, based on 2,001 occurrences of the two adverbs in the CREA, doesn't offer any direct answers about mood variation between Spain and Latin America. It reaffirms that temporal reference is the most critical factor group to consider in determining mood choice with *quizá* and *quizás*. Furthermore, it offers evidence that more frequent verbs appear in the subjunctive at a higher rate than less frequent verbs. Finanger (2011) confirms García's findings and lists the verbs that more frequently appear in the subjunctive. They are: *ser*, *tener* and *haber* (2011: 101).

11.3.10 Acaso

In DeMello's corpus, *acaso* is mainly used with the indicative. This matches what Woehr (1972: 320) said about this adverb and also what I found in the CORPES. In a spot check, here, *acaso* was used in around 75% of cases with the indicative in Spain, 79% in Mexico, 89% in Colombia, 82% in Venezuela, and 67% in Argentina. This contradicts Gili y Gaya (1980: 112), who wrote that when there is an adverb of doubt in an independent sentence, the verb is usually in subjunctive.[10] It also disputes the evaluation of Porto Dapena (1991: 60) who stated that *acaso* is used exclusively with the subjunctive, as well as Navas Ruiz (1990: 40), who qualified it as an adverb that calls for the subjunctive. The statistics also question the statement of Fente Gómez (1972: 58) who says that the use of the indicative with *acaso* sounds a little strange. Butt/Benjamin (2011: 248) write: "*acaso* is rather literary in the meaning 'perhaps', but it is found in all styles with the indicative in rhetorical, often sarcastic, questions, i.e. ones to which the speaker already knows the answer." They also offer two examples, one in subjunctive and one in indicative.

11.3.11   Ser posible que/ser probable que

In his study, DeMello confirms what has been said and written about these expressions: They are mainly used with the subjunctive.[11] However, DeMello (1995a: 355) and other authors also found a few examples (4%) in indicative. Blake (1987: 353) found that the indicative was possible in 2% of his examples from San Luis Potosí, Mexico. Anadón (1979: 38–39), in his study about South American Spanish, found that 12% of his 245 informants considered the sentence *Es posible que Francia comercia con Cuba* completely acceptable. Other evidence of the indicative in connection with *ser posible que/ser probable que* can be found in Bolinger (1956: 168), Bosque (1990b: 36), Cook (1975: 126), Lope Blanch (1958: 384–385) and others. The *Nueva gramática de la lengua española* (NGLE) (2009: 1884, §25.3v) repeats that predicates expressing necessity, possibility and 'suficiencia' are used with the subjunctive and list the adjectives *posible* and *probable*, as well as the nouns *posibilidad* and *probabilidad*. However, they note that in the colloquial speech of some Central American countries and in the Andean region, the use of the indicative with some of the expressions of this group has been registered and quote the example: *Es necesario que terminas el trabajo* (2009: 1886, §25.3v). A search in the CORPES for all occurrences of *es posible que* in the Andean region confirmed the latter assessment. Among the 263 cases, I could find 5 (1.9%) examples in indicative. Butt/Benjamin (2013: 246) write: "The future indicative, or, when the verb in the main clause is in the past, the conditional, are quite often found in informal Latin-American Spanish after such statements."

11.3.12   No sé si + SUB

In another article from 1995, DeMello compares comments about the modal usage after *no sé si*, with its occurrence in the PNCH. He finds that

> use of the present subjunctive following *no sé si* is revealed to be regional, occurring to a very high degree in Mexico City, to a lesser, but still high degree in Bogotá, to a fair degree in Caracas, to a very small degree in Santiago, and not at all in Buenos Aires, Havana, La Paz, Lima, Madrid, San Juan or Seville.

(1995b: 570)

In the same article he also describes modal usage with *quién sabe si* and finds

> that this expression is followed by the subjunctive only in the Mexico City
> corpus, with a total of six occurrences, divided equally between educated and
> uneducated speech; examples of *quién sabe si* followed by other verbal modes
> do not occur in the Mexican corpora.
>
> (1995b: 571)

The authors of the NGLE point out that the subjunctive use in this context was
very common in Old Spanish and indicate that the subjunctive use was extended
to verbs of possession and acquiring of knowledge (2009: 1901, §25.50). Furthermore, they write that this use is currently more frequent in Spanish spoken in
America, but with some restrictions. According to the NGLE, the sentence *No sé
si te guste (SUB) esta comida* today is normal in Mexico, Central America, Chile,
the Caribean and the Andes. In the Rio Plata region and Spain people say *No sé
si te [gusta – gustará] (IND) esta comida*. However, the indicative is also possible in
the countries where the subjunctive is normally used if the speaker thinks that the
listener already knows the food in question. On the other hand, the subjunctive
is not used in the second group even in a hypothetical situation.

11.3.13   *Expressions of emotion*

In yet another study, DeMello (1996) offers statistics from the PNCH to refute
the rule that expressions of emotion must be followed by the subjunctive in modern Spanish.[12] Until then, there was only anecdotal and sporadic evidence for
the use of these expressions with the indicative. DeMello shows that the use of
the indicative is not limited to specific regions and that the frequency clearly is
higher in Hispano-America. This is not surprising. Already in 1958 Lope Blanch
described this phenomenon, especially in Mexico.[13] He also pointed out that this
was not exclusively an American phenomenon and quoted examples from Spain.
This is echoed by the NGLE in 2009.[14]

DeMello's examples from Madrid, Sevilla and 10 Latin American cities
revealed a higher indicative frequency in Spanish America (a total of 50%) than
in Spain (33%). The exact geographic distribution is summarized in Table 11.13.

He also found that the preposition *de* after verbs of emotions (for example
alegrarse de, indignarse de, horrorizarse de, etc.) favours indicative use. Referring
to another article from 1995, DeMello explains this with the degree of semantic
independence that the speaker wants to give to the clause headed by *de que*.[15] This
confirms my definition of the subjunctive as a marker of syntactic and semantic
subordination under a main predicate.

DeMello also refers to the fact that, in Old Spanish, expressions of emotions
were often used with the indicative and quotes examples by Keniston (1937:
§ 28.26) and Tarr (1922: 137, 160). Jensen/Lathrop (1973), in a descriptive study
based on 900 examples of subjunctive use from 26 works, both literary and non-
literary, centring around the thirteenth century, showed that the "generalization

of the subjunctive mood after verbs of emotion is to be considered a trend towards unification of a semantic group, which, from the onset, shows relatively little cohesion" (1973: 54). "Fear is related to volition, astonishment is related to uncertainty, and verbs as *gozar* and *folgar* are closely tied up with subjective judgement" (1973: 54).

Table 11.13 Cuadro 1

Distribución geográfica de casos de indicativo/subjuntivo con expresiones de reacción personal

Ciudad	Indicativo	Subjuntivo
Bogota	16 (53%)	14 (47%)
Buenos Aires	8 (67%)	4 (33%)
Caracas	12 (60%)	8 (40%)
La Habana	2 (40%)	3 (60%)
La Paz	6 (46%)	7 (54%)
Lima	3 (75%)	1 (25%)
Madrid	3 (30%)	7 (70%)
Mexico	8 (40%)	12 (60%)
San Jose	9 (56%)	7 (44%)
San Juan	10 (43%)	13 (57%)
Santiago	21 (45%)	26 (55%)
Sevilla	2 (40%)	3 (60%)
Total	100 (49%)	105 (51%)

It is interesting to note that precisely for *alegrar* DeMello didn't find any instance of the indicative. In the five examples that he found, this verb was always followed by a clause in subjunctive. This confirms pretty much the result for Spain in the Varigrama corpus, where only one out of the 184 speakers from Madrid would have used the indicative in the sentence: Me *alegro de que has venido/hayas venido*. In Latin America, on the other hand, the indicative was accepted by more speakers, between 4% in Venezuela to 29.4% in Cuba.

The difference between the frequency of the indicative with 'expressions of personal reaction' in general (49%) and the verb *alegrar* in DeMello (1996) (0%) and in Varigrama (16.3%) confirms that there is little cohesion in this group and that there are many elements – for example, the lexical meaning of the expressions and their syntax (rection) – that must be taken into consideration. This has also been confirmed by the results of the Varigrama corpus.

With reference to DeMello's study of 1996, Butt/Benjamin (2013: 255) write:

> In spontaneous language in Latin America, and to a lesser extent in some parts of Spain, an emotional reaction to a past, present or habitual event may be expressed by the indicative. Some speakers accept *me alegra/molesta que estás aquí* for *estés aquí* 'I'm glad/annoyed you're here', other speakers reject

the indicative. This tendency to use the indicative is rather stronger with verbs followed by *de que*.

11.4 The studies by Gallego and Alonso-Marks: subjunctive versus infinitive

The article by Gallego/ Alonso-Marks (2014) is in line with others that claim that the subjunctive is disappearing or that there is a tendency to use it less, especially in (Latin) America. The analysis is based upon 934 utterances of semi-spontaneous oral production solicited from 112 adult monolingual native speakers of Spanish (56 from Rosario, Argentina; and 56 from Toledo, Spain). It "seeks to establish whether there are dialectal differences in the frequency of use of the present subjunctive in complement clauses in oral semi spontaneous production" (97). Here, the frequency of the subjunctive, however, is not compared with the indicative, but with the infinitive that is viable after many verbs of influence.[16] Butt/Benjamin write: "Spanish-speakers avoid the subjunctive when the rules of grammar allow it" (2013: 251). They make a division between "verbs that can be constructed with an indirect object, as in *te ayudaré a conseguir/a que consigas lo que quieres* 'I'll help you to get what you want'" (2013: 251). With these verbs, "the infinitive is almost always then used in preference to the subjunctive" (2013: 251). Then they divide "verbs not followed by *a*" (2013: 251) into two categories: one group "usually followed by the infinitive, although the subjunctive is also found" (2013: 251) (for example *dejar, hacer, impedir, mandar permitir*); and verbs that "are in a transitional state. The older construction is with the subjunctive and is safer for foreigners, but the infinitive construction is often heard and is creeping into the written language" (2013: 251) (for example, *aconsejar, recomendar* and *sugerir*). According to Butt/Benjamin:

> *pedir* and other verbs of similar meaning, e.g. *rogar* 'to request', seem to be in a complex transitional state with respect to the use of the infinitive. . . . when the subjects differ [the infinitive] is not normally accepted as correct in standard language, but it is heard in familiar Latin-American speech and sometimes appears in Latin-American writing: *piden restituir a empleados de Correos que fueron despedidos* (La Prensa, Panama) *(unions) ask for reinstatement of dismissed Post Office workers* . . . This infinitive construction is rejected in Spain, but it is increasingly common in journalistic styles, especially headlines.
>
> (2013: 253)

Gallego/Alonso-Marks solicited those noun clauses that according to Butt/ Benjamin were in a transitional state from the finite verb in subjunctive to the infinitive; for example, *Le recomiendo que hable con su jefe* versus *Le recomiendo hablar con su jefe*. They came to the conclusion:

> The pervasiveness of constructions with the infinitive among younger speakers is noteworthy. For participants from Toledo, complement clause-triggering

questions were mainly answered with complement clauses; however, constructions with the infinitive were the second most frequent choice. In Rosario, on the other hand, young and middle-aged participants primarily answered complement clause-triggering questions with constructions using the infinitive.

(2014: 102)

The authors point out that their article "represents the first study that reports results concerning the use and vitality of the present subjunctive in complement clauses among speakers of Argentina and Spain in oral semi-spontaneous production" (2014: 103) versus the infinitive.

Much earlier, in 1984, A. Morales presented the first quantitative text analysis with the infinitive as a mood variation in this kind of sentences, using language material from Puerto Rico, to study the influence of English on the Spanish of this country, at the VII Simposio de Dialectología del Caribe Hispano. The paper was published in 1988. Her analysis as well as the one carried out by Rivera (1986) show that the reason for the lower frequency of the subjunctive in Puerto Rico is not so much because speakers prefer the indicative, but because of the abundance of infinitive constructions.[17] I am reproducing Rivera's chart 3 (1986: 115) in Table 11.14.

Table 11.14

Modos	Mon.	X	Bil.
IND	87/890 (9.77%)	40/626 (6.38%)	69/1104 (6.25%)
SUB	144/890 (16.17%)	112/626 (17.89%)	148/1104 (13.40%)
Infinitive	659/890 (74.04%)	474/626 (75.71%)	887/1104 (80.34%)

The data shows that bilinguals are using the infinitive more often than monolinguals. However, the difference is not as significant as one might assume. These results were confirmed by Yamín in 1991.

Gallego/Alonso-Marks "argue that semantically both constructions are almost identical: *Le recomiendo hablar con su jefe* versus *Le recomiendo que hable con su jefe*, and the use of the infinitive does not posit a meaning loss" (2014: 102). In an article from 2014, I argued that "because the subjunctive is a grammatical, specifically a morphological category, there is no need to assign it a single conceptual meaning, but just a very general (grammatical) one." This meaning, that Ahern's (2008) calls "procedural", is activated to express that a predicate should not be taken as an absolute statement, but as something that must be interpreted or processed according to the context. In the case of the subjunctive this means as something that signals a "contextual alternative" (119). It is my understanding that the subjunctive as a dependent mood signals that the dependent predicate must be interpreted according to the context and not taken as a literal statement. The infinitive shares this contextual dependence with the subjunctive and therefore subjunctive and infinitive are interchangeable in specific contexts. Dietrich (1981) wrote:

> If the subjunctive excludes taking into consideration the realization of the action and if the indicative includes it specifically with the help of a grammatical specification, the infinitive is much more unspecific, and, due to its meaning as a grammatical category, only expresses the action in the most virtual form possible.
>
> (404–405)[18]

11.5 Conclusions and outlook

The studies that I have analyzed in this section show the following:

1   Mood variation is subject to the same syntactic, semantic and pragmatic mechanisms in all varieties of Spanish. This means that, on both sides of the Atlantic, speakers make use of the subjunctive to signal semantic and pragmatic subordination of a dependent noun clause under the meaning of a main clause or even in a larger context.

2   There are quantitative differences in the use of subjunctive and indicative in certain geographical areas. In Latin America, in general, the indicative is used more often in contexts where Spaniards would use the subjunctive, namely where the content of a subordinated clause could be seen as an absolute and independent fact. The best examples are probably the so-called expressions of emotions or personal reaction. The main reasons might just lie in the higher prescriptive pressure that exists in Spain and that was exercised by the Spanish Royal Language Academy and, subsequently, other social institutions (for example, schools, mass media, families, etc.) for many years. The NGLE is much less prescriptive and reflects the big shift that took place in the Spanish Royal Academy. Even though the authors were not able to present a unifying analysis of all the contexts that determine the election of the subjunctive and clear practical rules, they tried to paint a very detailed and diverse picture of the subjunctive and showed that, in many cases both the subjunctive and the indicative produce grammatically correct sentences, such as after 'expressions of emotions or personal reaction'. Studies show that there is indeed little cohesion in this group and that there are many elements that have an influence on the choice of mood. The only verb of this group that is almost exclusively followed by the subjunctive in Spain is *alegrarse*. With all the other expressions in this group there was a higher percentage of indicative use.

3   There are also quantitative differences in the use of subjunctive and indicative among the national and regional varieties of Spanish and therefore it is not possible to reduce the differences to European and American Spanish. In some aspects, the Mexican Spanish is more similar to the Spanish spoken in Spain than in other places in Spanish America. In other instances, the

subjunctive is used more often in Venezuela and Puerto Rico than in Spain. Contrary to popular belief as well, in the entire Spanish speaking world, even in Spain, the majority of speakers favour the indicative after *el hecho de que*. The same goes for *acaso*.

4   The diatopic (geographical) differences are not as pronounced as the differences between written and spoken colloquial Spanish. One analysis found that the spoken language in Mexico City was very similar to the spoken and written language in Madrid and Sevilla.

5   It is clearly not true that the subjunctive is disappearing in Latin America. The subjunctive is very much alive in all the contexts where it is also used in Spain. After *querer que*, the subjunctive is the only choice on both sides of the ocean. The subjunctive is also used very frequently in formulaic speech. In other contexts, for example, after *¿crees que . . .?* studies even found a higher frequency of the subjunctive in Latin America than in Spain. Following *no sé si*, researchers found a very high degree of present subjunctive use in Mexico City, to a lesser but still high degree in Bogotá, to a fair degree in Caracas and to a very small degree in Santiago. This is something that cannot be found at all in Buenos Aires, Havana, La Paz, Lima, San Juan or Spain, even though this use was very common in Old Spanish.

6   There are also studies that point out that some verbs (especially very popular, irregular verbs, such as *ser*, *tener* and *haber*) more frequently appear in the subjunctive than other, less common verbs.

7   A few studies also show that the reason for the lower frequency of the subjunctive (for example in Puerto Rico, but not only there) is not so much because speakers prefer the indicative, but because of the abundance of infinitive constructions which share common characteristics with the subjunctive.

Notes

1 See: Alcina/Blecua (1983: 989), Aleza/ Enguita (2010), López Morales (1992: 311), Mendoza Quiroga (1992: 467), NGLE (25.14b, 1951) and Ocampo (1990: 450).
2 For the complete list, see De Sterck (2000: 12, footnote 4).
3 The first interviews for the corpus were conducted in April of 1997. By 2015 the researchers had published the transcript of 108 interviews with speakers from the entire sociolinguistic spectrum of society. For more information, see: http://lef.colmex.mx/index.php/investigaciones/corpus-sociolingueistico-de-la-ciudad-de-mexico-cscm
4 See also chapter 9.3.2.3.
5 See: Lope Blanch (1986).
6 See also Butt/ Benjamin (2013: 246–248, chapter 16.3.2) – Subjunctive after words meaning 'perhaps', 'possibly', 'probably'.
7 Fente Gómez (1972: 58), Gili y Gaya (1980: 112), Togeby (1953: 33) and Woehr (1972: 323).
8 See also Butt/ Benjamin (2013: 246–248, chapter 16.3.2) – Subjunctive after words meaning 'perhaps', 'possibly', 'probably'.
9 ibid.
10 Original quote: "Cuando en una oración independiente figura algún adverbio de duda, el verbo suele estar en modo subjuntivo: . . . acaso estuvieseis mejor allí"

11 Examples are Bosque (1990b: 35–36), Butt/ Benjamin (2013: 16.3.1), Esbozo (1973: 458) and Guitart (1984: 172).
12 Esbozo (1973: 457, §d), Gili y Gaya (1980: § 10) and Vogel (1979: 22–25).
13 Original quote: "En el español de México no es raro – aunque desde luego es poco frecuente- encontrar expresiones de estas clases construidas con verbo subordinado en indicativo . . . Seguramente también en otros países de América podrán hallarse construcciones semejantes aunque nada diga Kany sobre ello"(1958: 383).
14 "Casi todos los predicados de afección que admiten argumentos oracionales se construyen con subjuntivo" (2009: 1881, §25.3q). "Se ha observado, no obstante, que algunos de ellos se usan en ocasiones en indicativo. . . . las subordinadas encabezadas por *que* introducen a veces el indicativo con los verbos mencionados, más frecuentemente en el español americano que en el europeo" (2009: 1895, §25.5b). "Los casos con indicativo son más numerosos en el coloquio que en los textos narrativos o descriptivos, pero se documentan también en los últimos . . . En algunos de estos casos, el empleo del indicativo deja en suspenso la factividad del predicado . . . por tanto la asunción de que se da por cierta la situación de la que se habla, como en *Se lamentaba de que ganaba muy poca plata, lo que no era cierto*"(2009: 1895–1896, §25.5c).
15 "El empleo de la preposición 'de' liga la cláusula a la expresión de reacción personal sin subordinarla a ésta" (1996: 382).
16 See: Butt/ Benjamin (2013: 5th ed., 251–253, §16.5.2 & 16.5.3).
17 Morales (1992) writes: "Estos datos son un índice de que la variación más significativa habrá que buscarla en esta oposición y no tanto en la alternancia subjuntivo/indicativo. Efectivamente los datos de Rivera 1986 en ella no fueron siempre reveladores en términos de Ia alternancia subjuntivo vs. infinitivo, tanto en cuanto a los datos totales que observamos en el cuadro 3, como en los obtenidos en cada una de las categorías semánticas verbales" (346).
18 Translation from French by the author of this book.

12 Synopsis

12.1 How can we describe the essence of the subjunctive?

With the subjunctive we are not making a declarative statement about something that exists or happens independently – but about the dependent object, subject or attribute of a higher predicate that characterizes it as its result and something non- or counterfactual: a wish, the object of an emotion, a doubt or an alternative.

12.2 Step-by-step instructions to explain the use of the subjunctive in modern Spanish

1 We have sentences with one predicate (verb or verbal expression) and sentences with two or more predicates. Generally, in **sentences with only one predicate** we can only use the INDICATIVE (present indicative, preterit, imperfect, future, etc.):

    a   Yo <u>hablo/hablé/hablaba/hablaré/</u> . . . español.
    b   Juan <u>cree/creyó/creía/creerá/</u> . . . en la razón.

2 Only in very specific communicative situations is it possible to use subjunctive forms in sentences with one predicate. These utterances can only be interpreted as commands or expressions of wishes.

    a   Profesora, por favor, <u>hable</u> español.
    b   Amigos, <u>díganme</u> la verdad.
    c   <u>Hablemos</u> con Juan.
    d   ¡<u>Viva</u> el pueblo!
    e   Que <u>hable</u> María primero.
    f   Ojalá <u>venga</u> pronto.

3 If there are several predicates (verbs), these can be coordinated or subordinated.

4 Coordinated predicates have pretty much the same level of importance and are connected with commas or coordinating conjunctions; for example *and, but, for, nor, or, so* and *yet* in English and *y, pero, o, ni* and *ya* in Spanish:

    a   Juan habla español, Pablo habla chino Y María habla francés.

b Juan habla español, PERO María habla francés.

c Juan vendrá mañana O se quedará en Madrid.

5 Coordinated predicates or clauses are relatively independent and can be made into independent sentences. They are always in INDICATIVE:

a Juan habla español. Pablo habla chino. María habla francés.

b Juan habla español. María habla francés.

c Juan vendrá mañana. Juan se quedará en Madrid.

6 **Subordinated predicates** are, as their name suggests, subordinated under another predicate that is called the main predicate.

7 The most common conjunction to mark subordination is *that* in English and *que* in Spanish. Others are *después de que*, *aunque*, *cuando* and many more.

a **Sé** que Juan **está** enfermo.

b Te **digo** que Juan **está** enfermo.

c Juan **vino** a la reunión, aunque **estaba** enfermo.

d **Empecé a viajar** cuando **tuve** 13 años.

8 Syntactically, subordinated clauses have the function of objects, subjects or attributes of main clauses:

a Sé que Juan está enfermo. (= object)

b Lo sabe todo el mundo que Juan lo ha hecho. (= subject)

c Juan vino a la reunión, aunque estaba enfermo. (= attribute)

d Tengo un amigo que siempre me dice la verdad. (= attribute)

9 The mood in the **main clause** is always INDICATIVE.

10 If the subordinated clause is in the indicative, it is only syntactically subordinated. Semantically and pragmatically, however, it is coordinated. We have two absolute statements or assertions:

a Yo sé lo que Juan ha hecho. → Yo sé algo. and Juan lo ha hecho.

b Te digo que Juan está enfermo. → Te digo algo. and Juan está enfermo.

c Juan no vino a la reunión porque estaba enfermo. → Juan no vino a la reunión. and Él estaba enfermo.

d Empecé a viajar cuando tenía 13 años. → Empecé a viajar. and Tenía 13 años.

e Tengo un amigo que siempre me dice la verdad. → Tengo un amigo. and Siempre me dice la verdad.

11 **The INDICATIVE is an ABSOLUTE MODE.**

12 The **SUBJUNCTIVE**, on the other hand, is a **DEPENDENT** and **RELATIVE MODE**. The subjunctive forms always signal that a predicate is not only syntactically subordinated, but that it depends semantically and pragmatically on a higher predicate. This means that predicates in subjunctive can only be interpreted as expressing the intention or personal attitude of the main subject or speaker at the time of utterance. Without the main predicate, they are agrammatical and cannot be interpreted:

a   Quiero que Juan vaya al cine. → *Juan vaya al cine.
b   Juan, te digo que vayas al cine. → *Juan, vayas al cine.
c   Dudo que Juan esté enfermo. → *Juan esté enfermo.
d   Me alegro que salga el sol. → *Salga el sol.
e   Veré a Juan, aunque sea tarde. → *Sea tarde.
f   Busco un amigo que siempre me diga la verdad. → *Siempre me diga la verdad.

13   Semantically and pragmatically we have just one absolute statement (the main clause) and one dependent predicate (the subordinate clause):

a   **Quiero** algo que es el contenido de lo que digo.
b   **Dudo** algo que es el contenido de lo que digo.
c   **Me alegro** de algo que es el contenido de lo que digo.
d   **Veré a Juan**, aunque pase algo que digo.

14   Because the subjunctive verb forms cannot stand alone or be used as absolute statements, the speaker is unable and not required to express that whether s/he says actually exists, happens, happened or will happen independently from him/her and other circumstances. With the subjunctive the speaker cannot refer directly to extra-linguistic facts, but only indirectly through the expression of his attitude.

a   Busco una secretaria que <u>hable</u> inglés, ruso, chino, árabe, alemán, swahili y a la que le <u>guste</u> trabajar sin dinero.

15   Therefore, with a sentence such as the following, a speaker does not refer directly to the obvious fact that Juan came to the party. He only states his attitude towards it.

a   [JUAN IS STANDING IN FRONT OF THE SPEAKER] Me alegro (de) que <u>hayas venido</u> a mi fiesta.

16   The subjunctive gives the speaker the opportunity to say things without committing to their actual existence or truth. Therefore, it is mostly used to express the opposite of what is actually said:

a   Quiero que Juan vaya al cine. = (Actualmente) <u>Juan no va al cine</u>.
b   Dudo que Juan tenga razón. = (Pienso que) <u>Juan no tiene razón</u>.
c   Vendré cuando tenga tiempo. = (Actualmente) <u>no sé si tengo tiempo</u>.
d   Me molesta que venga Juan. = <u>Quiero que no venga</u>.
e   Me alegro que Juan haya venido a la fiesta. (Pensaba que) <u>Juan no iba a venir</u>.

17   Consequently, the subjunctive is often used to present information as known, presupposed, less important or to be polite or non-committal.

18   The use of the subjunctive is mandatory in Spanish after indirect commands and expressions of wishes:

a   El capitán manda que el soldado corra treinta kilómetros.

b   El profesor sugiere que los estudiantes hagan todas las tareas.

c   Es necesario que me digas la verdad.

19 After expressions of doubt, uncertainty and personal preferences, the indicative or the subjunctive – theoretically – both can be used:

a   Me alegro (de) que Juan no está enfermo. = Me alegro. and Juan no está enfermo.

b   Me alegro (de) que Juan no esté enfermo. = Yo quiero pensar que Juan no esté enfermo, no importa que esté o no enfermo en realidad.

20 In modern Spanish, however, the norm is to use the subjunctive as the standard mode after these expressions and represent the content of the embedded clause as expressing a personal attitude rather than an objective and absolute fact.

12.3 Some examples

Now we can explain the use of the subjunctive or the indicative in the following examples:

1   *Quiero que Juan me <u>da</u> el libro que está en la mesa.

a   Are you saying that this actually happens, and that Juan gives you the book? If you drop *quiero que*, are you still communicating the same message: *¿Juan me da el libro que está en la mesa?* If this is NOT the case, then this is NOT an absolute statement. It is not a fact but the speaker's wish. Therefore, you have to use the **SUBJUNCTIVE**. → **Quiero que Juan me <u>dé</u> el libro que está en la mesa.**

2   *Sin embargo, creo que ambos <u>compartan</u> la responsabilidad y la culpa.

a   Are you saying that this actually happens, and that they actually do share the responsibility and the blame? If you drop *creo que*, are you still communicating the same message: *(Ellos) comparten la reponsabilidad y la culpa?* If this is the case, then this is an absolute statement and you have to use the **INDICATIVE**. → Sin **embargo, creo que ambos <u>comparten</u> la responsabilidad y la culpa.**

3   *Es probable que ella <u>se involucró</u> con las drogas.

a   Are you saying that this actually happened and that she was involved with drugs? If you drop *es probable que*, are you still communicating the same message: *(Ella) se involucró con drogas?* If this is NOT the case, then this is NOT an absolute statement. *Involucrarse con drogas* is only the expression of your personal presumption, guess or speculation. Therefore you have to use the **SUBJUNCTIVE**. → **Es probable que ella se <u>haya involucrado/involucrara</u> con las drogas.**

4   *Por último, cada miembro de la sociedad tiene que luchar por cambiar una ley que es injusta, para que los criminales <u>serán</u> castigados por sus acciones.

   a   Are you saying that this will actually happen and that the criminals will be punished for their actions, no matter what? If you drop the rest of the sentence, are you still communicating the same message: *(Los) criminales serán castigados?* If this is NOT the case, then this is NOT an absolute statement, but the expression of the speaker's wish, which is contrary to the actual situation. Therefore you have to use the **SUBJUNCTIVE**. → **Por último, cada miembro de la sociedad tiene que luchar por cambiar una ley que es injusta, para que los criminales <u>sean</u> castigados por sus acciones.**

5   *Esta falta de acción disciplinaria promueve el consumo de alcohol por menores de edad porque los estudiantes sienten que nunca <u>vayan</u> a ser arrestados.

   a   Are you saying that this is what they actually feel, that they are not going to be arrested? If you drop the rest of the sentence, are you still communicating the same message: *Nunca van a ser arrestados?* Then this is an absolute statement and you have to use the **INDICATIVE**. (May be you were thinking about the more specific meaning of 'feeling sorry', which is mostly followed by subjunctive.) → **Esta falta de acción disciplinaria promueve el consumo de alcohol por menores de edad porque los estudiantes sienten que nunca <u>van</u> a ser arrestados.**

6   *Si todavía <u>tenga</u> dinero, iré al cine contigo mañana.

   a   Are you saying that you do have or will have money? If you drop the rest of the sentence, are you still communicating the same message: *Tengo dinero?* Then this is an absolute statement and you have to use the **INDICATIVE**. (*Si* is never followed by the present subjunctive in Standard Spanish.) → **Si todavía <u>tengo</u> dinero, iré al cine contigo mañana.**

7   *Si tenía dinero, iría al cine contigo mañana.

   a   Are you saying that you do have or had money? If you drop the rest of the sentence, are you still communicating the same message: *Tenía dinero?* If this is NOT the case, then this is NOT an absolute statement but a counterfactual adverb clause, and you have to use the **SUBJUNCTIVE**. (In combination with the conditional in the main clause, you always use the past subjunctive.) → **Si <u>tuviera</u> dinero, iría al cine contigo mañana.**

8   *Desafortunadamente, mucha gente <u>use</u> su estrés como razón de tomar mucho alcohol.

   a   Are you saying that many people use stress as a reason to drink alcohol? Then this is an absolute statement and you have to use the

INDICATIVE. Could you also use the subjunctive here? No, because 'mucha gente usa su estrés como razón de tomar mucho alcohol' is a main clause and not syntactically subordinated by 'que'. Furthermore, in a 'pseudo-independent clause, the subjunctive can only be interpreted as a command or a wish. → **Desafortunadamente, mucha gente <u>usa</u> su estrés como razón de tomar mucho alcohol.**

9   Es una lástima que mucha gente <u>usa</u> su estrés como razón de tomar mucho alcohol.

   a   Are you saying that many people use stress as a reason to drink alcohol? Then this is an absolute statement and you have to use the **INDICA-TIVE**, even if the clause is syntactically subordinated. Semantically and pragmatically it is coordinated. Your sentence is correct, even if Spanish speakers, especially in Spain, usually use the **SUBJUNCTIVE** after most impersonal expressions and expressions of emotions. → **Es una lástima que mucha gente <u>usa</u> su estrés como razón de tomar mucho alcohol.**

   b   The subjunctive, however, marks semantic and pragmatic subordination under the main predicate and the speaker, who expresses his/her personal attitude but doesn't state whether the content of the subordinate clause is a fact or something else. → **Es una lástima que mucha gente <u>use</u> su estrés como razón de tomar mucho alcohol.**

10   *La lluvia hizo que se <u>desbordaron</u> los ríos.

   a   Are you saying that this actually happened and that the rivers spilled over? If you drop *la lluvia hizo que*, are you still communicating the same message: *Se desbordaron los ríos?* The answer is YES. However, *se desbordaron los ríos* here is presented as an effect or result of something that causes it, and therefore it is NOT an absolute statement, and you must use the **SUBJUNCTIVE**. → **La lluvia hizo que se <u>desbordaran</u> los ríos.**

11   Iré a España, aunque no <u>tengo</u> dinero.

   a   Are you saying that you don't have money? Then this is an absolute statement and you have to use the **INDICATIVE**, even if the clause is syntactically subordinated. Semantically and pragmatically, however, it is coordinated. Your sentence is correct. → **Iré a España, aunque no <u>tengo</u> dinero.**

   b   If, on the other hand, you didn't want to say that you don't have money, but that by the time you are going to Spain, you may not have money, you would have to use the **SUBJUNCTIVE**. → **Iré a España, aunque no <u>tenga</u> dinero.**

12   *No tengo ningún compañero de cuarto que <u>limpia</u> el baño.

   a   Are you saying that you do have a flatmate that cleans the bathroom? If you drop *the negation*, are you still communicating the same message:

Tengo un compañero de cuarto que limpia el baño? If this is NOT the case, then this is NOT an absolute statement. You are not talking about something that exists but something that is not existent for you, something counterfactual. Therefore you have to use the **SUBJUNCTIVE**. → **No tengo ningún compañero de cuarto que <u>limpie</u> el baño.**

13 [Juan is standing in front of me and I am saying:] *Juan, me alegro que <u>has</u> venido.

Are you saying: "Juan, you came to my party"? If you drop *me alegro que*, are you still communicating the same message: *Juan, has venido a mi fiesta?* Juan would probably say: "Yes, of course, are you blind? I am standing in front of you." What you wanted to do here was not to state a fact, which is very obvious in this situation, but to express your attitude towards that fact. Therefore, you have to use the **SUBJUNCTIVE**. → **Juan, me alegro que <u>hayas</u> venido.**

13 Alphabetic list of conjunctions that are used with the subjunctive or both moods[1]

a (period of time) **de que** = *after* → después de que (→ 9.3.2.5)

    SUB (present subjunctive) (hypothetical) • Ahora damos una pensión a los 37 días de que el trabajador **cause** derecho.

    SUB (past or past perfect subjunctive instead of past perfect indicative) • Nunca se me olvidará el viaje que hicimos David y yo a la India. Mucho antes del desastre de su boda, claro, a poco de que tu padre **mandara** saquear nuestra casa del muelle. No sé cuántos años hace, diez o dieciocho.

    IND • Esfumáronse a su turno aquellas bestias mitológicas, y a poco de que una relativa bonanza **había tornado a afirmar** su efímero gobierno en la espelunca, los demonios reanudaron el ataque, . . .

    a (period of time) **de** → después de INF • Holyfield tocó una vez más con su cabeza la ceja ya abierta de Tyson por otro golpe a poco de **iniciarse** el asalto anterior.

a cambio de que (→ 9.3.2.4) SUB = *if in exchange* • En el tercer programa de bonos escolares las compañías que deben al menos un millón de dólares al estado de la Florida tienen la opción de pagar un porcentaje de su deuda a cambio de que el resto lo **entreguen** a la agencia Florida Child para becas y asistencia educativa. • En los meses siguientes, el subsecretario de Gobernación, doctor José Narro Robles, acudió al reclusorio y me propuso dejarme libre a cambio de que **saliera** al extranjero del 15 de noviembre de 1994 al 15 de enero de 1995, . . .

    a cambio de (→ 9.3.2.4) INF = *in exchange for* • Estaba dispuesto a decir dónde la había enterrado a cambio de **ser juzgado** por la pena mínima correspondiente, homicidio en primer grado.

a condición de que (→ 9.3.2.4) SUB = *on the condition that* • Toubon insistió en que "no hay límites en el manejo de las palabras, a condición de que se **sepa** leer". • Luego se descubrió que la propaganda podría valer a condición de que nadie **supiera** que era propaganda.

    a condición de (→ 9.3.2.4) INF = *on the condition of* • El gimnasio estaba bien para algunos a condición de **ser** jóvenes y aun así el deporte no se practicaba con intensidad.

a costa de que = *at the cost of* → a expensas de **SUB** •. . . otras provincias y regiones que recibirán más a costa de que **se dé** menos a otros. • Silvino Navarro, que había sido partidario de buscar capital fresco para sanear la entidad, aún a costa de que la Iglesia **perdiera** la mayoría.

> **a costa de INF/NOUN** • Sí, pero usted ha formado parte de esa política de reforzar el Madrid a costa de **irle quitando efectivos** a Estudiantes.

a efecto(s) de que → para que (→ 9.3.1.1) **SUB** • Yo presenté una iniciativa a efectos de que estos delitos **se declaren imprescriptibles**. • Tan sólo tenían que registrar sus nombres, a efectos de que nuestro censo **quedara saneado**, y pagar una tasa simbólica por los gastos de la travesía.

> **a efecto(s) de** → para **INF** • Sin embargo, se mantendrá a efectivos de la Policía Nacional a efectos de **preservar** el orden y la seguridad.

a expensas (estar/quedar/seguir ~) **de que** = *to be dependent upon* → a la espera de que → dependiendo de que (→ 9.3.1.1) **SUB** • Todo queda a expensas de que el jugador **esté** o no **de acuerdo** en la operación. • Ellos tenían que estar a expensas de que **viniera**, pues, o un primo, pues, que **tuviera acceso** a un club, a una piscina, ¿verdad?

> **a expensas de** = *at the expense of* **NOUN** • . . . que este acuerdo se suscribió a expensas de **los palestinos**.

a fin de que = *so that, with the purpose of, in order to, so as to* → para que (→ 9.3.1.1) **SUB** •. . . para que su Anteproyecto de Ley pase a discusión ante el plenario de la Asamblea, a fin de que **sea aprobado** lo más pronto posible. • Ayer, Javier . . . habló con el representante para España del jugador a fin de que **se pusiera en contacto** con el Palmeiras.

> **a fin de** → para **INF** • Había suficiente número de programadores a fin de **hacer** las tareas con rapidez, . . .

a la espera de que = *waiting for* → hasta que → esperando que **SUB** • . . . compartimos una botella de rakia de cereza a la espera de que le **llamen** para la comida. • Allí, en medio de la lluvia y el frío, y a la espera de que **se pudieran llevar a cabo** las competencias aplazadas por el mal clima, estaban Miguel Enrique Rueda y Carlos Alberto Penagos, . . .

> **a la espera de** → esperando **INF/NOUN** • Y que están a la espera de **ver** cómo se confirman las buenas expectativas de los indicadores de julio, . . . • Javi Prendes, tras su paso por el Figueres, retornó al Langreo, el equipo de su pueblo, para echarle una mano a la espera de **un equipo** de superior categoría.

a medida que → según

> **SUB** = *to the extent that* (intention) • Todos estos servicios iniciales se irán ampliando a medida que se **vaya desarrollando** el Campus.

> **IND** = *as, at the same time that* (fact) • Esta navegación se produce a medida que **se van seleccionando** los documentos que nos interese consultar.

a menos (+ period of time) **de que** = *less than . . . before* → antes de que (→ 9.3.1.2) **SUB** • La denuncia se produce a menos de 24 horas de que el juez Guzmán **interrogue** a Pinochet acerca de los 57 homicidios y 18 secuestros atribuidos a La Caravana de la Muerte, . . . • Su publicación, a menos de una semana de que Jacques Chirac **anunciase** su candidatura como presidenciable del RPR, supone . . . una forma de contrarrestar el efecto mediático del candidato neogaullista. • El jefe del ejército, general Augusto Pinochet Ugarte, fue invitado a tomar parte a menos de una semana antes de que **tuviera lugar**.

a menos (+ period of time) de = *less than . . . before* → antes de INF • Los incidentes se precipitaron en horas de la mañana, cuando las ventanillas de expendio de localidades del estadio sobre la calle Brandsen se cerraron a menos de una hora de **ponerse** en venta las generales.

a menos (de) que = *unless* → a no ser que (→ 9.3.2.4) **SUB** • Según el informe presentado ayer, los 5.660 millones de habitantes de la Tierra se multiplicarán por cinco en 150 años a menos que **se tomen medidas** eficaces de control demográfico. • Al Gore concluyó que perdería a menos que **se detuviera** el proceso.

a nada que = *as long as* → basta con que → es suficiente con que (→ 9.3.2.4) **SUB** (possibility) • Este tipo de corridas, las llamadas de los banderilleros, a nada que los empresarios les **echaran** unos toros con ciertas posibilidades de lucimiento, resultarían divertidas, porque el público se embala en el segundo tercio. • El hombre lo creerá, por supuesto, a nada que la mujer **ponga un poco de empeño**, . . .

IND (fact) {rare} • Si el castillo de naipes se ha desmoronado a nada que **ha soplado el viento** de la crisis, es porque sobre unos cimientos históricos muy endebles . . . no han cesado de engañarnos empleando materiales inconsistentes y ensamblándolos de forma chapucera y apresurada, procurando más por sus intereses gremiales que por la solvencia de la obra.

a no ser que = *unless* → si no es que → a menos que (→ 9.3.2.4) **SUB** • El poder es absolutamente efímero y no hay que abusar de él a no ser que **se utilice** de forma responsable. • Algunos años más tarde, estas presiones se repitieron, al negarle el suministro de tabaco para un estanco que tenía, a no ser que **entregara** los originales de la obra completa de su marido.

a pesar de que = *even though, in spite of, despite* → aunque → pese a que (→ 9.3.2.3)

SUB (possibility or counterfacticity) • -No quiero ganar batallas a través de las primeras páginas de los periódicos. Los ciudadanos tienen derecho a la intimidad a pesar de que **defrauden**. Al defraudador hay que ponerlo en su sitio, pero no en la primera página de los diarios. • Sí, tengo muy claro lo que quiero, pero hay ciertas cosas que no haría a pesar de que **supusiera** un gran paso en mi vida profesional.

IND (fact) • El tío abuelo del muchacho cubano encontrado por unos pescadores en las costas de Fort Lauderdale en el día de Acción de Gracias, trata de conseguir la custodia del niño de 6 años, a pesar de que su padre **está vivo** y al parecer deseoso de educar a su hijo en Cuba.

a pesar de **INF** • Frecuentemente estos actos se van hasta el término a pesar del hecho de que no quiere verdaderamente hacerlos, y a pesar de **querer resistirlos**.

a poco que → si se hace un poco (de la acción el verbo en subjuntivo) → a nada que → bastar con que → ser suficiente con que (→ 9.3.2.4)

    SUB (possibility) = *as long as; provided that* • Pero a poco que **sigas** una rutina, que **cojas** el metro a determinada hora o **pases** por ésta o esta otra calle en un determinado momento del día, no es difícil que comiences a reconocer a perfectos desconocidos. • Mi taller quedaba, por tanto, a poco que **dejara la puerta abierta**, prácticamente en el camino de cualquiera que fuera o viniera de los cuartos al resto del palacio.

    IND (fact) {rare} = *if* (+ imperfecto); *whenever* • Eran tiempos de revistas que, a poco que **te descuidabas**, las cerraban porque descubrían sus mensajes de libertad.

a punto de que = about *when; just before* → justo antes de que (→ 9.3.1.2)

    SUB • Juana: -En medio de la muchedumbre y a punto de que se **me acabe** el milenio, no oigo otra cosa que el latido de mi corazón. • A punto de que el Land Cruiser **cruzara** el Pacífico hasta su destino, sentía como si el horizonte, las estrellas limpias, nítidas, centelleantes del desierto australiano fueran a cerrarse sobre mí. • También, claro, las botellas de vino -blanco y tinto- y las latas de cerveza. Cuando terminó de servirse una -a punto estuvo de que la espuma **desbordara** el vaso- . . .

    a punto de = *about to* → antes de **INF** • Rodrigo Paz, presidente del CONAM, estuvo a punto de **tirar** la toalla y de retirarse del cuadrilátero.

a que = *so that; until* → para que (→ 9.3.1.1) **SUB** • No hay duda de que Valdivieso está jugando a que **crean** que existe la posibilidad de que se lance. • -Obliga a que **nos hagamos una pregunta**, perdón por la expresión, estúpida: ¿podremos creerle esta vez? → hasta que (→ 9.1.5) **SUB** • No hay necesidad de esperar a que **lleguen** todos los helicópteros. • Entonces empezamos a disparar para que no se nos fueran a meter a la base, y a esperar a que **llegara** un apoyo.

a raíz de que

    SUB = *as an (immediate) result of, due to* → a consecuencia de que → después de que • . . . que ha reabierto recientemente a raíz de que Amedo **haya decidido confesar** datos que durante el juicio en el que fue condenado no quiso revelar. • ¿Ha pasado apuros económicos a raíz de que su antigua compañía no **confiara** en usted?

    IND = *because* → porque • Además yo me inscribí también en la UTU, en administración de empresas, pero hice un año nomás. Y todo a raíz de que **tenía** una novia que se había inscrito ahí, esas cosas que uno hace de joven . . .

a riesgo de que (often used with ***aun***) = *at the risk that* **SUB** • Mejor dejar que el tiempo corra, aún a riesgo de que en el camino **encontremos** obstáculos o gratas sorpresas. • El muchacho picó, aun a riesgo de que su madre **tuviera un ataque de nervios**.

a riesgo de (often used with *aun*) = *at the risk of* **INF** • Aun a riesgo de **repetirme** les quiero decir que no hay el menor problema y que los ciudadanos de Canarias pueden estar tranquilos, . . .

acaso → por si acaso

además de que = *besides the fact that*

    IND (fact) • "Ese día además de que **aumentan** los clientes, también se incrementa el número de parejas del mismo sexo, . . .

    SUB (intention) • PSOE y PP también acordaron solicitar al Ejecutivo la realización inmediata de campañas informativas . . ., además de que **impulse** estudios generales sobre la influencia de la televisión en los niños y los jóvenes, . . .

    además de **INF/NOUN** • Pues exactamente, el pasado día siete de julio, además de **celebrar** los sanfermines, pues muchas parejas tenían que celebrar o no esta ley de divorcio,

ahí → de ahí que

al margen de que = *apart from; independently from* → independientemente de que

    SUB (present) (possibility) • "ETA debe dejar las armas al margen de que **haya o no diálogo**."

    SUB (past instead of the conditional or preterit) • De esa actitud de Freddy vino el cariño inmenso que siempre se tuvieron, y eso al margen de que luego los dos **se distanciaran** algo -pues según creo en los últimos meses ya Freddy y él no congeniaban mucho . . .

    IND (fact) • Espelosín afirmó que los 500.000 viandantes que diariamente pasan por la Puerta del Sol son un argumento suficiente para solucionar el problema de las zonas reservadas a viandantes, al margen de que el proyecto **tiende a mejorar** la utilización del espacio.

antes de que → (9.3.1.2)

aparte de que = *apart from, besides*

    SUB (possibility) • Sé que mi gente, mi público, irá a verme cantar, aparte de que luego **se encuentren** a una Isabel Pantoja actriz, interpretando un papel.

    IND (fact) • Ya está bien de minimizar a Aznar, aparte de que la izquierda **necesita** dejar el poder.

apenas = *as son as* → en cuanto → (9.3.2.5)

    SUB (hypothesis) • -Estamos planteando que la etapa de digitalización debe empezar en las primeras semanas del próximo año. Apenas **esté finalizada**, ya podríamos ir hacia la etapa de cedulación de los venezolanos.

    IND (fact) • Apenas **supo** del cartel, el alcalde mandó a un par de funcionarios municipales a sacarlo.

aun cuando → aunque

aun a costa de que (→ 9.3.2.3) = *even though* **SUB** • Una buena madre se
realiza si su hija evoluciona, aun a costa de que ella no lo **haga**. • Pero
bueno, ¿no querían que ganara aun a costa de que **fallaran** las estrategias
del señor Azcargorta?

aun a costa de **INF** = *even at the expense of* • La realidad actual del acoso
moral en general, es satisfacer la necesidad de dominio, aun a costa de
destruir el objeto de su interés.

aun en el caso de que → en el caso de que → (9.3.2.4)

> **SUB** (possibility) • Segundo, ocultando que, aun en el caso de que no
> **pueda establecerse** si la Ejecutiva del PSOE contrajo responsabilidades
> penales, es obvio que las tiene en el plano político. • Por tanto, aun
> en el caso de que alguien **pudiera sostener** que Vera gozó de ese fuero
> mientras fue secretario de Estado, lo habría perdido cuando cesó.
>
> **IND** (fact) {rare} • Pero aun en el caso de que esa voluntad no **se explici-**
> **tará** en forma política, la dinámica propia de la Comunidad la forzaría.

aunque → (9.3.2.3)

bajo la condición de que = *under the condition that*

> **SUB** (intention) • El alivio es otorgado bajo la condición de que los
> ahorros **sean usados** en proyectos de educación y salud, y que se absten-
> gan de participar en conflictos militares. • Entre otras cosas dijo, que
> las instituciones de educación superior mexicanas (como la UNAM)
> podrían tener apoyo financiero bajo la condición de que **se cobrara** por
> lo menos el 30% del costo promedio por estudiante (. . .).
>
> **IND** (fact) • La intervención de los diputados del PSOE . . . fue decisiva
> para que una nueva comisión de trabajadores . . . pudiera negociar con
> la patronal bajo la condición de que no **hay** ningún **despedido**.
>
> condición (bajo la ~) de **INF/NOUN** • Ambas modalidades mantienen
> el denominador común de ser utilizadas por personas distintas del titu-
> lar original de la marca, bajo la condición de **observar** el reglamento
> de uso.

cada vez que = *every time that* → siempre que → (9.3.2.5)

> **SUB** (possibility/intention) • Tú te encuentras perfectamente bien, y así,
> como ahora, podrás encontrarte cada vez que **repitas** los precedentes
> ejercicios cada vez que repitas los precedentes ejercicios. • O sea, es
> que Robson tenía la lámpara y con frotarla salía cada vez que **quisiera**
> un genio.
>
> **IND** (fact) • Mejor es no hablar con nosotros porque cada vez que **habla-**
> **mos** es un problema.

cambio → a cambio de que

caso (en el ~ de) que = *in the case that* → (9.3.2.4)

> **SUB** (possibility) • ¿Existe alguna sanción en el caso de que no **se cancele**
> la información? • . . . de alguna manera se reservaba el derecho a ini-
> ciar nuevas acciones en el caso de que **aparecieran** nuevas pruebas.
>
> **IND** (fact) {rare} • En el capítulo XXIV describe un instrumento para
> conocer la altura de las montañas, la distancia que nos separa de una

cumbre cualquiera y también la distancia entre dos picos o dos puntos dominantes visibles en el caso de que esta distancia no **puede ser medida** sobre la superficie del suelo.

caso (en el ~ de) **INF/NOUN** • ¿Qué hubiera sido de mí en el caso de haber proseguido mis estudios en Zaragoza?

como

→ causal conjunction → porque → (9.3.2.2)

SUB (negation) (Only used with the past subjunctive; written Spanish) {rare} • Como no **respondiese** a sus nuevos llamados, se propuso subir a ayudarle.

IND (fact) • Como estos cambios fiscales **son trascendentes** y seguramente tienen impacto recaudatorio, consideramos conveniente proponer sean agendados para su discusión en la posterior reforma fiscal.

→ conditional conjunction → en el caso de que (no) **SUB** → cuando (no) **SUB** → (9.3.2.2) **SUB** • Como no **te comportes**, te quito el nombre y te llamo otra cosa cualquiera . . . • Como no **fuera** en sentido figurado, ya nadie podría hablar de Imperio. • Podría modernizar sus fuerzas armadas, comprar productos industriales y tecnología, atraer una eficaz inversión capitalista de Estados Unidos, Alemania Occidental, Suecia o Suiza, como **hiciera falta**.

→ modal conjunction → tal como → de acuerdo a como

SUB (hypothetical) • Multiplicamos cada cifra por la base del número tantas veces como **indique** el número que hemos asignado a la cifra. • Se trabajó la primera por capítulos, aunque teníamos también la opción de seguir un orden cronológico, de acuerdo a como **fueran produciéndose** los materiales.

IND (fact) • El equipamiento interno de este equipo está ubicado en el laboratorio de Equipos Electrónicos Popa, como **puede verse** en la imagen. • Esta empresa típicamente ilustrada, en la que no se reparó en gastos, estuvo al servicio exclusivo de la Corona, ya que los intentos que se hicieron para comercializar su producción fracasaron estrepitosamente, tal y como **ocurrió** en el caso de otros establecimientos similares.

como para que → para que → **SUB** • "Todavía no hemos recibido suficiente lluvia como para que **se alivien** los embalses. • Cuando la ventaja de Cortés era suficientemente grande como para que nadie **pudiera alcanzarle**, Nieto y Tormo forzaron su ritmo, superando en pocas vueltas la desventaja, para luego rodar ambos en solitario.

como si

SUB (past subjunctive) (counterfacticity) = *as if* • O sea, aquí resulta que la humanidad va por un lado y las prisiones van por otro, como si en las prisiones no **hubiera** hombres y mujeres, como si no **tuvieran** las limitaciones de conocimiento de toda comunidad humana.

IND (comparison of two fact) = • Esta carta han de enviarla ustedes por correo o depositarla en cualquier Administración de Lotería. Tanto si la envían por correo, como si la **depositan** en una administración, deben consignar en su interior o en el remite los siguientes datos: . . .

con el criterio de que

SUB (purpose) = *with the idea, purpose that* → con el fin de que → para que → (9.3.1.1) • . . . el Poder Judicial deberá diseñar e implementar sus programas de reingeniería con el criterio de que el mismo **modernice** la Administración de Justicia para que se convierta en foco de confianza el clima de Estado de Derecho, . . . • Entretanto, el gobierno dispuso, . . . , la recomposición de los ayuntamientos y de las diputaciones con el criterio de que las corporaciones **se formasen** en un 50 por 90 con concejales a partir de los mayores contribuyentes, y la otra mitad con aquellos que fueron elegidos desde 1917 con mayor número de votos.

IND (fact) (relative clause) = *criterion* → (9.2) • La propiedad y disposición de la tierra cultivable debe examinarse con el criterio de que **se trata** de un bien necesario y un factor de trabajo, . . .

criterio (con el ~) de INF/NOUN • . . . se están contratando y construyendo con el criterio de **iniciar** los tramos fáciles y sin problemas y postergar los que presentan dificultades.

con el fin de que = *with the intention, purpose of* → para que SUB (intention) • Esto lo informo con el fin de que las autoridades **puedan atrapar** esta banda de delincuentes y para que la gente se alerte y evite caer en esta trampa. • . . . los extorsionistas no cumplieron las citas que le pusieron al ciudadano extorsionado con el fin de que **pagara**.

con el fin de → para INF/NOUN • UNESA podrá realizar una auditoría extraordinaria y/o ensayos, a cargo de la empresa licenciataria, con el fin de **decidir** sobre el mantenimiento del certificado.

con la finalidad de que → con el fin de que SUB (intention) • Así como por la prestación de servicios del Programa a sus usuarios de todo el mundo, con la finalidad de que **se intercambien** experiencias. • También tenían que examinar los cernidores con la finalidad de que la harina no **se mezclara** con materias perjudiciales.

con la finalidad de INF/NOUN • Idearon la nueva firma con la finalidad de **rescatar** obras inencontrables . . .

con el objetivo de que → con el fin de que SUB (intention) • Son 140 cuadros en total los que han sido diseñados con el objetivo de que **se conozca** más sobre nuestra historia, . . . • . . . el Juez de Jinotepe y varios civiles, quienes llegaron a la finca con el objetivo de que **se devolviera** la propiedad a sus legítimos dueños . . .

con el objetivo de INF/NOUN • La STT dijo que tomó la medida con el objetivo de **descongestionar** la carrera 11, . . .

con el propósito de que → con el fin de que SUB (intention) • El encuentro ha sido convocado por la Universidad Simón Bolívar, . . . , con el propósito de que los ex presidentes **dialoguen y opinen** acerca de los avatares de la democracia en nuestro continente. • La Unión Soviética trabajó simultáneamente al menos en cuatro frentes distintos con el propósito de que sus cosmonautas **llegaran** a la Luna.

  con el propósito de **INF/ NOUN** • El pintor francés Heri Josset se encuentra en Bogotá, . . . , con el propósito de **permanecer** una larga temporada en Colombia.

con miras a que = *in view of* → para que **SUB** (intention) • Ahora me estoy desempeñando como modelo, pero con miras a que **me tomen en cuenta** para otros proyectos. • Por ejemplo, que el Presidente se vería obligado a llamar al expresidente Pastrana para negociar, con miras a que el país **siguiera siendo "gobernable"**.

  con miras a → para **INF/ NOUN** • Por otro lado, ayer se reanudaron los entrenamientos de la plantilla, con miras a **preparar** el próximo compromiso de Copa del Rey, el 4 de enero en Palamós.

con tal de que = *so that* → para que **SUB** (intention) • Se da la bienvenida a cualquier pirata extranjero con tal de que **comparta** su botín. • Los palestinos podrían aceptar la fórmula con tal de que la declaración **incluyera** sus conocidas reservas y esperar a la Administración Bush, . . .

  con tal de → para **INF/ NOUN** • No es de quienes acostumbran empeñar lo que sea con tal de **ir** a una excursión o una fiesta de quince años.

con que → con tal de

condición → a condición de que; bajo la condición de que

conforme = *as, just as, just like this* → según → como → del mismo modo que

  SUB (possibility) {rare} • Además, cada forma de opinar depende de ciertos condicionamientos, conforme **se haga** oralmente o por escrito, solo o acompañado. • Cada vez que golpee, acomode la cadena en su mano de manera distinta, para que la marca que haga siempre sea diferente. Siga entintando la cadena conforme lo **necesite**, hasta que toda la superficie que quiera quede marcada.

  SUB (past subjunctive) (negation?) {rare} • Pero contra lo que parece, no se trata tanto de banalidad cómica como de una respuesta a la angustia que producen los grandes interrogantes, enfrentándose a ella con su opuesto el humor, conforme **señalara** Freud (1986).

  IND (fact) • . . . -las relaciones de la alquimia con la astrología siempre fueron íntimas conforme **demuestra** la propia terminología heredada en parte de la antigua Babilonia- . . .

costa → a costa de que; aun a costa de que

criterio → con el criterio de que

cual si {literary} → como si **SUB** (counterfactual) • Por ese camino se comprendía su exterminación, cual si de una alimaña **se tratara**.

cuando = *when*

  SUB (time) → (9.3.2.5) • "Cuando **tengamos** información detallada sobre el caso estaremos abiertos a cualquier cooperación", manifestó Vitali Nasonov, portavoz de ese ministerio. • Víctor Ullate soñó que algún día, cuando **tuviera** su propia compañía, montaría Giselle, . . .

SUB (condition) → (9.3.2.4) • Cuando **tenga** que hablar de mis cosas personales, yo los cito". (= Si tengo que hablar de mis cosas, . . .) • Los afiliados de "La Boicotizadora" juramentaban, al ingresar en esta agrupación, comprar exclusivamente en establecimientos cuyos dueños pertenecieran a la sociedad o fueran puertorriqueños, aun cuando **tuvieran que pagar** un precio más alto por las mercancías. (= . . . si tuvieran que pagar . . .)

IND (time) • Cuando **tuve** hijos volví a encontrarme con mis propios orígenes judíos

IND (time/ condition) • No soy en absoluto austera. Cuando **tengo** dinero me voy al mejor restaurante y pido caviar. Pero si no tengo ni para tabaco, no fumo.

cuanto

SUB (hypothetical) = *as much as* → tanto como • Por eso, todo cuanto **podamos** analizar acá esta materia es poco para preservar un derecho tan trascendental como el de que todos los chilenos dispongan de agua potable.

SUB (hypothetical) = *as many as* → tantos/as como → (9.2) • y amenazar a cuantos se les **dé** la gana o permiso unos minutitos más, con quitarles lo traía muy bien, . . .

IND (fact) = *as many as* → tantos/as como → (9.2) • . . . y en representación de cuantos hoy día **están luchando** por el derecho al trabajo, a rechazar este proyecto.

SUB (hypothetical) = *as many* **NOUN** *as* → tantos/as **NOUN** como → (9.2) • Se trata del Quinto Premio de Poesía Ciudad de Córdoba Ricardo Molina, al que pueden concurrir cuantos poetas lo **deseen** de cualquier nacionalidad, siempre que las obras que se presenten sean originales e inéditas y estén escritas en castellano. • . . . sino a presentar cuantos documentos **pudiera requerir** el Senado como la Cámara de Diputados que también así lo solicitó sobre esa materia.

IND (fact) = *as many* **NOUN** *as* → tantos/as **NOUN** como → (9.2) • . . . y lo dicen cuantos juristas y constitucionalistas serios **hay** en el país. • éste llamó por teléfono a toda la familia, a los amigos, a cuantos números **se acordó** de memoria, . . .

IND (fact) = *all that* → todo lo que • Es cuanto **quería** agregar, señor Presidente, a lo mencionado por el Honorable señor Andrés Zaldívar.

cuanto antes = *as son as possible* → lo más pronto posible → (9.3.2.5)

SUB • Cuanto antes **reciba** un paciente tratamiento adecuado en un hospital, más posibilidades tendrá de recuperarse plenamente", afirma Amy S. Hurwitz, . . . • Cuanto antes **llegara** a las anchuras de la calle Ocho, antes dejarían de perseguirle las frituras y las tentaciones.

cuanto (en ~) (que) → tan pronto como → cuando → (9.3.2.5)

SUB • También ayer se esperaba la llegada. . . para evacuar a los tres observadores españoles en cuanto **sean liberados**. • Sólo me dijo que procurara evitar, en cuanto **fuera posible**, la efusión de sangre. • Pero la república y sus históricos partidarios que la sobreviven, en cuanto que lo **sigan siendo**, sí que han entrado ya en la historia.

IND • Ya, pero en cuanto vas a una boda, ya no te cobran eso, mamá.

• . . . y, en cuanto que **pudo**, dio el chivatazo a la policía.

de ahí que = *and therefore, hence* → deberse a que

SUB ([dependent] cause) → así que → (9.3.2.1) • Después de que todos los rumores de su posible colaboración con REM a finales de los ochenta no produjeran ningún fruto, Young afirma que está decidido a no dejar pasar ninguna oportunidad, y de ahí que ahora **colabore** con Pearl Jam. • En Cataluña no, y de ahí que ayer **manifestase su voluntad** de darle carácter prioritario a esta cuestión.

IND ([independent] cause) → *and this is the reason why* → por eso → (9.3.2.1) • EL TIEMPO conoció que los dos coroneles llevan consigo los registros decadactilares de Perafán, señalado por la Policía, como jefe de los carteles de Bogotá y Cauca y contra quien pesa una orden de captura por narcotráfico expedida por autoridades de Estados Unidos. "Hay una alta probabilidad de que se trate de él -Perafán-, de ahí que **se hizo urgente** viajar a la mayor brevedad",

de (tal) forma que

SUB (purpose) = *so that* → para que → (9.3.1.1) • El secretario general del Partido Popular, Francisco Alvarez Cascos, es partidario de que se convoquen elecciones generales para el próximo 28 de mayo, de tal forma que **coincidan** con las autonómicas y municipales, debido a la actual crisis política. • Para conseguir este "rejuvenecimiento", las profesionales optaron por conservar los elementos y materiales usados durante años en todos los locales, pero combinándolos con otros, de tal forma que **se actualizaran**.

IND (fact) = *in a way that* → tal que • Las obras de la línea 2 que ejecuta la Generalitat se han disparado de tal forma que **han generado** un altísimo sobrecoste.

de (tal) manera que → de (tal) forma que

de tal modo que → de (tal) forma que

desde que

IND (fact) = *since, given that* → causal conjunction → porque → (9.3.2.2) • Desde que el gobierno no **envió** asesores ni invitados para discutir asuntos tan importantes como la democracia y la justicia, . . ., sentimos que algo se había roto en las pláticas.

IND (actual cause or starting point) = *since someone did something* • Desde que **perdió** el plebiscito de 1988, el general se ha dedicado con especial tenacidad a consolidar la institucionalidad que su régimen diseñó.

SUB (past subjunctive) (possible cause or starting point) = *since someone would do something* → (9.3.2.5) • La lingüística moderna está dominada por la idea de "estructura". Desde que Saussure **desarrollara** su concepción del lenguaje como "sistema" organizado de elementos interdependientes, el estudio de las relaciones entre los elementos es más significativo que el de los elementos en sí. • Desde que **comenzaran** las audiencias legislativas sobre el escándalo Irán-Contras, Reagan ha guardado un estricto silencio.

después de que → (9.3.2.5)

efecto → a efecto(s) de que

encima → por encima de que

espera → a la espera de que

expensas → a expensas (estar/ quedar/ seguir ~) de que

fin → a fin de que; con el fin de que

finalidad → con la finalidad de que

forma → de (tal) forma que

forma (la ~) de que → de forma que

forma (de ~) que = *in a way that* → dependiendo de que

función (en) de que→ dependiendo de que

hasta que = *until* → (9.3.2.5)

> SUB (purpose, intention) • Son gafas que favorecen la elasticidad de los músculos ciliares. Pueden ser muy útiles. Se usan sin ninguna corrección (cristales o lentillas) durante una hora o dos al día, hasta que **se produzca** la corrección natural en el ojo. • Esto se conocía en noviembre, se formó ese comité, luego ha ido un fotógrafo y un hombre que manejaba un vídeo, también de la Diputación de Álava y al parecer incluso ellos, han tenido que firmar un escrito por el que se comprometían a no decir nada, absolutamente nada hasta que **se hubiera comprobado** todo esto que acabamos de decir y **se diera a conocer,** que tuvo lugar ayer el conocimiento de esta noticia, a nivel, digamos mundial, a las doce y unos minutos se daba a conocer el hallazgo.

> IND (fact, existing) • Y lo que digo aquí es que luego el terapeuta, en base a sus ideas previas, ajusta lo que dice el paciente hasta a estas ideas hasta que el paciente **queda convencido** de ello, con lo cual se ha superado la terapia. • Y curioso lo que ha dicho que hasta que no **vio** en la pantalla el rótulo de Laurent Jalabert ganador de la Vuelta no se lo había creído.

> hasta **INF/ NOUN** • . . . No descansaré hasta **ver** a los conspiradores en la cárcel.

luego de que = *after* → después de que SUB • Llerena explicó a Vistazo que los inmuebles los empezó a comprar luego de que **vendieran** varios almacenes de llantas importadas y zapatos para niños que poseían desde años atrás.

> luego de **INF/ NOUN** • Pero le brillaban los ojos luego de **hablar** con los periodistas, . . .

manera → de (tal) manera que

margen → al margen de que

medida → a medida que

menos → a menos (+ period of time) de que; a menos (de) que

mientras = *while* → (9.3.2.5)

IND (fact) = *while; at the same time as; when* → al mismo tiempo que → cuando • El Profesor Yunus justifica que el banco busque sus usuarios entre las mujeres por la capacidad que ellas demuestran para planificar el futuro de la familia, mientras los hombres **piensan** más **en disfrutar** del dinero día a día. • Hay que lograr que desaparezca esa enorme sima que tiene condenados a países pobres a ser cada día más pobres, mientras los países ricos **son** cada vez **más ricos**. • Ahora, cuando estaba en el banquillo, mientras tu **comentabas** esto, parecía buscar algún tipo de golpe en la parte derecha de su cuerpo, no sé si a la altura de la cadera o de la pierna.

SUB (hypothetical) = *as long as, whenever, if* → si (no) + IND → (9.3.2.4) • Entonces, la Constitución Española tiene algo muy importante muchísimas cosas, pero hay un artículo, el artículo veinticuatro concretamente, donde se habla de la tutela efectiva de jueces y magistrados, y la presunción de inocencia mientras no **se demuestre** lo contrario. • No le importa mientras no se lo **cuenten**. • Picasso, que quería ver su cuadro colocado en el Museo del Prado, se opuso a que se trasladara a España mientras **estuviera vigente** la dictadura. • Bini era de las que se entregaba; y mientras **estuviera** con un tipo, cliente o no, actuaba como una mujer enamorada.

mientras que = *while* → (9.3.2.5)

IND (fact) = *while, at the same time/ on the other hand, something is happening* • Todo esto se ha visto venir, y se ha denunciado con todo lujo de detalles mientras que el Madrid **iba ganando** partidos. • Spassky utilizó la defensa siciliana, mientras que Fischer **eligió** la variación cerrada, tal como hizo en la partida 17 que ganó.

SUB (hypothetical) {rare} = *while, at the same time, something might be happening* • El picador debe mantener la puya, sin golpear con ella, mientras que **esté en contacto** con el toro y debe "abrir la salida" para permitir al torero sacar rápidamente al toro. • Ni la originalidad literaria cabe, ni la libertad política subsiste mientras que no **se asegure** la libertad espiritual. • Los tratados no serán tratados; no recibirán esta consideración jurídica. . . . Constituirían, mientras que **fueran necesarios**, compromisos políticos sin valor normativo alguno, ni siquiera de rango legislativo y así también reservado al poder propio. No eran, sin más, tratados. No obligaban a una parte, la nación, México.

miras → con miras a que

modo → de tal modo que

nada → a nada que

objetivo → con el objetivo de que

para que = *so that* → con el fin de que → (9.3.1.1) **SUB** • La salida inmediata de la guerra, pide la paz, y alienta a todos los países para que **se haga** lo mismo y **se vuelva** a las fronteras de 1914. • Estos y otros eran los engaños que usaban para que todo **pareciese perfecto**.

para **INF/ NOUN** • Y para **escribir** una novela, primero hay tener un buen argumento.

pesar → a pesar de que

pese a que

    IND (fact) = *even though* → aunque → (9.2.3) • Pese a que la popularidad del primer ministro **es** todavía **alta**, el problema de la participación de España en la OTAN es un tema todavía muy controvertido. • Pese a que durante seis horas Conde **repitió** los argumentos en defensa de su . . . , el ex banquero no convenció a los miembros de la comisión parlamentaria . . .

    SUB (possibility) {rare} *even though* → aunque → (9.2.3) • La Administración Clinton logró ayer un crucial, aunque reticente compromiso de apoyo del líder de la mayoría del Senado, Bob Dole, quien hizo un llamamiento al Congreso para que respaldara el despliegue de las tropas norteamericanas en Bosnia. . . . Clinton, dijo, quiere enviar ahora a unos 20.000 soldados pese a que **exista**, o no, objeción del Congreso. • Pese a que su pasado **nos parezca** sumamente **oscuro** [we could insert 'o no'], como sus propias tonalidades, la introducción del chocolate en el mundo de la repostería representó un jalón fundamental para los hábitos alimenticios del ser humano. • De no haber iniciado el invierno antes del 15 de este mes, se hubieran reportado pérdidas del 20 por ciento de la producción nacional de maíz y siete por ciento de la producción nacional de frijoles. • La reforma de la LOPJ no impide que nadie se dirija en castellano a la administración de justicia, sino que garantiza que pueda hacerlo en catalán. Recurrir por inconstitucionalidad dicha reforma significa recurrir el uso del catalán en Cataluña. Y pese a que con ello **ganen** [we could insert 'o no'] votos en otras comunidades, es vergonzante que el señor Trillo pretenda mostrarnos en qué casos es apropiado el uso de nuestra lengua.

    SUB (counterfactual) {rare} = *despite the fact that* → (9.2.3) • Pese a que INETER **señalara** que ya están las condiciones dadas para un buen invierno, el titular del MAG indicó que hay muchos productores que aún tienen temor de sembrar, principalmente los que tienen grandes manzanas de tierra en lugares secos y donde no ha llovido hasta la fecha como el caso del norte del país. • Convergència i Unió (CiU) rompió la disciplina de voto que venía manteniendo con el grupo socialista y apoyó las enmiendas presentadas por el PP, IU y el PNV para incrementar el control del gasto público. El portavoz catalán, Francesc Homs, explicó que, . . ., su grupo "apoyó estas iniciativas porque creemos que es necesario un mayor rigor en el control del gasto público, pese a que el Partido Socialista **no estuviera de acuerdo**". • Zapatero se refirió entonces a la propuesta sobre un plan de catedrales para Castilla y León que el Ministerio y la Junta trataron de consensuar en 1989.2. Según el proyecto, durante algún tiempo sería el Gobierno quien se haría cargo de la catedral pese a que la competencia **correspondiera** -desde 1983- a la comunidad autónoma.

pese a INF/ NOUN • . . . dijo Bachelet, . . . que ella más que nadie puede opinar sobre el tema en vista de que su padre murió detenido en la Cárcel Pública en 1974, pese a **ser** general de aviación.

poco → a poco que

por (~ mucho/ más/ poco) que = even though . . . → aunque → (9.3.2.3)

SUB (hypothetical) • No sabrán nada hasta el día que yo quiera, si quiero. Pero nadie lo sabe, por mucho que **se escriba**. • Dentro de un tono monótono, la faena tampoco terminó de arrancar de verdad, por mucho que el torero lo **intentara**. • Es que esto está tan malo que por poco que yo **haga** se va a mejorar. • El encuentro en las Azores fue, así, por más que **intentara desmentirlo** alguno de los participantes, un auténtico consejo de guerra.

IND (fact) {rare} • En la candidatura de Gómez Pintado el optimismo se parece al de las demás, por mucho que las encuestas **sitúan** al presidente de Otaysa en tercer lugar. • Y de cualquier modo, lejos de ser una iniquidad perpetrada por el Capitalismo contra el Tercer Mundo, más bien refleja, por poco que **se piensa** en ello, una notable mejora en las condiciones de vida de esas poblaciones. • En la práctica recreativa los dos quedaron en diferentes equipos, y por más que **intentó** no pudo anotarle gol al espigado portero.

por encima de que {rare} = even though . . . → aunque → (9.3.2.3)

por lo que

IND = *and therefore; and that is why, and that is the reason why* → y por eso → (9.3.2.1) • Parece que el cuerpo está recuperando un lugar en la sociedad chilena, por lo que la danza **empieza a verse** como una eficaz herramienta de expresión, tanto artística como terapéutica.

IND (fact) = *for what* → en cuanto a lo que → (9.2) • Y no sólo por lo que **significa reunir** el dinero para traslados, estadía y alojamientos, sino por las barreras de incomprensión cultural que hay que romper.

SUB (hypothetical) = *for what* → en cuanto a lo que → (9.2) • "La idea -cuenta Rosario- es que cada uno muestre al resto el estado en que se encuentra el teatro de su zona, no sólo a través de una obra de teatro, sino además por lo que **puedan decir** sociólogos, críticos, dramaturgos, directores u otros.

por que = *so that* → para que → (9.3.1.1) **SUB** (intention) • Clamamos por que **se proscriba** la violencia, la pobreza, el abandono secular, la miseria, por que **haya** carreteras, puentes, salud, comercialización, adecuada, buenas semillas y precios. • . . .el artista barroco se esforzaba por que el cuadro **fuese verosímil** para la mirada del espectador, . . . (The use of 'por que' instead of 'porque' is very frequent but, nevertheless, considered wrong: *¿Te vas a dedicar a la pasarela o prefieres hacer cine? A la pasarela no por que **soy tímida** y no **tengo** la suficiente estatura. By the same token, the use of 'porque' instead of 'por que' is also considered wrong: * Hasta la familia -un poco tarde- pugna porque **sea declarado loco** de remate.)

porque = *because* → (9.3.2.2) (The indicative characterizes the content of a dependent clause as a fact and the link between related clauses as real and effective, no matter what. With the subjunctive we question and criticize the effectiveness, validity and exclusivity of the causal relation.)

IND (cause, fact) • "Es prudente no dar precisiones, porque no **estamos seguros**", agregó.

SUB (hypothetical, possibility) → por la posibilidad de que • El Romanticismo artístico es un movimiento difícil de definir <u>tal vez</u> porque **sea** más un movimiento social y espiritual, "un modo de sentir" que un estilo en el más estricto sentido del término. • Quizá porque esté más lejos del poder que en ningún otro momento de su carrera, Sharon se pone filosófico, si bien de forma poco profunda y muy militar.

SUB (a fact not being sufficient or adequate to conclude what is stated in the main clause) → solo porque → •. . .y añadió que porque **esté fugado** "no quiere decir que esté diciendo mentira o verdad. No se le puede desacreditar porque **esté huido**. • Es cuestión de suma importancia, porque si se pretende la libre circulación de capitales y mercancías entre Estados Unidos y América Latina, los seres humanos valen mucho más que capitales y mercancías. En un mundo globalizado y cada vez más integrado económicamente, es criminal que hombres, mujeres y niños mueran porque **esté prohibido** para ellos la misma libertad de circulación. • Mi primo Ricard me explicó que para aquella noche le había preparado a su padre una cama aparte, pues el cadáver de la tía María reposaba en la cama de matrimonio, pero que el tío Manel se emperró en dormir en el mismo sitio de siempre. "¿No hemos dormido media vida juntos?, pues ahora, porque **esté un poco más fría**, no pienso cambiar de cama", y así lo hizo.

SUB (counterfactual) • El partido será histórico. <u>No</u> porque **sea** el primer enfrentamiento entre ambas, que no lo es. Sino porque es la primera vez en la historia de los torneos del Grand Slam que dos españolas disputarán una semifinal de tan alto nivel.

SUB (intention or felling of the main subject) → 'porque' = 'que' → (9.) • El propio Nicolás Redondo, afirmó ayer que la postura del sindicato era a favor de mantener los complementos de pensiones existentes como una conquista irrenunciable de los trabajadores. El secretario general <u>mostró su preocupación</u> porque **fuera** precisamente en las empresas públicas donde se estaba intentando hacer desaparecer los complementos de pensiones. (= *Al secretario general le preocupaba que fuera. . .*) • <u>Llama</u> ésto <u>la atención</u>, no porque se equivocara Hayek, sino porque **fuera** precisamente un filósofo político y economista de su calibre quien incurriera en tal error. (=*Llama la atención que fuera. . .*)

por si = *in case that; if* → si → (9.3.2.4)

IND (present, imperfect) (fact) • Los más pequeños, como Silvia, madrileña de 7 años, han preferido mandar su autorretrato, por si alguien, allá arriba, siente curiosidad por saber, algún día, qué aspecto tenían las niñas del planeta Tierra a finales del siglo XX. • "Yo estaba haciendo fotos a los daños causados <u>por si</u> **era necesario** para el seguro o una posible denuncia y Maradona me dijo que mi trabajo era una puta mierda", . . .

IND (conditional) (hypothetical) • Varias patrullas de policía han rastreado el fondo de la costa por si los ladrones **habrían arrojado** algún lienzo al mar.

SUB PAST (hypothetical) • A la vez, hay que mantener la capacidad de producir estas armas por si **hubiera** otra guerra. • Y por si **fuera poco**, en el abuso contra la niña también participó un amigo de éste.

por si acaso = *in case that may be; if* → si → (9.3.2.4) por si = *in case that; if*

pronto → tan pronto como

propósito → con el propósito de que

punto → a punto de que

raíz → a raíz de que

riesgo → a riesgo de que

salvo que

SUB = *unless* → a no ser que → (9.3.2.3) • Por otra parte, en los contratos de los directores los estudios suelen imponer una cláusula que les obliga a montar una versión que como máximo obtenga el calificativo R (restringida a menores de 17, salvo que **vayan acompañados** por un adulto). • Gómez Redondo aseguró, al ser preguntado sobre la posibilidad de reciclar el programa para semanas posteriores, que "se podría emitir, salvo que **perdiera actualidad**".

IND = *only (for the fact) that* → solo que • López de Ayala aportó un documento colegial que es idéntico en todo a las cartas recibidas por muchos colegiados, salvo que en la polémica frase **se puede leer** que los cuatro magistrados se enfrentan a la "posibilidad de ser procesados por una presunta flagrante prevaricación". • Luego de un viaje de siete horas por caminos de tierra y tres horas de caminata nocturna en los bosques, sin luces para guiarse, los reporteros se encontraron con los rebeldes, quienes no indicaron su posición exacta, salvo que **se encontraban** en algún lugar de las montañas oaxaqueñas, dijo AP.

según que = *according to [an alternative]* → dependiendo de que **SUB**

• Las reacciones químicas pueden entonces clasificarse en exotérmicas o endotérmicas, según que **haya** desprendimiento o absorción de calor.

• Tal puede ser el caso respectivo de. . . la persistencia o desaparición de conductas psicopáticas, según que éstas **fueran autóctonas o simuladas** por la enfermedad alcohólica.

ser → a no ser que

siempre que = *every time that*

IND (fact) → cada vez que → siempre • "Los expertos dicen que siempre que se produce una mejora económica, viene acompañada por un aumento de la siniestralidad", dijo. . .

SUB (hypothetical) → siempre y cuando → con tal de que → a condición de que → (9.3.2.4) • En definitiva, la tele no es mala. El problema es cómo se ve: . . . Los puntos de referencia de la vida deben ser las personas de carne y hueso, y siempre que **exista** un padre y/o una madre que se ocupe de sus hijos y que les guíe en su uso, la tele será positiva.

•. . . tenían unos bosques maravillosos donde campar a sus anchas siempre que **tuvieran** cuidado de los osos.

siempre y cuando = *if and when* → con tal de que → a condición de que → (9.3.2.4) **SUB** Como tantas otras cosas en el mundo árabe, la homosexualidad está tolerada en Egipto, siempre y cuando no **se exhiba**, siempre y cuando **se desarrolle** de puertas para adentro, en el ámbito privado, no en el público. • La soprano se reservó el derecho de autorizar la biografía siempre y cuando **pudiera leer** el texto final y tener el derecho de aclarar las posibles "fantasías, en el sentido de que ellos imaginaran lo que yo pensara".

sin que = *without* → (9.3.1.4) **SUB** • A las urnas acuden más votantes que nunca, sin que **se produzca** el menor incidente. • Pero aquí están los libertarios andaluces, luciendo por las calles de Jaén banderas verdiblancas, negras y rojas, sin que **ocurriera** el más mínimo incidente, . . .

sin **INF/ NOUN** • Al preguntarles por qué no había nadie allí, uno de esos soldados levantó la mano y abrió los cinco dedos sin **decir** palabra.

tal → con tal de que

tan pronto como = *as son as* → (9.2.5)

SUB (hypothetical) • Tan pronto como **tengamos** elecciones . . . entonces la inestabilidad política va a desaparecer. • Tan pronto como **aparecieran**, se apagaron aquellas palabras en la ventana.

IND (fact) • Tan pronto como **me ha sido posible** he ido a ver la nueva película de Luis García Berlanga. • Tan pronto como Bucaram **ganó** las elecciones, el Poder Judicial absolvió a la hermana del presidente, sindicada por peculado en la municipalidad de Guayaquil.

una vez que = *once* → después de que

SUB (hypothetical) • Una vez que el usuario **obtenga** la información deseada, sólo tendrá que asegúrese de anotar el Código Bibliográfico y el Número de Inventario, para solicitar su préstamo en la biblioteca. . .

IND (fact) • Empecé a hablar inglés y luego aprendí a leer. Una vez que **pude leer**, me convertí totalmente al inglés.

vez → cada vez que; una vez que

Note

1 All the examples are taken from the REAL ACADEMIA ESPAÑOLA: Banco de datos (CREA) [en línea]. Corpus de Referencia del Español Actual. <http://www.rae.es> [September 2013-September 2014]

Bibliography

Bibliography of works cited in this book

Achard, Michel (2000). Seleccción de modo en construcciones oracionales de comple-mento. In: R. Maldonado/ M. Sanaphre (eds.), *Estudios cognoscitivos del español. Revista Española de Lingüística Aplicada* (Spec. Issue). Logroño, 153–74.

Ahern, Aoife (2008). *El subjuntivo: contextos y efectos.* Madrid: Arco/ Libros.

Alarcos Llorach, Emilio (1994). *Gramática de la lengua española.* Madrid: Espasa.

Alarcos Llorach, Emilio (1978). *Estudios de gramática funcional del español.* Madrid: Gredos.

Alcoba Rueda, Santiago (1991). Después de que se aprobara . . . , recurso de un antepre-térito necesario en el lenguaje periodístico. In: C. Barrera/ M. A. Jimeno (eds.), *La información como relato.* Pamplona: Universidad de Navarra, 521–34.

Aleza Izquierdo, Milagros/ Enguita Utrilla, José Mª. (coords.) (2010). *La lengua española en América: Norma y usos actuales.* Valencia: Universitat de València. https://www.uv.es/aleza/esp.am.pdf

Alonso Cortés, Angel M. (1981). *Gramática del subjuntivo.* Madrid: Cátedra.

Anadón Rojas, S. (1979). *El subjuntivo en el español de Sudamérica.* Unpublished doctoral dissertation. Ann Arbor: University of Michigan.

Anderson, Gunnar Jay (1995). *The Spanish Subjunctive in Context.* Lanham, MD: University Press of America.

Badía Margarit, Antoni Maria (1953). El subjuntivo de subordinación en las lenguas romances y especialmente en iberorromance. *Revista de Filología Española,* 37, 95–129.

Bally, Charles (1944). *Linguistique générale et linguistique française.* Geneve: A. Francke.

Beardsley, Wilfred A. (1925). The Psychology of the Spanish Subjunctive. *Hispania,* 8.2, 98–108.

Becker, Martin G./ Remberger, Eva-Maria (eds.) (2010). Modality and Mood in Romance: Modal Interpretation, Mood Selection, and Mood Alternation. *Linguistische Arbeiten,* 533.

Bejarano, Virgilio (1962). Sobre las dos formas del imperfecto de subjuntivo y el empleo de la forma en -se con valor de indicativo. In: *Strenae. Estudios de filología e historia dedicados al profesor Manuel García Blanco.* Salamanca: Universidad de Salamanca, 77–86.

Bell, Anthony (1980). Mood in Spanish: A Discussion of Some Recent Proposals. *Hispania,* 63.2, 377–90.

Bello, Andrés (1981). *Gramática de la lengua castellana destinada al uso de los americanos.* Ed. Ramón Trujillo. Tenerife: Cabildo Insular e Instituto Universitario Lingüístico Andrés Bello.

Bergen, John J. (1978). One Rule for the Spanish Subjunctive. *Hispania,* 61.2, 218–34.

Blake, Robert (1987). El uso del subjuntivo con cláusulas nominales: regla obligatoria o variable. In: H. López Morales/ M. Vaquero (eds.), *Actas del I Congreso Internacional sobre el español de América*. San Juan: Academia Puertorriqueña de la Lengua Española, 351–60.

Blake, Robert (1985). From Research to the Classroom: Notes on the Subjunctive. *Hispania*, 68.1, 166–73.

Bolinger, Dwight L. (1976). Again-One or Two Subjunctives? *Hispania*, 59.1, 41–9.

Bolinger, Dwight L. (1974). One Subjunctive or Two? *Hispania*, 57.3, 462–71.

Bolinger, Dwight L. (1956). Subjunctive -ra and -se: "Free Variation"? *Hispania*, 39.3, 345–9.

Bolinger, Dwight L. (1953). Verbs of Emotion. *Hispania*, 36.4, 459–61.

Borrego, Julio/ Ascencio, J. G./ Prieto, E. (2003). *El subjuntivo. Valores y usos*. Madrid: SGEL-Educación. Ninth edition.

Bosque, Ignacio (ed.) (1990a). *Indicativo y subjuntivo*. Madrid: Taurus.

Bosque, Ignacio (1990b). Las bases gramaticales de la alternancia modal: repaso y balance. In: Ignacio Bosque (ed.) (1990a), *Indicativo y subjuntivo*. Madrid: Taurus, 13–65.

Bosque, Ignacio/ Demonte, Violeta (eds.) (1999). *Gramática descriptiva de la lengua española*. Madrid: Espasa Calpe.

Busch, Hans-Jörg (2014). The Subjunctive, a Marker of "Subordinance"? A Comparison between German and Spanish. *Borealis: An International Journal of Hispanic Linguistics*, 3.1, 103–23.

Bustos Tovar, Eduardo (1986). *Pragmática del español. Negación, cuantificación y modo*. Madrid: U.N.E.D.

Butt, John/ Benjamin, Carmen (2013). *A New Reference Grammar of Modern Spanish*. New York: Routledge. Fifth edition.

Cano Aguilar, Rafael (1990). Sobre la historia del subjuntivo en español. In: M. A. Alvarez Martínez (ed.), *Actas del Congreso de la Sociedad Española de Lingüística: XX Aniversario : Tenerife, 2-6 de abril de 1990*. Gredos. 340–53.

Carbonero Cano, Pedro (1990). Usos de las formas verbales -ra y -se en el habla de Sevilla (nivel popular). *Filosofía y Letras*, 120, 45–58.

Castronovo, Brian J. (1984). *A Critical Analysis of Interpretations of the Spanish Subjunctive from Bello to the Present Day*. Doctoral Dissertation. University of Wisconsin-Madison.

Chiquito, Ana B. (2012). *A Handbook of Contemporary Spanish Grammar*. Boston: Vista Higher Learning Inc.

Collentine, Joseph (2010). The Acquisition and Teaching of the Spanish Subjunctive: An Update on Current Findings. *Hispania*, 93.1, 39–51.

Collentine, Joseph (2003). The Development of Subjunctive and Complex-Syntactic Abilities among FL Spanish Learners. In: B. Lafford/ R. Salaberry (eds.), *Studies in Spanish Second Language Acquisition: The State of the Science*. Washington, DC: Georgetown University Press, 74–97.

Collentine, Joseph (2002). On the Acquisition of the Subjunctive and Authentic Processing Instruction: A Response to Farley. *Hispania*, 85.4, 879–88.

Collentine, Joseph (1998). Processing Instruction and the Subjunctive. *Hispania*, 81.3, 576–87.

Collentine, Joseph (1995). The Development of Complex Syntax and Mood-Selection Abilities by Intermediate-Level Learners of Spanish. *Hispania*, 78.1, 122–35.

Cook, Gerard LeStrang (1975). *Mode, Code, and Performance: Analyses and Discussions of the Indicative/Subjunctive Contrast in Spanish with Reference to a Theory of Language Use*. Dissertation Abstracts International, 36: 2775A–6A.

Cristofaro, Sonia (2003). *Subordination*. Oxford: Oxford University Press.

De Jonge, Bob (2006). Significado y uso del subjuntivo en español: una alternativa relevante. In: M. Sedano/ A. Bolívar/ M. Shiro (coords.), *Haciendo lingüística: homenaje a Paola Bentivoglio*. Universidad Central de Venezuela, 163-76.

De Jonge, Bob (2004). The Relevance of Relevance in Linguistic Analysis: Spanish Subjunctive Mood. In: E. Contini-Morava/ R. S. Kirsner/ B. Rodriguez-Bachiller (eds.), *Cognitive and Communicative Approaches to Linguistic Analysis*. Amsterdam/Philadelphia: John Benjamins, 205–18.

De Jonge, Bob (2001). Spanish Subjunctive Mood: One Form, More Than One Meaning? In: Reineke Bok-Bennema/ Bob de Jonge/ Brigitte Kampers-Manhe/ Arie Molendijk (eds.), *Adverbial Modification, Selected Papers from the Fifth Colloquium on Romance Linguistics, Groningen, 10–12 September 1998*. Amsterdam/ Atlanta: Rodopi, 79–92.

De Jonge, Bob (1999). El uso del subjuntivo: ¿un problema para los hablantes de lenguas germánicas? In: Fermín Sierra Martínez/ Carmen Hernández González (eds.), *Las lenguas en la Europa comunitaria III, Diálogos Hispánicos 23*. Amsterdam: Rodopi, 75–84.

De Kock, Josse (coor.) (2001). *Lingüística con corpus. Catorce aplicaciones sobre el español*. Salamanca: Ediciones Universidad de Salamanca.

Delbecque, Nicole/ Lamiroy, Béatrice (1999). La subordinación sustantiva: las subordinadas enunciativas en los complementos verbales. In: I. Bosque/ V. Demonte (eds.), *Gramática descriptiva de la lengua española*, Vol. 2. Madrid: Espasa Calpe, 1931–65.

DeMello, George (1996). Indicativo por subjuntivo en cláusula regida por expresión de reacción personal. *Nueva Revista de Filología Hispánica*, 44.2, 365–86.

DeMello, George (1995a). Alternancia modal indicativo/subjuntivo con expresiones de posibilidad y probabilidad. *Verba*, 22, 339–61.

DeMello, George (1995b). Tense and Mood after No sé si. *Hispanic Review*, 63.4, 555–73.

DeMello, George (1993). -Ra vs. -se Subjunctive: A New Look at an Old Topic. *Hispania*, 76.2, 235–44.

Demonte, Violeta (1977). *La subordinación sustantiva*. Madrid: Cátedra.

De Sterck, Goedele (2000). *Registros y áreas geográficas en lingüística. Valores y usos de las formas verbales en -RA, -SE, -RÍA y – RE*, Vol. 2, 7 of a series edited by Josse De Kock, Gramática española: enseñanza e investigación. Salamanca: Ediciones Universidad de Salamanca.

Dietrich, Wolf (1981). Actualité et inactualité de l' action: Les fonctions modales dans le système verbal des languages romanes. *Logos semantikos*, 4, 395–416.

Farley, Andrew P. (2004). Semantic and Syntactic Perspectives on Mood Selection in Spanish: An Analysis of Presupposition, Government, and Binding. *Estudios de Lingüística Aplicada*, 22, 13–35.

Farley, Andrew P. (2002). Processing Instruction, Communicative Value, and Ecological Validity: A Response to Collentine's Defense. *Hispania*, 85.4, 889–95.

Farley, Andrew P. (2001). Authentic Processing Instruction and the Spanish Subjunctive. *Hispania*, 84.2, 289–99.

Fauconnier, Gilles (1985). *Mental Spaces*. Cambridge: MIT.

Fente Gómez, Rafael (1972). *El subjuntivo. Valores y usos*. Madrid: Sociedad General Española de Librería.

Fernández Alvarez, J./ Fente Gómez, Rafael (1992). *El subjuntivo*. Madrid: Edelsa.

Ferrell, Julia E. (1999). *The Development of Subjunctive Use with Expressions of Emotion from Latin to Spanish*. Thesis. University of Michigan. Ann Arbor.

Finanger, Elizabeth (2011). Time Reference, Adjacency, and Lexical Effects in Mood Choice Following Spanish Epistemic Adverbs Quizá(s): A Dialectal Comparison. In: Jim Michnowicz/ Robin Dodsworth (eds.), *Selected Proceedings of the 5th Workshop on Spanish Sociolinguistics*. Somerville, MA: Cascadilla Proceedings Project, 90–102.

Flamenco García, L. (1999). Las construcciones concesivas y adversativas. In: I. Bosque/ V. Demonte (dirs.), *Gramática descriptiva de la lengua española*. Madrid: Espasa Calpe, 3805–78.

Fontanella de Weinberg, María B. (1997). El uso del futuro de subjuntivo en el español bonaerense (siglos XVI a XVIII). *Lingüística*, 9, 87–95.

Frege, Gottlob (1892). Über Sinn und Bedeutung. *Zeitschrift für Philosophie und philosophische Kritik*, *100.1*, 25–50.

Fukushima, Noritaka (2013), El español y el japonés. Monograph Series in Foreign Studies, 53. Universidad de Estudios Extranjeros de Kobe, Kobe.

Fukushima, Noritaka (2008). The Mood in the Appositive Clause Preceded by el hecho de que in Spanish. *Lingüística Hispánica*, 31, 1–22.

Fukushima, Noritaka (2001a). El modo subjuntivo en el español de América. *Lingüística Hispánica*, 24, 79–92.

Fukushima, Noritaka (2001b). En busca del valor del modo subjuntivo (desde el punto de vista de la lingüística japonesa). *Hispanica Polonorum*, 3. Lodz, 102–13.

Fukushima, Noritaka (1981a). Frecuencia del subjuntivo en el español actual. In: *Lingüística Hispánica*, Vol. 5. Hirakata: Círculo de Lingüística Hispánica de Kansai, 47–72.

Gallego, Muriel/ Alonso-Marks, Emilia (2014). Degrees of Subjunctive Vitality among Monolingual Speakers of Peninsular and Argentinian Spanish. *Borealis: An International Journal of Hispanic Linguistics*, 2.2, 95–105.

García, Christina (2011). Distinguishing Two "Synonyms": A Variationist Analysis of Quizá and Quizás in Six Spanish Dialects. In: J. Michnowicz/ R. Dodsworth (eds.), *Selected Proceedings of the 5th Workshop on Spanish Sociolinguistics*. Somerville: Cascadilla Proceedings Project, 103–12.

Gili y Gaya, Samuel (1980). *Curso superior de sintaxis española*. Barcelona: Bibliograf. Decimotercera edición.

Goldberg, Barbara Ruth S. (1991). A Semantic Analysis of the Spanish Subjunctive with a Special Consideration of the Endings -ra and -se. *Dissertations Abstracts International*, 52.5, 1731A.

Goldin, Mark G. (1974). A Psychological Perspective of the Spanish Subjunctive. *Hispania*, 57.2, 295–301.

Gordon, Calvin Gustav (1964). *The Subjunctive Mood in Representative Spanish Words from the Twelfth to the Eighteenth Century*. Dissertation. Michigan: Ann Arbor.

Gragera, Antonio (2002). *L1 Attrition and L2 Acquisition of Spanish Subjunctive: A Functionalist Approach*. Colección Cultura Iberoamericana, 9. Valladolid: Universitas Castellae.

Gragera, Antonio (2000). *The Role of Typological Markedness in the Acquisition of Spanish Subjunctive and in Language Change*. University of Massachusetts Amherst.

Gregory, Amy E./ Lunn, Patricia (2012). A Concept-Based Approach to the Subjunctive. *Hispania*, 95.2, 333–43.

Guitart, Jorge M. (1987). Sobre el uso del subjuntivo español en dos dialectos caribeños: análisis pragmático. *Thesaurus*, 42.1, 141–8.

Harris, James (1765). *Hermes or a Philosophical Inquiry Concerning Universal Grammar*. London, Printed for F. Wingrave.

Haverkate, Henk (2002). *The Syntax, Semantics and Pragmatics of Spanish Mood*. Amsterdam: John Benjamins.

Heim, I. (1992). Presupposition Projection and the Semantics of Attitude Verbs. *Journal of Semantics*, 9, 182–221.

Hermerén, Ingrid (1992). *El uso de la forma en RA con valor no-subjuntivo en el español moderno*. Lund: Lund University Press.

Hernández Alonso, Cesar (1984). *Gramática funcional del español*. Madrid: Gredos.

Hummel, Martin (2001). Der Grundwert des spanischen Subjuntivs. *Tübinger Beiträge zur Linguistik*, 459. Tübingen: Narr.

Hunnius, Klaus (1976). *Der Modusgebrauch nach den Verben der Gemütsbewegung im Französischen*. Heidelberg: Winter.

Jary, Mark (2004). Indicative Mood, Assertoric Force and Relevance. *Philosophica*, 4.2, 237–46.

Jegerski, J./ VanPatten, B. (2014). *Research Methods for Second Language Psycholinguistics*. New York: Routledge.

Jelinski, Jack B. (1977). A New Look at Teaching the Spanish Subjunctive. *Hispania*, 60.2, 320–6.

Jensen, Frede/ Lathrop, Thomas (1973). *The Syntax of the Old Spanish Subjunctive*. The Hague: Mouton.

Keenan, Eduard L. (1971). Two Kinds of Presupposition in Natural Language. In: Charles J. Fillmore/ D. Terence Langendoen (eds.), *Studies in Linguistic Semantics*. New York: Holt, Rinehart and Winston, 45–54.

Keniston, Hayward (1937). *The Syntax of Castillian Prose*. Chicago: University of Chicago Press.

Kiparsky, Paul/ Kiparsky, Carol (1971). Fact. In: D. D. Steinberg/ L. A. Jakobovits (eds.), *Semantics: An Interdisciplinary Reader in Philosophy, Linguistics and Psychology*. Cambridge: Cambridge University Press, 345–69.

Kirk, Rachel W. (2013). The Effects of Processing Instruction with and without Output: Acquisition of the Spanish Subjunctive in Three Conjunctional Phrases. *Hispania*, 96.1, 153–69.

Klein-Andreu, Flora (1994). The Painless Subjunctive. In: P. Hashemipour (ed. and preface)/ R. Maldonado (ed. and preface)/ M. Van Naerssen (ed. and preface)/ T. Dorwick (foreword), *Studies in Language Learning and Spanish Linguistics*. New York: McGraw-Hill, 419–31.

Knauer, Gabriele (1998). *Der Subjunctive im Spanischen Mexikos, sein Wechselverhältnis zwischen Syntax, Semantik und interaktionalen Faktoren*. Beihefte zur Zeitschrift für Romanische Philologie, 292. Tübingen : M. Niemeyer.

Krakusin, Margarita (1992). Selección del modo después de *el hecho de que*. *Hispania*, 75.5, 1289–93.

Krashen, Stephen (1990). Some Factors in the Acquisition of the Present Subjunctive in Spanish: A Re-Analysis. *Hispania*, 73.3, 805–6.

Kronning, Hans (1999). Les subordonnées temporelles introduites par «après que». Aspects distributionnels et quantitatifs. In: K. Jonasson/ S. Swahn. (eds.), *Résonances de la recherche. Festskrift till Sigbrit Swahn*. Uppsala : Acta Universitatis Upsaliensis, 225–34.

Laca, Brenda (2010a). Mood in Spanish. In: B. Rothstein/ R. Thieroff (eds.), *Mood in the Languages of Europe*. Amsterdam: John Benjamins, 198–220.

Langacker, Ronald (2009). *Investigations in Cognitive Grammar*. Berlin: de Gryter.

Langacker, Ronald (2008). *Cognitive Grammar: A Basic Introduction*. Oxford: Oxford University Press.

Langacker, Ronald (1991). *Foundations of Cognitive Grammar*, Vol. 2. Stanford: Stanford University Press.

Langacker, Ronald (1987). *Foundations of Cognitive Grammar*, Vol. 1. Stanford: Stanford University Press.

Lastra, Yolanda/ Butragueño, Pedro (2012). Aproximación al uso del modo subjuntivo en el Corpus sociolingüístico de la ciudad de México. *Boletín de Filología*, 47.2, 101–31.

Lavandera, Beatriz R. (1990). El cambio de modo como estrategia de discurso. Indicativo y subjuntivo. In: I. Bosque (ed.), *Indicativo y subjuntivo*. Madrid: Taurus, 330–57.

Lavandera, Beatriz R. (1983). Shifting Moods in Spanish Discourse. In: F. Klein-Andreu (ed.), *Discourse Perspectives on Syntax*. New York: Academic, 209–36.

Lee, James F. (1987). Comprehending the Spanish Subjunctive: An Information Processing Perspective. *The Modern Language Journal*, 71.1, 50–7.

Lee, James F./VanPatten, Bill (1995). *Making Communicative Language Teaching Happen*. Nueva York: McGraw Hill.

Lehner, Bianca (2009). *Der Subjuntivo im Spanischen Lateinamerikas*. Munich: GRIN Verlag GmbH.

Lemon, Francis J. (1925). The Relative Frequency of the Subjunctive Forms in -se and -ra. *Hispania*, 8.5, 300–2.

Lenz, Rodolfo (1935). *La oración y sus partes*. Publicaciones de la Revista de filología española, 5. Madrid: Junta para ampliación de estudios e investigaciones científicos.

Leonetti, M. (1999). El artículo. In: I. Bosque/ V. Demonte (dirs.), *Gramática descriptiva de la lengua española*. Madrid: Espasa, 787–890.

Lope Blanch, Juan M. (1986). *Estudio del español hablado culto. Historia de un proyecto*. Ciudad de México: UNAM.

Lope Blanch, Juan M. (1958). Algunos usos del indicativo por el subjuntivo en oraciones subordinadas. *Nueva Revista de Filología Hispánica*, 12, 383–5.

López Morales, Humberto (1992). *El español del Caribe*. Madrid: MAPFRE.

Lozano, Anthony G. (1975). In Defense of Two Subjunctives. *Hispania*, 58.2, 277–83.

Lozano, Anthony G. (1972). Subjunctives, Transformations and Features in Spanish. *Hispania*, 55.1, 76–90.

Lunn, Patricia V. (1995). The Evaluative Function of the Spanish Subjunctive. In: J. L. Bybee/ S. Fleischmann (eds.), *Modality in Grammar and Discourse*. Typological Studies in Language, 32. Amsterdam: John Benjamins, 429–49.

Lunn, Patricia V. (1989a). The Spanish Subjunctive and "Relevance": Studies in Romance Linguistics. In: C. Kirschner/ J. DeCesaris (eds.), *Selected Proceedings from the XVII Linguistic Symposium on Romance Languages*. Current Issues in Linguistic Theory, 60. Amsterdam: John Benjamins Publishing Company, 249–60.

Lunn, Patricia V. (1989b). Spanish Mood and the Prototype of Assertability. *Linguistics: An Interdisciplinary Journal of the Language Sciences*, 27.4, 687–702.

Lunn, Patricia V./ Cravens, Thomas D. (1991). A Contextual Reconsideration of the Spanish – ra "Indicative". In: S. Fleischman/ L. R. Waugh (eds.), *Discourse Pragmatics and the Verb*. London:Croom Helm, 147–63.

Maldonado, Ricardo (1994). Middle-Subjunctive Links. In: P. Hashemipour (ed. and preface)/ R. Maldonado (ed. and preface)/ M. Van Naerssen (ed. and preface)/ T. Dorwick (foreword), *Studies in Language Learning and Spanish Linguistics in Honor of Tracy D. Terrell*. New York: McGraw-Hill, 399–418.

Mallo, Jerónimo (1947). El empleo de las formas del subjuntivo terminadas en "ra" con significación de tiempos del indicativo. *Hispania*, 30.4, 484–7.

Manteca Alonso-Cortés, Angel (1981). *Gramática del subjuntivo*. Madrid: Ediciones Cátedra.

Martinell Gifre, Emma (1985). *El subjuntivo*. Madrid: Editorial Coloquio.

Matte Bon, Francisco (1992). *Gramática comunicativa del español*. Madrid: Difusión.

McKay, Douglas R. (1976). *Understanding the Spanish Subjunctive: A Simplified Student Guide to the Mood of Uncertainty*. Colorado Springs: Centenial Editions.

Mejías-Bikandi, Errapel (2016). Entailments, Pragmatic Asertion and Mood in Spanish Complements. *Borealis: An International Journal of Hispanic Linguistics*, 5.1, 107–22. http://dx.doi.org/10.7557/1.5.1.3730

Mejías-Bikandi, Errapel (2014). A Cognitive Account of Mood in Complements of Causative Predicates in Spanish. *Hispania*, 97.4, 651–65.

Mejías-Bikandi, Errapel (2009). Conditional Sentences and Mood in Spanish. *Journal of Pragmatics*, 41, 163–72.

Mejías-Bikandi, Errapel (2002). Space Accessibility and the Pragmatic Status of Propositions. In: J. Gutiérrez-Rexach (ed.), *From Words to Discourse: Trends in Spanish Semantics and Pragmatics*. Oxford: Elsevier, 145–58.

Mejías-Bikandi, Errapel (1998a). Pragmatic Presupposition and Old Information in the Explanation of Use of Subjunctive Mood in Spanish. *Hispania*, 81.4, 941–7.

Mejías-Bikandi, Errapel (1998b). Space Accessibility and Mood in Spanish. In: G. Fauconnier/ E. Sweetser (eds.), *Spaces, Worlds and Grammars*. Chicago: University of Chicago Press, 157–78.

Mejías-Bikandi, Errapel (1994). Assertion and Speaker's Intention: A Pragmatically Based Account of Mood in Spanish. *Hispania*, 77.4, 892–902.

Mejías-Bikandi, Errapel (1993). *Syntax, Discourse and Acts of the Mind: A Study of the Indicative/Subjunctive Contrast in Spanish*. Dissertation Abstracts International, 54, 4: 1343A.

Mendoza Quiroga, José G. (1992). Aspectos del castellano hablado en Bolivia. In: César Hernández Alonso (coor.), *Historia y presente del español de América*. Valladolid: Junta de Castilla y León, 437–99.

Merrill, Judith S. (1987). "Fuese" and "Fuera". *The Language Quarterly*, 26, 8–10.

Metz, Jens (2013). *Morphologie und Semantik des Konjunktivs im Lateinischen und Spanischen: eine vergleichende Analyse auf der Grundlage eines Literaturberichts*. Romanische Sprachen und ihre Didaktik, 42. Stuttgart: Ibidem Verlag.

Molina, Inmaculada (2006). *Practica tu español. El subjuntivo*. Madrid: Sociedad General Española de Librería.

Molitor, Eva (2000). *Sprachgefühl und Sprachbewusstsein am Beispiel des Subjonctif nach après que. Eine empirische Untersuchung*. Göttingen: Peust & Gutschmidt.

Morales, Amparo (1992). Variación dialectal e influencia lingüística: el español de Puerto Rico. In: C. Hernández Alonso (ed.), *Historia y presente del español de América*. Valladolid, España: Junta de Castilla y León, Pabecal, 333–54.

Morales, Amparo (1988). Infinitivo con sujeto expreso en el español de Puerto Rico. In: R. Hammond/ M. Renick (eds.), *Studies in Caribbean Spanish Dialectology*. Washington: Georgetown University, 85-96.

Navas Ruiz, R. (1990). El subjuntivo castellano. Teoría y bibliografía crítica. In: I. Bosque (ed.), *Indicativo y subjuntivo*. Madrid: Taurus, 107–41.

Navas Ruiz, R. (1986). *El subjuntivo castellano*. Salamanca: Colegio de España.

Nieves Vázquez Núñez, María de las (1999). *Tempus, Modus und Aspekt im Spanischen des 16. Jahrhunderts: die Chronik von Alonso Borregán*. Dissertation. Freiburg (Breisgau): University of Freiburg.

Ocampo, Francisco (1990). El subjuntivo en tres generaciones de habitantes bilingües. In: J. Bergen (ed.), *Spanish in the United States: Sociolinguistic Issues*. Washington, DC: Georgetown University Press, 39–48.

Oro, C. (1975). *El subjuntivo en la "Primera Crónica General de España"*. Dissertation Abstracts International, 36, 868A–9A.

Pérez, Petronilo/Süss, Kurt (2010). *Diccionario de uso del subjuntivo*. Erlangen: Marpes-Verlag.

Pérez-Leroux, Ana Teresa (1988). The Acquisition of Mood Selection in Spanish Relative Clauses. *Journal of Child Language*, 25.3, 585–604.

Pérez Saldanya, Manuel (1999). El modo en las subordinadas relativas y adverbiales. In: I. Bosque/ V. Delmonte (eds.), *Gramática descriptiva de la lengua española*. Madrid: Espasa Calpe, 3253–322.

Porto Dapena, J. Alvaro (1991). *Del indicativo al subjuntivo: valores y usos de los modos del verbo.* Madrid: Arco/ Libros.

Puente-Schubeck, Elsa B. de la (1992). *La pérdida del modo subjuntivo en el español chicano de Nuevo México.* Dissertation Abstracts International, 52, 8: 2906A.

Ramirez Luengo, Jose Luis (2001). Notas sobre el futuro de subjuntivo en la primera mitad del siglo XIX: el caso de Bolivar. *Estudios de Lingüística,* 15, 393–405.

Real Academia Española (2010). *Nueva gramática de la lengua española / Manual (NGLE/M).* Madrid: Espasa Libros, S.L.U.

Real Academia Española (2009). *Nueva gramática de la lengua española (NGLE).* Madrid: Espasa Libros, S.L.U.

Real Academia Española (1973). *Esbozo de una nueva gramática de la lengua española.* Madrid: Espasa-Calpe.

Renaldi, Thomas W. (1977). Notes on the Functions of "Acaso", "Quiza(s)" and "Tal Vez" in American Spanish. *Hispania,* 60.2, 332–6.

Ridruejo, Emilio (1999). Modo y modalidad. El modo en las subordinadas sustantivas. In: I. Bosque/ V. Delmonte (eds.), *Gramática descriptiva de la lengua española.* Madrid: Espasa Calpe, 3209–52.

Rivera, Álamo R. (1986). *Alternancia de modo en el español de Puerto Rico: análisis de lenguas en contacto.* Unpublished master's thesis. San Juan: University of Puerto Rico.

Rivero, María L. (1979). *Estudios de gramática generativa del español.* Madrid: Cátedra.

Rivero, María L. (1975). Referential Properties of Spanish Noun Phrases. *Language,* 51.1, 42–8.

Rivero, María L. (1972). La concepción de los modos en la gramática de Andrés Bello y los verbos abstractos en la gramática generativa. *Revista de Lingüística Teórica y Aplicada,* 10, 55–74.

Rivero, María L. (1970). Mood and Presupposition in Spanish. *Foundation of Language,* 7, 305–36.

Rodriguez-Ford, Pilar/ Georgalas, Sotiri (1983). El uso periodístico de las formas -ra y -se del imperfecto de subjuntivo. *Canadian Modern Language Review/La Revue Canadienne des Langues Vivantes,* 39.4, 895–9.

Rojo, Guillermo (1996). Sobre la distribución de las formas llegara y llegase en español actual. In: M. Casado Velarde (ed.)/ A. Freire Llamas (ed. & bibliography.)/ J. E. López Pereira (ed. & tribute)/ J. Pérez Pascual (ed.)/ A. Zamora Vicente (biographical note)/ M. Regueiro Tenreirol (tribute), *Scripta Philologica in Memoriam Manuel Taboada Cid,* Vol. 1–2. Servicio de Publicaciones, Universidade da Coruña, 677–91.

Rosemond, Fritz (1996). *Hacia una mejora pedagógica en la presentación del modo subjuntivo español a los estudiantes de la escuela secundaria de Haiti.* Dissertation Abstracts International, 56, 7: 2593A–4A.

Rothstein, Björn/ Thieroff, Rolf (eds.) (2010). *Mood in the Languages of Europe.* Studies in Language Companion Series, 120. Amsterdam: John Benjamins.

Ruiz Campillo, José Plácido (2008). El valor central del subjuntivo: Informatividad o declaratividad? *marcoELE. Revista didáctica ELE,* 7, no page numbers.

Ruiz Campillo, José Plácido (2007). El concepto de no-declaración como valor del subjuntivo. Protocolo de instrucción operativa de la selección modal en español. In: C. Pastor (coord.), *Actas del programa de formación para profesorado de ELE 2006–2007.* Múnich: Instituto Cervantes, 89–146.

Sastre Ruano, Ma. Angeles (1997). *El subjuntivo en español.* Salamanca: Colegio de España.

Schifko, Peter (1967). *Subjonctif und subjuntivo. Zum Gebrauch des Konjunktivs im Französischen und Spanischen.* = Wiener romanistische Arbeiten, 6. Wien [etc.]: Wilhelm Braumüller.

Schmidely, Jack (1992). Los subjuntivos -ra y -se en Cinco horas con Mario. In: A. Vilanova (ed.), *Actas del X Congreso de la Asociación de Hispanistas*, Vol. 1–4. Barcelona: Promociones y Publicaciones Universitarias, 1301–139. http://cvc.cervantes.es/literatura/aih/pdf/10/aih_10_4_052.pdf

Serrano, María José (1996). El subjuntivo -ra y -se en oraciones condicionales. *Estudios Filologicos*, 31, 129–40.

Serrano, María José (1992). El subjuntivo en Canarias y América. *Cauce*, 14–15, 241–51.

Stalnaker, Robert (1984). *Inquiry*. Cambridge, MA: MIT Press.

Stalnaker, Robert (1978). Assertion. In: P. Cole (ed.), Syntax and Semantics, vol 9: Pragmatics. New York: Academic Press, 315-332.

Stokes, Jeffery D. (1988). Some Factors in the Acquisition of the Present Subjunctive in Spanish. *Hispania*, 71.3, 705–10.

Stokes, Jeffery D./ Krashen, Stephen (1990). Some Factors in the Acquisition of the Present Subjunctive in Spanish: A Re-Analysis. *Hispania*, 73.3, 805–6.

Stokes, Jeffery D./ Krashen, Stephen/ Kartchner, John (1988). Factors in the Acquisition of the Present Subjunctive in Spanish: The Role of Reading and Study. *ITL: Review of Applied Linguistics*, 121–2, 19–25.

Tarr, F. C. (1922). Prepositional Complementary Clauses in Spanish with Special Reference to the Works of Pérez Galdós. *Revue Hispanique*, 56, 1–264.

Terrell, Tracy/ Hooper, Joan (1974). A Semantically Based Analysis of Mood in Spanish. *Hispania*, 57.3, 484–94.

Togeby, K. (1953). *Mode, aspect et temps en espagnol*. Historisk-filologiske Meddelelser udgivet af Det Kgl. Danske Videnskabernes Selskab 34.1. Copenhagen: Munksgaard.

Trujillo, Ramón (1996). Sobre el uso metafórico de los modos en español. In: G. Wotjak (ed.), *El verbo español: aspectos morfosintácticos, sociolingüísticas y lexicogenéticos*. Frankfurt a. M. [etc.]: Vervuert Iberoamericana, 9–39.

Tyo, Suzanne E. (1993). *An Analysis of the Spanish Subjunctive and Its Pedagogical Presentation*. Rochester: University of Rochester.

VanPatten, Bill (1995). Cognitive Aspects of Input Processing in Second Language Acquisition. In: P. Hashemipour/ R. Maldonado/ M. van Naerssen (eds.), *Studies in Language Learning and Spanish Linguistics: In Honor of Tracy D. Terrell*. New York: McGraw-Hill, 170–83.

VanPatten, Bill/ Dvorak, T./ Lee, J. F. (1987). Foreign Language Learning: An Overview. In: B. VanPatten/ T. R. Dvorak/ J. F. Lee (eds.), *Foreign Language Learning: A Research Perspective*. Cambridge, MA: Newbury House, 1–16.

VanPatten, Bill/ Lee, James F. (eds.) (1990). *Second Language Acquisition/Foreign Language Learning*. Clevedon, Philadelphia: Multilingual Matters Ltd.

VARIGRAMA. Variación Gramatical del Español en el Mundo. http://lecture.ecc.u-tokyo.ac.jp/~cueda/varigrama/index.html

Veiga, Alexandre (1996a). *La forma verbal española "cantara" en su diacronía*. Santiago de Compostela: Universidade de Santiago de Compostela.

Veiga, Alexandre (1993). Sobre a reorganización das oposicións temporais en subxuntivo e subxuntivo irreal na diacronía do verbo hispánico. In: A. Lorenzo (ed.), *Actas do XIX Congreso Internacional de Lingüística e Filoloxía Románicas*. Santiago de Compostela: Universidade de Santiago de Compostela, 1989, 435–66.

Veiga, Alexandre (1992b). Una discrepancia en cuanto a la sustitución histórica del futuro de subjuntivo castellano. *Verba: Anuario Galego de Filoloxia*, 19, 409–29.

Veiga, Alexandre (1989). La sustitución del futuro de subjuntivo en la diacronía del verbo español. *Verba: Anuario Galego de Filoloxia*, 16, 257–338.

Villalta, Elisabeth (2008). Mood and Gradability: An Investigation of the Subjunctive Mood in Spanish. *Linguistics and Philosophy*, 31.4, 467–522.

Vogel, Lynn Cheryl (1979). *A Contribution to the Study of the Subjunctive in Spanish*. Los Angeles: University of California.

Vogt, Eric W. (2008). *The Spanish Subjunctive Up Close*. New York: McGraw-Hill Primis Custom Publishing.

Wasa, Atsuko (2006). Supeingo to Nihongo no jouken hyougen. Johou to jisei no kanten kara. (= Expresiones consicionales en español y japonés. Desde el punto de vista del modo y tiempo). In: Takashi Masuoka (ed.), *Jouken hyougen na taishou*. Tokio: Kuroshio Shuppan, 151–71.

Woehr, Richard (1975). Grammar of the Factitive Nominal in Spanish. *Language Science*, 36, 13–16.

Woehr, Richard (1972). Acaso, "Quiza(s)," "Tal vez": Free Variants? *Hispania*, 55.2, 320–7.

Wright, Leavitt O. (1933). The Earliest Shift of the Spanish -ra Verb Form from the Indicative Function to the Subjunctive: 1000–1300 A.D. *Language: Journal of the Linguistic Society of America*, 9.3, 265–8.

Wright, Leavitt O. (1929). The Indicative Function of the -ra Verb Form: I. Its Disappearance in Pre-Golden Age Prose. *Hispania*, 12.3, 259–78.

Wright, Leavitt O. (1926a). The Indicative Forms in -ra in Spanish America. *Hispania*, 9.5, 288–93.

Wright, Leavitt O. (1926b). The Subjunctive Forms in -ra and -se in Spanish-American Speech. *Hispania*, 9.3, 170–3.

Yamín, I. (1991). *Análisis sintáctico de la lengua escrita de estudiantes universitarios: Influencia del inglés*. Doctoral Thesis. San Juan: Universidad de Puerto Rico.

Zamorano Aguilar, Alfonso (2005). *El subjuntivo en la historia de la gramática española (1771–1973)*. Madrid: Arco/ Libros.

Additional subjunctive bibliography

Ahern, Aoife (2005). Mood Choice and Sentence Interpretation in Spanish. *Cahiers Chronos*, 13, 201–14.

Ahern, Aoife (2004). *El subjuntivo: significado e inferencia. Un análisis basado en la Teoría de la Relevancia*. PhD thesis. Madrid: U.N.E.D, Departamento de Lengua Española y Lingüística General.

Ahern, Aoife/ Leonetti, Manuel (2004). The Spanish Subjunctive: Procedural Semantics and Pragmatics Interference. In: R. Marquez Reiter/ M. Placencia (eds.), *Current Trends in the Pragmatics of Spanish*. Amsterdam/ Philadelphia: John Benjamins Publishing Company, 35–56.

Aliaga, Francisco/ de Bustos, Eduardo (2002). Mental Spaces and Epistemic Attitudes: On the Spanish Subjunctive/ Indicative Alternation. In: J. Gutiérrez-Rexach (ed.), *From Words to Discourse: Trends in Spanish Semantics and Pragmatics*. Oxford: Elsevier, 135–44.

Aliaga, Francisco/ Escandell, Maria Victoria (1988). Cuando + SN: Algunos problemas sintácticos. *Lenguajes naturales y lenguajes formales*, 3, 389–401.

Arce, Germán (1980). La motivación del subjuntivo. *Linguistica Hispánica*, 3, 3–40.

Ariyoshi, Shunzi (1981). A Note on the Spanish Subjunctive, with Special Reference to Its Use in the Subordinate Clause of Verbs of Belief. Diálogo de la lengua. *Lingüística Hispánica*, 4, 3–30.

Barolo Ottonello, Marta (2000). Presuposición en la interlengua española: El subjuntivo. *Actas de la Asociación para la Enseñanza del Español como Lengua Extranjera, 1*. Cádiz: Universidad de Cádiz, 97–106.

Bayerová, Marcela (1994). Alternancia indicativo – subjuntivo en oraciones independientes. *Studia minora Facultatis Philosophicae Universitatis Brunensis*, L 15 (Etudes romanes de Brno XXIV), 61–71.

Becker, Martin G. (2010). Principles of Mood Change in Evaluative Contexts: The Case of French. In: Martin G. Becker/ Eva-Maria Remberger (eds.), *Modality and Mood in Romance*. (= Linguistische Arbeiten 533) De Gruyter Mouton, 209–33.

Bell, Anthony (1990). El modo en español: consideración de algunas propuestas recientes. In: Ignacio Bosque/ Violeta Demonte (eds.), *Indicativo y subjuntivo*. Madrid: Taurus, 81–105.

Blake, Robert (1983). Mood Selection among Spanish-Speaking Children: Ages 4 to 12. *The Bilingual Review*, 10, 21–32.

Blake, Robert (1981). Some Empirically Based Observations on Adult Usage of the Subjunctive Mood in Mexico City. In: J. Lantolf/ G. B. Stone (eds.), *Current Research in Romance Languages*. Bloomington, IN: Indiana University Linguistics Club, 13–22.

Blanco Gómez, María Luisa (1996). ¿Por qué el subjuntivo es un problema para el anglófono? *Diálogos Hispánicos*, 17, 127–41.

Blas Arroyo, José Luis/ Porcar Miralles, M. (1997). Aproximación sociolingüística al fenómeno de la neutralización modal en las comunidades de habla castellonenses: Análisis de algunos contornos sintácticos. *Sintagma: Revista de Lingüística*, 9, 27–45.

Bolinger, Dwight L. (1970). Modes of Modality in Spanish and English. *Romance Philology*, 23.4, 572–86.

Bolinger, Dwight L. (1959). Gleanings from CLM: Indicative vs. Subjunctive in Exclamations. *Hispania*, 42.3, 372–73.

Borgonovo, Claudia (2001). Mood and Focus: Selected Papers from "Going Romance" Amsterdam, 6–8 December 2001, Amsterdam Studies in the Theory and History of Linguistic Science IV. *Current Issues in Linguistic Theory (CILT)*, 245, 17–30.

Borgonovo, Claudia/ Bruhn de Garavito, J./ Prevost, P. (2005). Acquisition of Mood Distinctions in L2 Spanish. *Proceedings of the Annual Boston University Conference on Language Development*, 29.1, 97–108.

Bosque, Ignacio (2012). Mood: Indicative vs. Subjunctive. In: J. I. Hualde/ A. Olarrea/ E. O'Rourke (eds.), *The Handbook of Spanish Linguistics*. Oxford: Wiley-Blackwell, 373–95.

Bosque, Ignacio (1990c). *Tiempo y aspecto en español*. Madrid: Cátedra.

Bow, Ernie L. (1996). *The Spanish Subjunctive*. Ernie L. Bow Books.

Busch, Hans-Jörg (2009). La enseñanza del subjuntivo en EE.UU. El subjuntivo en cláusulas nominales. *RLA: Revista de lingüística teórica y aplicada*, 47.1, 145–66.

Bybee, Joan L./ Fleischmann, Suzanne (eds.) (1995). *Modality in Grammar and Discourse*. Typological Studies in Language, 32. Amsterdam: John Benjamins.

Bybee, Joan L./ Terrell, Tracy D. (1990). Análisis semántico del modo en español. In: Ignacio Bosque (ed.), *Indicativo y subjuntivo*. Madrid: Taurus, 145–63.

Cano Aguilar, Rafael (1992a). Nuevas precisiones de como + subjuntivo. In: M. Ariza Viguera/ R. Cano Aguilar (eds.), *Actas del II. Congreso Internacional de Historia de Lengua Española*. Madrid: Pabellón de España, 333–45.

Cano Aguilar, Rafael (1992b). Tiempo y modo en el subjuntivo español. *Gramma-Temas*, 1, 65–90.

Carlsson, Lennart (1970). Sur l'usage des modes après (me) parece que en castilian et (em) sembla que en catalàn. *Studia Neophilologica*, 42, 405–32.

Castañeda Castro, Alejandro (1994). *Procesos de automatización y prácticas gramaticales comunicativas (de la adquisición del subjuntivo en español como lengua extranjera*. Thesis. Granada: Universidad de Granada.

Castañeda Castro, Alejandro (1993). *El subjuntivo: Su enseñanza en el aula de E/ LE*. Cuadernos del tiempo libre. Madrid: Colección Expolingua.

Castronovo, Brian J. (1990). La categoría gramatical de modo en la tradición gramatical española. In: I. Bosque (ed.), *Indicativo y subjuntivo*. Madrid: Taurus, 66–80.

Cathcart Roca, Mercedes L. (1986). Acerca de la expresión verbal de modalidad. *Actes du XVIIe Congrès Internationale de Linguistique et Philologie Romanes*, 4, 335–56.

Coles, Felice A. (2012). Stance and the Subjunctive in Isleño Spanish. *Hispania*, 95.2, 285–9.

Combe, Horst (2010). *Die Verwendung des spanischen Subjuntivo im Relativsatz. Untersuchungen zur Pressesprache der Gegenwart*. Dissertation. Tübingen: Universität Tübingen.

Cressey, William W. (1971). The Subjunctive in Spanish: A Transformational Approach. *Hispania*, 54.4, 895–6.

Dalbor, John B. (1969). Temporal Distinctions in the Spanish Subjunctive. *Hispania*, 52.4, 889–96.

Dale, G. I. (1925). The Imperfect Subjunctive. *Hispania*, 8.2, 127–9.

Deguchi, Atsumi (1980). Mood, Modal and Tense in Spanish. *Lingüística Hispánica*, 3, 87–101.

Donaire, María Luisa (1998). La insubordinación del subjuntivo: un ámbito polifónico y sus marcas. *Verba*, 25, 223–41.

Dunlap, Carolyn (2006). Dialectical Variation in Mood Choice in Spanish Journalistic Prose. *Language Variation and Change*, 18.1, 35–53.

Fabregas, Antonio (2014). A Guide to Subjunctive and Modals in Spanish: Questions and Analyses. *Borealis: An International Journal of Hispanic Linguistics*, 3.2, 1–94. http://dx.doi.org/10.7557/1.3.2.3064

Fabregas, Antonio (2009). Una contribución a la enseñanza del indicativo y del subjuntivo en ele. *Revista Espanola de Linguistica Aplicada*, 8, 151–73.

Faingold, Eduardo D. (2000). A Systematic Analysis of the Spanish Subjunctive. *Papiere zur Linguistik*, 62–3.1–2, 89–104.

Farkas, Donka F. (1992). On the Semantics of Subjunctive Complements. *Current Issues in Linguistic Theory*, 91, 69–104.

Farkas, Donka F. (1985). *Intensional Descriptions and the Romance Subjunctive Mood*. New York: Garland.

Farley, Rodger A. (1970). Time and the Subjunctive in Contemporary Spanish. *Hispania*, 53.3, 466–75.

Farley, Rodger A. (1965). Sequence of Tenses: A Useful Principle? *Hispania*, 48.3, 549–53.

Fernández Alvarez, J. (1984). *El subjuntivo*. Madrid: Sociedad General Española de Librería.

Fernández González, Jesús (1991). Guía del subjuntivo castellano para anglohablantes e hispanohablantes que estudian inglés, II. *Analecta Malacitana: Revista de la Seccion de Filologia de la Facultad de Filosofia y Letras*, 14.2, 347–60.

Fernández Ramírez, S. (1937). Como si + subjuntivo. *Revista de Filología Española*, 24, 327–80.

Fish, Gordon T. (1963). Subjunctive of Fact. *Hispania*, 46.2, 375–81.

Florez, Oscar (1993). El correlato pragmáticode la alternancia indicativo-subjuntivo. *Lingüística Española Actual*, 15, 65–85.

Floyd, Mary Beth (1990a). Sentence Complexity and Clause Subordination in Children's Spanish. *Hispania*, 73.2, 488–97.

Floyd, Mary Beth (1990b). Development of Subjunctive Mood in Children's Spanish: A Review. *Confluencia: Revista Hispanica de Cultura y Literatura*, 5.2, 93–104.

Foster, David William (1982). Internal Contradictions of a Spanish Subjunctive. *International Review of Applied Linguistics in Language Teaching*, 22.2, 131–7.

Foster, David William (1973). The Spanish Subjunctive as a Non-Semantic Category. *English Language Journal*, 4, 191–200.

Frounick, Ross Gilbert (1932). *The Spanish Subjunctive*. New York: Globe Book Co.

Fukushima, Noritaka (1990). Sobre la cláusula superregente. In: I. Bosque (ed.), *Indicativo y subjuntivo*. Madrid: Taurus, 164–79, 435–6.

Fukushima, Noritaka (1981b). La modalidad de las oraciones independientes y de las cláusulas sustantivas en español. *Lingüística Hispánica*, 4, 63–81. Hirakata: Círculo de Lingüística Hispánica de Kansai.

Fukushima, Noritaka (1978). La aserción y el modo español. *Lingüística Hispánica*, 2, 75–95. Hirakata: Círculo de Lingüística Hispánica de Kansai.

García, Mary Ellen/ Terrell, Tracy (1977). Is the Use of Mood in Spanish Subject to Variable Constraints? In: M. P. Hagiwara (ed.), *Studies in Romance Linguistics: Proceedings of the Fifth Linguistic Symposium on Romance Linguistics*. Rowley, MA: Newbury House Publishers, 214–26.

Giannakidou, Anastasia (2009). The Dependency of the Subjunctive Revisited: Temporal Semantics and Polarity. *Lingua*, 99, 1883–908.

Giorgi, Alessandra (2009). Toward a Syntax of the Subjunctive Mood. *Lingua*, 99, 1837–58.

Givón, Talmy (1994). Irrealis and the Subjunctive. *Studies in Language: International Journal Sponsored by the Foundation of Language*, 18.2, 265–337.

González Calvo, José Manuel (1995). Sobre el modo verbal en español. *Anuario de Estudios Filológicos*, 18, 177–203.

González Rodriguez, Raquel (2003). Tiempo y modo en las subordinadas sustantivas. *Dicenda: Cuadernos de Filología Hispánica*, 21, 35–58.

Graham, Malbone Watson (1926). The Imperfect Subjunctive in Spanish America. *Hispania*, 9.1, 46–9.

Granda, Germán de (1968). Formas en "-re" en español atlántico y problemas conexos. *ThBICC*, 23, 1–23.

Gregorio de Mac, María Isabel de (1968). El problema de los modos verbales. In: Amy E. Gregory (ed.) (2001), *A Cognitive Map of Indicative and Subjunctive Mood Use in Spanish: Pragmatics & Cognition*, Vol. 9.1. Amsterdam: John Benjamins, 99–133.

Gudmestad, Aarnes (2012). Acquiring a Variable Structure: An Interlanguage Analysis of Second Language Mood Use in Spanish. *Language Learning*, 62.2, 373–402.

Gudmestad, Aarnes (2010). Moving beyond a Sentence-Level Analysis in the Study of Variable Mood Use in Spanish. *Southwest Journal of Linguistics*, 29.1, 25–51.

Guitart, Jorge M. (1991). The Pragmatics of Spanish Mood in Complements of Knowledge and Acquisition-of-Knowledge Predicates. In: Suzanne Fleischman/ Linda R. Waugh (eds.), *Discourse Pragmatics and the Verb: The Evidence from Romance*. New York: Routledge, 179–93.

Guitart, Jorge M. (1984). Syntax, Semantics and Pragmatics of Mood in Spanish Noun Clauses. *Hispanic Journal*, 6.1, 159–74.

Guitart, Jorge M. (1982). On the Use of the Spanish Subjunctive among Spanish-English Bilinguals. *Word*, 33, 59–67.

Gutiérrez Araus, Maria L. (1986). La alternancia indicativo-subjuntivo en las proposiciones relativas del español actual. *Actes du XVIIe Congrès Internationale de Linguistique et Philologie Romanes*, 4, 365–78.

Gutiérrez-Rexach, Javier (ed.) (2002). *From Words to Discourse: Trends in Spanish Semantics and Pragmatics*. Oxford: Elsevier .

Haiman, John (1974). Concessives, Conditionals, and Verbs of Volition. *Foundations of Language*, 9, 341–59.

Harrington, Sophie/ Pérez-Leroux, Ana Teresa (2016). Subjunctive and Subject Pronoun Realization: A Study of "no creo que". *Borealis: An International Journal of Hispanic Linguistics*, 5.1, 87–106. http://dx.doi.org/10.7557/1.5.1.3726

Harris, Martin (1974). The Subjunctive Mood as a Changing Category in Romance. In: J. M. Anderson/ Ch. Johnes (eds.), *Historical Linguistics, II: Theory and Description in Phonology*. Amsterdam, Netherlands: North-Holland Publishing Company, 169–88.

Hengeveld, Kees/ Wanders, Gerry (1996). On the Use of Subjunctive and Indicative Verb-Forms in Adverbial Clauses. In: J. Gvozdanovic (ed.), *Language Change and Functional Explanations: Trends in Linguistics: Studies and Monographs*, Vol. 98. Berlin: Mouton de Gruyter, 249–72.

Igualada Belchí, Dolores A. (1989). Nueva hipótesis sobre el subjuntivo en español. *Estudios Románicos, 4*. Murcia: Universidad de Murcia, 643–62.

Ishizaki, Yuko (1985). The Tense of the Spanish Subjunctive. *Sophia Linguistica*, 18, 72–9.

Jiménez Juliá, Tomas (1989). Modalidad, modo verbal y modus clausal en español. *Verba*, 15, 175–214.

Kasper, Walter (1992). Presuppositions, Composition, and Simple Subjunctives. *Journal of Semantics*, 9.4, 307–31.

Kempchinsky, Paula (2009). What Can the Subjunctive Disjoint Reference Effect Tell Us about the Subjunctive? *Lingua*, 99, 1788–810.

Kempchinsky, Paula (1995). From the Lexicon to the Syntax: The Problem of Subjunctive Clauses. In: H. Campos/ P. Kemchinsky (eds.), *Evolution and Revolution in Linguistic Theory*. Washington, DC: Georgetown University Press, 228–50.

Kempchinsky, Paula (1987). The Subjunctive Disjoint Reference Effect. *Language Sciences*, 25, 123–40.

King, Larry D. (1992). *The Semantic Structure of Spanish: Meaning and Grammatical Form*. Amsterdam: John Benjamins.

Kirschner, Carl (1992). The Spanish Subjunctive and the Spanish-English Bilingual: A Semantically-Motivated Functional Shift. *Hispanic Linguistics*, 5, 1–2, 89–108.

Kleiman, Angela Bustos (1975). *A Syntactic Correlate of Semantic and Pragmatic Relations: The Subjunctive Mood in Spanish*. Dissertation Abstracts International, 35: 4481A–2A.

Klein, Flora (1975). Pragmatic Constraints on Distribution: The Spanish Subjunctive. *Papers from the Regional Meeting of the Chicago Linguistic Society*, 11, 353–65.

Klein, Philip W. (1977). Semantic Factors in Spanish Mood. *Glossa*, 9.1, 3–19.

Kloe, Donald R. (1977). *Understanding the Spanish Subjunctive*. Durham, NC: Moore Publishing Company.

Kowal, Jerzt (2007). La elección del modo subjuntivo en las subordinadas nominales. *Lingüística Española Actual*, 29.1, 45–72.

Laskurain, Patxi (2010). *Information Structure and Mood Distribution in Spanish Complement Clauses*. Dissertation. Austin: University of Texas at Austin.

Lemon, Francis J. (1927). A Psychological Study on the Subjunctive Mood in Spanish. *The Modern Language Journal*, 1.4, 195–9.

Lewis, H. Michael (1951). Some Notes on the Subjunctive. *The Modern Language Journal*, 35.5, 376–81.

Lipski, John M. (1978). Subjunctive as Fact? *Hispania*, 61.4, 931–4.

Lleó, Conxita (1979). *Some Optional Rules in Spanish Complementation: Towards a Study of the Speaker's Intent.* = Linguistische Arbeiten, 80. Tübingen: Niemeyer.

López Carrillo, R. (1986/87). Le subjonctif: Emplois en français et en espagnol (Études de contrastes). *Anales del Colegio Universitario de Almería*, 6, 197–228.

López Rivera, Juan J. (2002). *El modo: la categoría gramatical y la cuestión modal.* Santiago de Compostela: Universidad de Santiago de Compostela.

Lozano, Anthony G. (1995). Cognitive Development, Deontic and Epistemic Subjunctives. *Hispanic Linguistics,* 6–7, 93–5.

Lozano, Anthony G./ Takahara, Kumiko (1987). Politeness and Subjunctive in Spanish and Japanese. *Colorado Research in Linguistics,* 9, 38–44.

Lozano González, Lidia (2005). *Hacia una única explicación del subjuntivo aplicado a la adquisición de E/ LE (primera parte: no alternancia indicativo subjuntivo).* Cuadernos Cervantes, 56. Madrid: ELR Ediciones.

Lubbers Quesada, Margaret (1998). L2 Acquisition of the Spanish Subjunctive Mood and Prototype Schema Development. *Spanish Applied Linguistics,* 2, 1–22.

Lunn, Patricia V. (1988). Some Stops on the Modality Line. *Amsterdam Studies in the Theory and History of Linguistic Science IV: Current Issues in Linguistic Theory,* 69, 221–33.

Luquet, Gilles (1988). *Systematique historique du mode subjonctif espagnol.* Annexes des Cahiers de Linguistique Hispanique Médievale, 5. Paris: Klincksiek.

Lynch, Andrew (2000). *The Subjunctive in Miami Cuban Spanish: Bilingualism, Contact, and Language Variability.* PhD. dissertation. Minneapolis: University of Minnesota. Dissertation Abstracts International, 60, 8.

Mackenzie, Ian (2002). The Spanish Subjunctive: The Philosophical Dimension. *Bulletin of Hispanic Studies,* 79, 1–13.

Mansilla-García, M. (1973). El subjuntivo, escollo de la sintaxis verbal: análisis contrastivo de los usos del subjuntivo en las oraciones subordinadas sustantivas en español y en inglés. *Español Actual,* 24, 9–19.

Manteca Alonso-Cortés, Angel (1986). La temporalidad del subjuntivo en relación con el nodo "flexión". *Dicenda,* 5, 207–20.

Martin, John W. (1958). Some Uses of the Old Spanish Past Subjunctives (with Reference to the Authorship of La Celestina). *Romance Philology,* 12, 52–67.

Martínez Mira, María Isabel (2009). Position and the Presence of Subjunctive in Purpose Clauses in US-Heritage Speakers. *Sociolinguistic Studies,* 3, 61–91.

Matte Bon, Francisco (2007). El subjuntivo español como operador metalingüístico de gestión de la información. *MarcoELE: Revista de didáctica,* 5, 1–24.

Mikulski, Ariana (2010). Receptive Volitional Subjunctive Abilities in Heritage and Traditional Foreign Language Learners of Spanish. *The Modern Language Journal,* 94.2, 217–33.

Miyashita, K. (2008). ¿(Gimonshi) creer que . . .? gata na bun ni okeru juuzoku doushi no hou sentaku nin tsuite (= La selección del modo verbal en las oraciones sustantivas que se subordinan a la oración principal del tipo "¿Partícula interrogativa creer que . . .?". In: *Estudios Lingüísticos Hispánicos,* Vol. 23. Tokio: Círculo de Estudios Hispánicos Lingüísticos de Tokio, 41–60.

Miyoshi, J. (1981). Sobre el modo subjuntivo del español moderno. *Lingüística Hispánica,* 4, 97–117.

Moellering, William (1943). The Function of the Subjunctive Mood in como Clauses of Fact. *Hispania,* 26.3, 267–82.

Montrul, Sylvina (2009). Knowledge of Tense-Aspect and Mood in Spanish Heritage Speakers. *International Journal of Bilingualism,* 13, 239–69.

Montrul, Sylvina (2004). *The Acquisition of Spanish.* Monographs on the Acquisition of Specific Languages, Vol. 1. Amsterdam: John Benjamins.

Morales, Amparo (1989). Algunas consideraciones sobre la alternancia subjuntivo-infinitivo en las construcciones con "para". *Nueva Revista de Filología Hispánica,* 37.1, 27–42.

Moreno de Alba, José G. (1974). Transposiciones temporales y modales en las formas del indicativo. *Anuario de Letras*, 12, 205–19.

Moya Corral, Juan Antonio (1996). Valor modal del llamado "subjuntivo concesivo polémico". *Lingüística Española Actual*, 18.2, 161–74.

Murillo Medrano, Jorge (2000). Revisión de algunas propuestas teóricas en torno a la caracterización del modo subjuntivo. *Revista de Filología y Lingüística de la Universidad de Costa Rica*, 26.1, 99–112.

Nowikow, Wiaczeslaw (1995). El concepto de valoración en el subjuntivo español. *Moenia: Revista Lucense de Lingüística & Literatura*, 1, 203–17.

Obaid, Antonio H. (1967). A Sequence of Tenses? What Sequence of Tenses? *Hispania*, 50.1, 112–19.

Otaola Olano, Concepción (1988). La modalidad en español. *Revista de Filología Española*, 68.1, 97–118.

Oviedo, Tito Nelson (1974). *Mood and Negation in Spanish Noun Clauses*. Thesis. Los Angeles: University of California.

Pardo, José Felipe (1983). Sobre el subjuntivo español. *Thesaurus: Boletín del Instituto Caro y Cuervo*, 38.3, 593–602.

Parker, James F. (1928). Rationalizing the Subjunctive. *The Modern Language Journal*, 12.4, 292–4.

Pereira Rodríguez, Isabel (1999). The Impact of Teaching a Marked Element in the Acquisition of the Spanish Subjunctive. In: F. Sierra Martínez (ed. and introduction)/ C.Hernández González (ed. and introduction), Las lenguas en la Europa comunitaria, III: La adquisición/enseñanza de segundas lenguas y/o de lenguas extranjeras; Las lenguas de minorías; La traducción. *Diálogos Hispánicos*. Amsterdam: Rodopi Bv Editions, 361–77.

Pereira Rodríguez, Isabel (1997). *Markedness and Instructed SLA: An Experiment in Teaching the Spanish Subjunctive*. Dissertation Abstracts International, Section A: The Humanities and Social Sciences, 57, 9: 4720.

Porras, Jorge E. (1990). Análisis semántico del uso del subjuntivo español. *Discurso: Revista de Estudios Iberoamericanos*, 7.2, 387–94.

Powers, Michael (1983). Prodecimientos para seleccionar entre el modo indicativo o subjuntivo en castellano. *Lenguaje y Ciencias*, 23.3, 121–30.

Prado, Eduardo (1974). El subjuntivo (The Subjunctive). *Yelmo*, 15, 33–9.

Puryear, Arlene Lorraine (1991). *Semantics of the Spanish Subjunctive in Direct Object Clauses*. Dissertation Abstracts International, 51, 9: 3727A.

Reider, Michael (1990). Neg-Transportation, Neg-Trace, and the Choice of Mood in Spanish. *Hispania*, 73.1, 212–22.

Reyes, Graciela (1990). Tiempo, modo, aspecto y intertextualidad. *Revista Española de Lingüística*, 20.1, 17–53.

Sanchez-Naranjo, Jeannette (2014). Interpretation and Grammar Interaction in the Spanish Subjunctive Adjuncts. *Borealis: An International Journal of Hispanic Linguistics*, 3.1, 125–54.

Schane, Sanford (1994). Illocutionary Verbs, Subject Responsibility, and Presupposition: The Indicative versus the Subjunctive in Spanish. In: P. Hashemipour (ed. and preface)/ R. Maldonado (ed. and preface)/ M. Van Naerssen (ed. and preface)/ T. Dorwick (foreword), *Studies in Language Learning and Spanish Linguistics*. New York: McGraw-Hill, 360–74.

Seseña Gómez, Marta/ Sánchez Iglesias, Jorge J. (2009). A propósito del modo verbal: Orgullo o prejuicio? *Actas del XIX Congreso Internacional de la Asociación para la*

Enseñanza del Español como Lengua Extranjera (ASELE), Cáceres, 24–27 de septiembre de 2008, 793–806.

Shawl, James R. (1975). Syntactic Aspects of the Spanish Subjunctive. *Hispania*, 58.2, 323–9.

Shimoda, Yukio (1999). Sobre la alternancia modal en las oraciones sustantivas en español. *Studia Romanica*, 32. Tokio: Sociedad Japonesa de Romanistas, 44–55.

Silva-Corvalán, Carmen (1994). The Gradual Loss of Mood Distinctions in Los Angeles Spanish. *Language Variation and Change*, 6.3, 255–72.

Solano-Araya, José M. (1984). *Modality in Spanish: An Account of Mood*. Ann Arbor: University Microfilms International.

Solano-Araya, José M. (1980). *The Subjunctive in Spanish*. Thesis. Lawrence: University of Kansas.

Soler, Vicente Perez (1966). Construcciones con verbos de duda en español. *Hispania*, 49.2, 287–9.

Spaulding, Robert K. (1941). Two Problems of Spanish Syntax. *Hispania*, 24.3, 311–15.

Spaulding, Robert K. (1934). Two Elliptical Subjunctives in Spanish. *Hispania*, 17.4, 355–60.

Spaulding, Robert K. (1933). Infinitive and Subjunctive with "hacer", "mandar", "dejar", and the Like. *Hispania*, 16.4, 425–32.

Spaulding, Robert K. (1925). The Mood with "antes (de) que". *Modern Language Journal*, 10.3, 159–63.

Studerus, Lenard (1995). Some Unresolved Issues in Spanish Mood Use. *Hispania*, 78.1, 94–104.

Studerus, Lenard (1981). A Spanish Twilight Zone: Mood, Syntax, and Past Temporal Reference. *Hispania*, 64.1, 97–103.

Studerus, Lenard (1979). A Model of Temporal Reference for Spanish Verbs. *Hispania*, 62.3, 332–6.

Suñer, Margarita (1990). El tiempo en las subordinadas. In: I. Bosque (ed.), *Tiempo y aspecto en español*. Madrid: Cátedra, 77–105.

Suñer, Margarita/ Padilla-Rivera, José (1990). Concordancia temporal y subjuntivo. In: I. Bosque (ed.), *Indicativo y subjuntivo*. Madrid: Taurus, 185–201.

Suñer, Margarita/ Padilla-Rivera, José (1987). Sequence of Tenses and the Subjunctive again. *Hispania*, 70.3, 634–42.

Takagaki, Toshihiro (1984). Subjunctive as the Marker of Subordination. *Hispania*, 67.2, 248–56.

Travis, C. (2003). The Semantics of the Spanish Subjunctive: Its Use in the Natural Semantic Metalanguage. *Cognitive Linguistics*, 14.1, 47–69.

Uribe-Etxebarria, Myriam (1995). Subjunctive of Negation and [Neg(ative)] Complementizers. *Amsterdam Studies in the Theory and History of Linguistic Science IV: Current Issues in Linguistic Theory*, 133, 307–16.

Veidmark, Ronald Ross/ Umaña Aguiar, Jeanina (1991). La desaparición del subjuntivo español y sus implicaciones para el cambio lingüístico. *Revista de Filología y Lingüística de la Universidad de Costa Rica*, 17.1–2, 193–202.

Veiga, Alexandre (2006). *El modo verbal en cláusulas condicionales, causales, consecutivas, concesivas, finales y adverbiales de lugar, tiempo y modo*. Salamanca: Ediciones Universidad de Salamanca.

Veiga, Alexandre (1996b). Subjuntivo, irrealidad y oposiciones temporales en español. In: G. Wotjak (ed.), *El verbo español. Aspectos morfosintácticos, sociolingüísticos y lexicogenéticos*. Madrid: Iberoamericana, 41–60.

Veiga, Alexandre (1992a). *Condicionales, concesivas y modo verbal en español.* Santiago de Compostela: Universidade de Santiago de Compostela.

Verdonk, Robert A./ Vangehuchten, L. (1998). Te digo (de) venir; Me pide (de) salir. A propósito del uso erróneo del infinitivo en las sustantivas de régimen directo. *Revista de Filología Hispánica,* 14.2, 387–402.

Vijverman, Elmar (1971). Grammatikale analyse van het gebruik van de presente del subjuntivo (volgens de TGG) en zijn vertaling in het Nederlands. *Le Langage et l'Homme: Recherches Pluridisciplinaires sur le Langage,* 16, 36–45.

Villalta, Elisabeth (2007). *Context Dependence in the Interpretation of Questions and Subjunctives.* Thesis. Tübingen: Universität Tübingen.

Villalta, Elisabeth (2001). A Comparative Semantics for the Subjunctive Mood in Spanish. *Amsterdam Studies in the Theory and History of Linguistic Science: Series IV, Current Issues in Linguistic Theory,* 216, 227–42.

Wasa, Atsuko (2005). *Supeingo to Nihongo no modariti.* = La modalidad en español y en japonés. Tokio: Kuroshio Shuppan.

Wasa, Atsuko (2002). A lo mejor y el subjuntivo. *Hispania,* 85.1, 131–6.

Wasa, Atsuko (1999). El subjuntivo y la modalidad. *Hispania,* 82.1, 121–7.

Watson Graham, Malbone (1926). The Imperfect Subjunctive in Spanish America. *Hispania,* 9.1, 46–9.

Whalen, Gillian Hamer (1979). *A Study of the Two Imperfect Subjunctive Variants in Spanish.* Ann Arbor, MI: Dissertation Abstracts International, 40: 3275A–6A.

Wilson, Deidre/ Sperber, Dan (1988). Mood and the Analysis of Non-Declarative Sentences. In: A. Kasher (ed.), *Pragmatics: Critical Concepts,* Vol. 2. London: Routledge, 262–89. (Reprint of Wilson & Sperber 1988).

Wilson, Robert E. (1965). Polite Ways to Give Orders. *Hispania,* 48.1, 97/18.

Woehr, Richard (1975). Grammar of the Factitive Nominal in Spanish. *Language Science,* 36, 13–19.

Woehr, Richard (1973). Two Problems of Modal Syntax: The Superlative Construction and the Verb "Parecer". *Hispania,* 56, Spec. Issue, 318–25.

Zamorano Aguilar, Alfonso (2001). *Gramaticografía de los modos del verbo en español.* Córdoba: Servicio de Publicaciones de la Universidad de Córdoba.

Index

Made in the USA
Middletown, DE
31 May 2021

40774550R00117